In His Light

A Path into Catholic Belief

Rev. William A. Anderson, D.Min., Ph.D.

BROWN-ROA

A Division of Harcourt Brace & Company
Dubuque, Iowa

Nihil Obstat
Rev. Joseph F. O'Reilly, D.Min.
Imprimatur
✠ Bernard W. Schmitt, D.D.
Bishop of Wheeling-Charleston
November 9, 1994

The Nihil Obstat and the Imprimatur are official declarations that a book or a pamphlet is free of doctrinal or moral error. No implication is contained therein that those who have granted the Nihil Obstat or Imprimatur agree with the contents, opinions, or statements expressed.

Book Team
President—Matthew J. Thibeau
Executive Editor—Janie Gustafson
Production Editor—Marilyn Bowers Gorun
Production Manager—Marilyn Rothenberger
Marketing Manager—Ginny Schumacher
Design and Art Direction—Cathy A. Frantz

ISBN 0-697-17853-6

10   9

In Memory of
Bishop Joseph H. Hodges, D.D.
(1911–1985)

This book is dedicated to Bishop Joseph H. Hodges, D.D., who succeeded to the See of Wheeling-Charleston (West Virginia) on November 23, 1962, and served the diocese until his death on January 27, 1985.

Many of us in the Diocese of Wheeling-Charleston remember Bishop Hodges as a man of prayer and study, who worked day and night for the Lord and who was open to the direction taken by the Church in the wake of the Second Vatican Council.

I am especially indebted to him for his many suggestions made in the original manuscript for this book. Upon receiving the manuscript for the first edition, he read through it page by page and set aside a full day to discuss with me the many pages of notes he had compiled while reading the text. When he received the first revision, he was growing weak from his illness, but he still insisted on reading the text before giving the imprimatur. This was typical of the dedication he brought to every task of his ministry.

As his illness progressed, Bishop Hodges tired more quickly and was often too weak to stand for long periods of time, but he continued his ministry in the diocese until the day before his death. He did not want his illness to become an obstacle to those who sought his advice or needed a decision from him concerning the mission of the Church. He was a dedicated, prayerful man, and we, the people of the Diocese of Wheeling-Charleston, were fortunate to have had him as our bishop.

Contents

Introduction to Second Revision

Each day, an elderly man would take a three-mile walk into town. He would walk past several farm houses surrounded by fields of wheat or corn, and he would arrive in town about an hour before his son finished work. His son owned a hardware store, and the elderly man would sit on a stool behind the counter and talk with his son and the customers about any topic they wished. During the trip home, the man would tell his son about his new discoveries on his three-mile trip into town. The son was amazed that his father had walked that road for three years and could still make new discoveries each time he came to town.

A revision of a book can be like a stroll along a familiar road filled with new discoveries. What was written several years ago can now look a little different, perhaps be a little more important or a little better understood because of the experiences of the past few years. A new revision offers the opportunity to express these new insights which have come from the experiences of a living Church.

A major need for a new revision at this time centers on the significant publication of the *Catechism of the Catholic Church*. The Church published this Catechism as a resource for bishops and authors of catechisms in order to assure a unity in the presentation of the faith. The Catechism is not meant to replace existing catechisms. Although the teachings found in previous editions of *In His Light* reflect those found in the new Catechism, the *Catechism of the Catholic Church* was helpful and influential in providing new developments for this edition.

In this edition, as in the past, Scripture quotations are used extensively. Over the past several years, the use of the Rite of Christian Initiation of Adults has reached a deserved place in sharing the faith with those who wish to become members of our Catholic community. It has swept across the country with a force and power which no one would have imagined several years ago. The link between faith and our global concern cannot be ignored in any book such as this.

Over the past years, earlier editions of this book have been used in teacher training sessions, parish adult education sessions, high school classes, discussion groups, and as a basic text for those individuals entering the Catholic faith or for those persons wanting to know more about the faith. Several people have even found this book helpful for spiritual reflection. I am grateful for the many creative uses of this book and hope that this edition will find as welcome a place as earlier editions.

A book such as this plays an important role in the process of the Christian initiation of adults, but it does not attempt to replace the Bible, which is the major book for the initiation process. Nor does this book attempt to replace another important feature of the catechumenate, namely the shared, living stories of those involved in this process. The value of the initiation process lies in the relating of the stories of those sharing in the process to the revealed Word of God in the Scriptures. In the catechumenate, however, there is also a need for a basic text for reflection on the Catholic faith. This book offers such a text. The intent of this book has not changed since the first edition, namely to offer in a clear and concise language a presentation of the Catholic faith which shares the spirit and teachings of the faith without presenting an overwhelming amount of material. A common error in teaching the faith is the tendency to try to teach everything within the short period of a year or two. This book lays a foundation, realizing that there is much more to learn in the years ahead.

Because the Rite of Christian Initiation of Adults places such a great emphasis on the sharing of one's story in relationship to the Word of God, a companion book to *In His Light* has been published for the sake of this process. The book, entitled *Journeying in His Light*, is intended as the first book used in the initiation process. The opening chapters allow for reflection and sharing during the period of evangelization and precatechumenate, and the remaining chapters follow the periods of the catechumenate, purification and enlightenment, and post-baptismal catechesis or mystagogy. Where the chapters of this companion book follow the chapters from *In His Light*, we have so noted at the end of each chapter in this book.

Whether you are paging through this book for the first time or making a return journey, I pray that you will always find new and exciting insights into God's love and ways of responding to that love.

Using Journeying in His Light with In His Light

For those using *In His Light* and *Journeying in His Light* for the initiation process, the following schema might prove helpful. It lists those chapters where these two books parallel each other.

• • • • Evangelization and Precatechumenate • • • •

In His Light	*Journeying in His Light*
	Topic: Invitation
	Topic: Journey
	Topic: Insight—Faith
	Topic: Hope
	Topic: Love
Chapter 1 (God)	Topic: God
Chapter 2 (Knowing God Better—OT)	Topic: Knowing God Better—OT
Chapter 3 (Jesus)	Topic: Jesus
Chapter 4 (Holy Spirit)	Topic: Holy Spirit
Chapter 5 (Sin and Life)	Topic: Sin and Life

• • • • Catechumenate • • • •

Chapter 6 (Church)	Topic: Church
Chapter 7 (Sacraments)	Topic: Sacraments
Chapter 8 (Baptism)	Topic: Baptism
Chapter 9 (Confirmation)	Topic: Confirmation
Chapter 10 (Eucharist)	Topic: Eucharist
Chapter 11 (Reconciliation)	Topic: Reconciliation
Chapter 12 (Anointing)	Topic: Anointing
Chapter 13 (Marriage)	Topic: Marriage
Chapter 14 (Holy Orders)	Topic: Holy Orders
Chapter 15 (Last Things)	Topic: Last Things

Acknowledgments

The first edition of this book was originally written in 1978 at the urging of the Evangelization Commission of the Diocese of Wheeling-Charleston. The Commission was looking for a book which would express in a simple and timely fashion the developing thought taking place in Catholic belief. I am indebted to those past members of the Evangelization Commission for their time and encouragement.

I am most especially grateful to Sister Anne Francis Bartus SSJ, D.Min., for her many insights and corrections in the original edition and in each of the following revisions. I thank the Sisters of St. Joseph of the Diocese of Wheeling-Charleston who have contributed a great deal to this book, especially Sister Celestine Anderson SSJ, Sister Mary Grace Freeman SSJ, and Sister Immaculate Spires SSJ. I also thank Father Gary P. Naegele, M.A., and Father Anthony Cincinnati, Ph.D., who have offered helpful suggestions for this revision.

To these, and to so many others who in some way contributed to this book, I express my deepest gratitude.

Prologue

One night, a father decided that his son was now old enough to go out to the barn to feed the horses. The boy, however, told his father that he was afraid of the dark. The father stepped out onto the porch with the boy, lit a lantern, gave it to his son, and asked him how far he could see as he held up the lantern.

"I can see halfway down the path," said the boy. The father directed his son to carry the lantern halfway down the path. When the boy reached that point, the father asked the boy how far he could see now. The boy called back to the father that he could see to the gate. The father urged the boy to walk to the gate, and when the boy was at the gate, the father asked how far he could now see.

"I can see the barn," came the boy's reply. The father encouraged the boy to go to the barn and open the door. When the boy finally shouted back that he was at the barn and could see the horses, the father simply called, "Now feed the horses," and stepped into the house.

The point of this book and the point of the story are the same. The path this book attempts to light up is the path of understanding to God and the Church. As the boy walked with the lantern, he came to see the path, the gate, and the barn. He did not see the whole yard or the fields that surrounded him. Only daylight would provide that gift. Similarly, this book will shed light on only a portion of the topics it discusses.

Indeed, whole books have been written on each chapter. As a start, readers must first become familiar with the path of understanding. Having done that, they can look beyond to the wider context which other books illuminate.

In His Light consists primarily of questions in bold print and answers in italic print, followed by explanations of the answers in ordinary print. These questions and answers are stepping stones toward understanding the larger message. Wherever possible, technical words have been avoided so that readers may easily recognize what is at the heart of Christianity—deep joy and love—and may leave the reader with a desire to know more. If this happens and if it leads to further study of any topic, the book will have served its purpose well.

1 In Search of God

Introduction

A man and woman strolling along the beach stopped to look at a piece of sea-worn driftwood. The woman decided that the driftwood would fit in beautifully beside the fireplace at their bungalow. On another day, when her mood was more sullen, the woman might never have noticed the driftwood. But the morning sun, the sound of the waves, and the feel of the cool water and warm sand had lifted her to a greater awareness on this morning.

The man saw only a gnarled piece of wood, caked in mud and seaweed, that had drifted onto the beach with other pieces of sea litter. The sea shells, he decided, were pretty at least, but this old piece of wood had no place in anyone's home. However, he had promised his wife that this would be "her day," so he carried the driftwood back to the bungalow.

Some people view God with the same kind of eyes that the beachcombers turned on the driftwood. Some see God shining throughout the whole of life—in life's joyful, beautiful moments as well as in its sad, tragic moments. No matter what happens, God is there and God is still beautiful. Others see God only in the good moments. When a tragedy strikes, they say, "How can I believe in a good God when God allows this tragedy in my life?" But others live under the strong, fresh breeze of faith.

When we speak of God, we must also speak of how people experience God. This chapter will strive to share an insight into God that will help us to experience God at all moments of life—and perhaps to know God better.

1. Who are we?

a. We are members of the human family and the center of God's creation.

In the opening story of creation found in the book of Genesis, the author describes God's creation of the world, beginning with the separation of light from darkness and ending with the crowning event of creation, the creation of human beings. Only in the creation of human beings does God say that they are created ". . . in our image, according to our likeness" (Genesis 1:26). This does not mean that our shape is the shape of God, as though God has hands, legs, or a material body like ours, but it means that we share in some way in God's ability to think, act, judge, love, and choose freely. As members of the human family, we are special and central to God's creation.

The message found in the opening chapters of the Bible points out that every other detail of creation was created for the sake of human creation. The vast and intricate design of the universe not only tells us about the greatness of God, but it also tells of the importance of our human family in the eyes of God. In the Old Testament, or Hebrew Scriptures, we read the prayer of the psalmist who praises God for the goodness shown to human beings when he writes, "Yet you have made them a little lower than God, and crowned them with glory and honor. You have given them dominion over the works of your hands, and put all things under their feet" (Psalm 8:5–6, verses 6–7 in the NAB).

b. We are people who seek meaning and fulfillment in life.

Although we can live in happiness and contentment for many years, we finally discover that we have a restlessness of spirit which keeps us reaching out for a greater meaning and fulfillment in life. The woman on the beach in the opening story wanted a gnarled piece of wood as a decoration beside her fireplace, but, in time, she and her husband began to take the decoration for granted, and they would eventually be looking for other gifts in their lives. As members of the human family, we eventually discover that we become restless to continue our quest for something more deeply satisfying.

4

Many of us discover the answer to that quest in our response to the love of God in our lives. Augustine, a saint who lived around the late fourth and early fifth centuries, wrote that our lives are restless until they rest in God. A psalmist writing in the Old Testament spoke the same sentiments when he wrote, "My soul longs, indeed it faints for the courts of the Lord; my heart and my flesh sing for joy to the living God" (Psalm 84:2, verse 3 in NAB).

c. Our fulfillment lies in loving and serving God in this life and sharing eternal happiness with God.

As members of the human family, we are called to know, love, and serve God and one another. Our years on this earth are not given to us simply to test us for heaven, but we have a responsibility and call to help develop creation according to God's plan. In the New Testament, or Christian Scriptures, we read in the First Letter of John about the necessity of loving one another if we wish to claim that we love God. The author writes, "Those who say, 'I love God,' and hate their brothers or sisters, are liars" (1 John 4:20). Our fulfillment in this life lies in knowing, loving, and serving God and every member of the human family.

Our eternal fulfillment comes through happiness with God which surpasses all attempts to describe it. Paul, the great apostle of the early Church, writes in his letter to a Christian community at Corinth, ". . . no eye has seen, nor ear heard, nor the human heart conceived, what God has prepared for those who love him" (1 Corinthians 2:9).

In another letter, Paul faces the need for fulfillment both in this life and in the life hereafter. As he preaches the message of Jesus, he recognizes his special call on earth and his strong desire to be with God. He writes, "I am hard pressed between the two: my desire is to depart and be with Christ, for that is far better; but to remain in the flesh is more necessary for you" (Philippians 1:23–24). We have a mission and purpose here on earth, and we have a call to eternal happiness with God. In both of these lies our meaning and fulfillment as members of the human family.

d. We are a people who constantly seek to know more about God, our Creator.

As a group, human beings are curious, wanting to know the deep mysteries of the physical as well as the spiritual world. We strive to know the meaning of life, and we seek to understand the mind of a Creator who gave us such a creation. Some try to explain away the idea of such a Creator, while most of us accept it with lively faith. Faith consists in believing what we cannot see. Although we cannot see God as God truly exists, we continue to want to learn more about God so that we might love God more deeply. That is the purpose of beginning a study such as the one presented in this book.

2. Who is God?

a. We cannot fully understand the nature of God.

Even before we are born, we begin to experience life around us. Researchers of prenatal life tell us, for example, that a mother's stress can affect the infant in her womb. After birth, as our capacity for experiencing increases, so does our knowledge.

As children, we touch a hot stove and learn what the word "burn" means. Some years later, we enter school and our teachers make use of our past experiences to teach us. "Dry ice can burn us as badly as a hot stove," we are told. We remember how a hot stove burned us and we learn something new about dry ice by comparing it to something in our experience, namely, the hot stove.

Because we learn first through our senses, it's not surprising that, when we come to speak of God, we have a problem. We find nothing in our experience to compare with God. We learn that God has no limits, but we find nothing in our experience without limits. A house is limited by walls, a sea is limited by shores, and our very person is limited by a body. We learn that God is all powerful, but we know that even the strongest person or machine in the world can lift only so many pounds without breaking. We learn that God is all knowing, yet our experience tells us that even the most intricate computer cannot know everything. Ultimately, we must admit that a person without limits can never be understood by minds that are limited.

We cannot understand the nature of God because God has no limits. If someone challenged us with the words, "Tell me all about God so that I can know God perfectly," that person would be asking for something absurd. If we could know and describe God perfectly, God would not be God. God is limitless and far beyond our powers of understanding. The psalmist writes of God, "Great is the Lord, and greatly to be praised; God's greatness is unsearchable" (Psalm 145:3).

b. Ancient pagan cultures understood their gods by the way the gods touched their lives.

When a storm raged among people of ancient times, they would run to their altars to sacrifice animals and, at times, even human beings to appease the storm gods. Before a voyage, they would worship the sea gods. To these people, a god was the power or force who affected the mainstream of their lives. God was the sea who could either become angry or calm, depending upon the way the people treated their god. The summer god would hold back the refreshing rains when people ignored their god. Many of the unexplained mysteries that brought terror or tragedy into the lives of ancient people became gods to these peoples. They understood their gods through the very experiences of their lives. This was the way the gods touched them, and the only way they could speak of their gods.

c. The Old Testament authors often spoke of God as one who related to their lives.

In one of the stories of creation, the authors tell of God preparing the earth for the human family. Even when these people sinned, the love and mercy of God became apparent as God gave them other chances, over and over again. God showed a power greater than that of the Egyptian Pharaoh when Moses was able to lead the chosen people out of slavery. God showed a deep love in preparing a land for the people of Israel and in forgiving the sins of David, the great Hebrew king. When the writers of the Bible spoke of God, they spoke of God's love, power, mercy, anger, and overwhelming knowledge shown through God's dealings with the chosen people. The ancient Israelites worshiped the one God, not because they understood all about God, but because of the way God touched their lives with power and love. In a prayer from the Old Testament,

7

we read, "O come, let us worship and bow down, let us kneel before the Lord, our Maker! For he is our God, and we are the people of his pasture, and the sheep of his hand" (Psalm 95:6–7).

d. We can define God by understanding how God relates to us.

When we define God, we must accept our limitations. We have nothing in our experience to compare with God. But, like the people of the Scriptures, we too can speak of God who relates to us. When we experience love for our families, we know that a loving God has shared love with us. When we speak of an all-loving God, we reflect on our ability to love and realize that it merely hints at the love that the Creator of the world must possess. The human power of conceiving and constructing a great building points to a greater power that conceived and created our universe. When we stand in amazement at the knowledge that allows us to launch explorers off into space, we recall the creative knowledge that knew that space before it even existed. When we proclaim that God is all-loving, all-powerful and all-knowing, we declare that our experience of love, power, and knowledge reflects only a shadow of God's true person.

3. What do we mean by faith?

a. We call belief in God an act of faith.

In its broadest sense, faith is believing in that which we do not see. Each day, we live with a human expression of faith. When someone tells us that he or she loves us, we must take that on faith. We have no way of delving into that person's feelings to determine the truth of the statement. Through that person's actions, we find evidence of such a statement, but ultimately, we must "take it on faith."

In the same fashion, when our television depicts a man or woman walking on the moon or being in a space craft, we believe that a television crew is accurately reporting what is taking place. Since we ourselves are not on the moon nor in the space craft, we accept this news in faith. Because we ourselves cannot verify everything in life, we depend on other sources for the truth. We must have faith in the truthfulness of others. Every day, our decisions and opinions are often shaped by acts of faith in other human beings.

Faith in God reaches beyond our daily human endeavors to the source of all creation. We do not see God, but we see the wonderful works of God in creation. Faith in God moves us to action. Faith consists in believing that God exists and responding in accord with our belief. Our faith in God shapes our decisions and opinions and leads us to worship God whom we believe exists. When we encounter tragedies in creation, our faith is challenged.

b. Faith is a gift from God.

Human beings do not merit faith in God, but receive it as a gift. When Peter professed that Jesus was the Christ, the Son of the living God, Jesus told him that "flesh and blood" did not reveal this to him, but that he received this gift from God.

Although faith is a gift from God, the act of believing depends upon our human response. True belief demands that we pledge ourselves to that which we believe. Although we believe in God, we still have the free will to act according to that belief or to reject it. Belief in God does not take away our human ability to reason, nor does it limit our human freedom. Faith in God calls for a free assent to the whole truth given to us by God.

We can lose or weaken this gift of faith if we do not seek to learn more about God and to nourish faith by good works. The Scriptures teach us about God and how God calls us to respond to the gifts of creation. When we sin or ignore God, we can gradually reject this gift of faith in our lives and may even reach a stage where we lose our faith in God altogether.

c. Faith does not contradict true science or history.

The one and same God created the universe and reveals through creation as well as through the Scriptures. This means that our discoveries concerning the universe do not contradict faith, nor does faith contradict what is explicitly known about the universe. When an apparent contradiction occurs between faith and other fields of knowledge, scholars in these fields should investigate the question to arrive at the truth. God not only provides the gift of faith, but God enlightens minds in their search for truth.

4. What do the Scriptures tell us about God?

a. The Scriptures tell us that God is a loving, personal God.

Throughout the Old Testament, we read of God's continual concern and compassion for the chosen people. When they are in slavery, God frees them, and when they sin, God forgives them. When they seek a land and a kingdom, God grants it, and when they seem to lose all, God promises a savior. The psalms sing of the love and protection of God, and they continually proclaim the greatness of the God who has done so much for the people. In one of the psalms, we read, "For the Lord takes pleasure in his people, he adorns the humble with victory" (Psalm 149:4). Only a loving, living God could have led the people of the Old Testament to victory against all odds and given them hope when all seemed lost.

In the New Testament, Jesus tells us that he reflects the presence of God among the people. In the Gospel of John, we read, "Whoever believes in me believes not in me but in him who sent me. And whoever sees me sees him who sent me" (John 12:44–45). In the person of Jesus, we see the love, compassion, forgiveness, and concern of God for all people. Reflecting on the life and message of Jesus Christ, the author of the First Letter of John can write about the love of God, "In this is love, not that we loved God but that he loved us and has sent his Son to be the atoning sacrifice for our sins" (1 John 4:10).

A central, revealed theme of the Scriptures is that God is a God of love who lives and invites us to respond with love.

b. The Scriptures tell us that God is a spirit who knows all and is present to all.

The Scriptures tell us that God cannot be confined to space and time, since God has no limitations such as a body. God is a spiritual being, present in all places and for all time. No matter where we go or try to hide, we can never escape from the presence of God. Because God is a spiritual being, God is able to know all and see all. The psalmist expresses this belief when he writes, "O Lord, you have searched me and known me. You know when I sit down and when I rise up; you discern my thoughts from far away" (Psalm 139:1–2). A few verses later, the same psalmist speaks of the continual presence of God's spirit when he writes, "Where can I go from your spirit? Or where can I flee from your presence? If I ascend to heaven, you are there; if I make my bed in She'ol, you are there" (Psalm 139:7–8).

When Jesus tells the people to fast, pray, and offer alms in secret, he reminds them that God sees their hidden actions and will reward them for these good deeds. Matthew records these words of Jesus when he writes, ". . . so that your alms may be done in secret; and your Father who sees in secret will reward you" (Matthew 6:4).

God not only created the world, but God remains present to the world, knowing all and guiding those who respond in faith to this presence. The Spirit of the Lord fills the whole world.

c. The Scriptures tell us that God is without beginning and without end.

Although we live in time, we believe that God had no beginning and will have no end. This is difficult for us to understand since we are familiar with lives that begin and end (at least on this earth). From the Scriptures, we learn that God has neither beginning nor end. The psalmist again puts into words the living faith of the people when he prays, "Before the mountains were brought forth, or ever you had formed the earth and the world, from everlasting to everlasting you are God" (Psalm 90:2). The people of Israel believed that God always existed and would continue to exist into eternity.

In the opening verses of the Gospel of John, in the New Testament, we read about the creation of the world. When the author uses the expression, "In the beginning . . . ," he is actually speaking of God's existence before the beginning. The author of this Gospel writes, "In the beginning was the Word, and the Word was with God, and the Word was God. He was in the beginning with God" (John 1:1–2). The New Testament speaks not only of the presence of God before the beginning of time, but it speaks of the continued presence of God at the end of time. This presence is one we too will share—the eternal presence of God. The author of the First Letter of John writes, "God gave us eternal life, and this life is in His Son" (1 John 5:11).

God is eternal, and we have a hope of sharing in this eternal glory.

d. The Scriptures reveal these and many other insights into God.

Throughout the Scriptures, we are continually learning more about God through the people of the Old Testament and through Jesus Christ. To say that God is a living, loving, personal God who exists eternally, and who, as a spiritual being, is able to know all and be present to all is only the tip of the iceberg. We must reflect upon these truths, apply them to our lives, and understand how they touch us in our desire to know and love God more deeply. Our journey consists not only in knowing about God, but of a desire to serve and love God and every member of the human family.

5. Can we know about God from our human experience alone?

a. We can know some things about God through human experience alone.

Nature provides us with many signs of God's presence and powers. Although we have natural proofs of God's existence in creation, we still need the gift of faith to respond to these gifts. Without faith, we can simply keep saying, "Maybe we have not discovered the answer yet. We know a lot more now than we did a century ago, and perhaps in the next century we shall learn the answer to these mysteries in nature." With faith, the natural proofs of God's existence help to reinforce our faith by showing that belief in God's existence is not contrary to our human experience.

Paul, in writing to the Romans, reminds them that the pagans among them had faith in God through the "things he has made," but they refused to accept this as an incentive to worship the one true God. The basic faith was there, but they ignored the evidence of the world around them. Paul writes, "For what can be known about God is plain to them, because God has shown it to them. Ever since the creation of the world his eternal power and divine nature, invisible though they are, have been understood and seen through the things he has made. So they are without excuse; for though they knew God, they did not honor him as God or give thanks to him, but they became futile in their thinking, and their senseless minds were darkened" (Romans 1:19–21). In Paul's eyes, the sin of the pagans was their unwillingness to develop their faith, despite the evidence given by God in the world around them.

b. Our human experience supports our faith by showing that God must always have existed, without beginning.

When a baby is born, we congratulate the parents. The baby did not just suddenly appear in the world; every infant came from parents. When we see a painted picture, we ask the name of the artist. The painting did not suddenly fall together on the canvas. Everything in our experience had something or someone preceding it. Even the first parents had to come from someone, along with the earth they stood on and the food they ate. We keep going back in our experience until we stand alone with God who has no beginning but who put all this in mo-tion. At some point, our experience tells us that someone must have ex-isted with no one before that person. And if this is so, that person, God, always existed, with no beginning. The psalmist writes, "Before the mountains were brought forth, or ever you had formed the earth and the world, from ever-lasting to everlasting you are God" (Psalm 90:2).

c. Our human experience supports our faith by showing that God is an intelligent God.

As we look at the universe that surrounds us, we smile in wonder that anyone could ever suggest that it happened by chance. The perfect nervous system that a child shows at the moment of birth astounds the greatest minds. The many stars and planets of the universe that hold each other in place by varying forces of gravity could never be fully understood or repeated, even on a minor scale. Only a perfect, powerful, intelligent God could have planned so intricate a universe and a creation that works so well. The psalmist writes, "You made the moon to mark the seasons; the sun knows its time for setting. You make darkness, and it is night, when all the animals of the forest come creeping out" (Psalm 104:19–20).

d. Our human experience supports our faith by showing that God is a loving God.

Love is central to our creation. When we experience love, we experience lightheartedness, tenderness, simple contentment, and happiness. When we lack the experience of love, we grow sad, lonely, and deeply unhappy. Since love affects the whole of human experience so deeply, we look to the Creator, namely, God, and conclude from our experience that only a loving person can share love. For this reason, we believe in a loving God, not only because of the message of God's love learned from the Scriptures, but also because of our own human experience of loving.

6. How does God show concern for the world God created?

a. God keeps the world in existence.

Not only did the world need God for its creation, it also needs God to continue in existence. God created a world that is continually developing and growing. For this to happen, God must keep the world and all its creatures in mind, or the world ceases to exist. The mere fact of our existence tells us that God is showing concern for the world God created.

In the Gospel of Matthew, we read about God's concern for creation. The author of the Gospel gives us a message of Jesus who says, "Are not two sparrows sold for a penny? Yet not one of them will fall to the ground apart from your Father. And even the hairs of your head are all counted. So do not be afraid; you are of more value than many sparrows" (Matthew 10:29–31).

b. God shared with us the dignity of being co-creators.

God shared with us all the gifts of creation. We are called to understand these gifts more fully and use them more effectively in building up the world. By understanding the process of healing in the human body, doctors are able to help people heal more quickly and painlessly. By understanding the laws of gravity and stress, great minds achieve spectacular results that allow large bridges to span rivers and tall buildings to stretch skyward. As co-creators, we reach out in the universe to explore God's gifts and discover greater uses for these gifts. Because of the hope God had for human creation, God placed in our hands the ability to struggle with an incomplete world and to help God bring it to the completion God has planned. By doing so, human beings share in the dignity of being co-creators with God.

From the very beginning, human beings were destined to share in God's creative work. The message found in the first book of the Bible speaks of God's creation of human beings with a special co-creative task. The author writes, ". . . male and female he created them. God blessed them, and God said to them, 'Be fruitful and multiply, and fill the earth and subdue it; and have dominion over the fish of the sea and over the birds of the air and over every living thing that moves upon the earth' " (Genesis 1:27–28). The mission to work does not come to us as a result of sin, but, as the opening book of the Bible tells us, it comes to us from God's creative plan. From the beginning, we have been called to the dignity of being co-creators with God.

c. God gives help and guidance as we seek it.

God helps and guides us in our quest to understand and develop the world. God is an inviting God. God does not force this help and guidance upon us, but allows us to respond to an invitation to call upon God. With our belief in God's help in our lives, we dare to attempt more than we would attempt alone. We do not depend solely upon our talents or knowledge; rather we learn to depend upon God for help. The prayer of the psalmist reminds us of our need to call upon God: "On the day I called, you answered me, you increased my strength of soul" (Psalm 138:3).

d. God loves the world.

Some portray God as a condemning God, just waiting for people to step out of line in order to punish them. This unfortunate image of God has caused many to deny or to fear God. The Scriptures do not portray this image of God. The Scriptures speak of a God who continually seeks to forgive and to show love. Throughout the Scriptures, we learn that God will never abandon God's people, even if they should abandon God. A psalmist again captures the true image of God when he writes, "They feast on the abundance of your house, and you give them drink from the river of your delights. For with you is the fountain of life; in your light we see light. O continue your steadfast love to those who know you, and your salvation to the upright of heart!" (Psalm 36:8–10, verses 9–11 in NAB).

7. What name do we give people who deny or doubt God's existence?

a. An agnostic is a person who claims ignorance of God's existence.

An agnostic neither denies nor accepts the existence of God. The agnostic simply says, "I do not know if God exists." Some who do not know whether God exists make an honest effort to try to discover an answer to their questions concerning God. Others, however, make use of their ignorance to avoid facing the question of God and all it involves. Although they seem to become indifferent, they are often living with an atheistic attitude toward life without admitting it.

b. An atheist is a person who claims that God does not exist.

For the atheist, there is no doubt. Belief in God is absurd. Many atheists feel so strongly about their denial of God that they spend a great deal of time and money spreading their message. Atheism is not something new in our modern world. In the Old Testament, we read the words of a psalmist who proclaims the foolishness of the atheist. The psalmist writes, "Fools say in their hearts, 'There is no God.' They are corrupt, they do abominable deeds; there is no one who does good" (Psalm 14:1).

Atheism takes many forms. Along with an outright denial of God, some atheists practice a form of materialism which limits their needs and desires only to this world. Human beings become the center and controllers of their own life and responsible for their own destiny which is limited to this world alone. Some believe that true liberty comes through social and economic freedom. Such an attitude views religion as a means of deceiving human beings with a false hope for a future life, thus discouraging them from seeking a better life on earth.

c. Some people who proclaim a belief in God live as though God does not exist.

Some people who glibly say that God exists often betray a disbelief in God by their daily lives. By their actions and their lack of advert-ing to God's presence in life, these people lead lives that some refer to as the life of a "practical atheist." Life moves along with all its decisions, tragedies, joys, and pleasures with no thought of God. The fact of God's existence has no effect on their lives—to the point that in the real day-to-day living of their lives, God does not exist. Because their lives lack the awareness of God's presence, we could say that such people are atheists in practice.

d. A person who believes in God may pass through periods of doubt or nonbelief.

As we grow and mature throughout life, we relate to people around us in different ways. As children, we fully depend upon our parents. To approach God with child-like dependence comes easily in our early years. During the teenage years and early twenties, breaking away from the authority of the Church comes as easily as breaking away from the authority of the home. Just as parents no longer have wise answers to all the problems in life, so apparently God no longer has wise answers. In the process of learning how to relate to God in a new way during these years, many pass through stages of doubt or nonbelief. During the years when we struggle to break away from the nest and all images of authority, we change our way of relating to God. Some never learn how to relate as a mature adult to God. Others will gradually move from rejection to a greater understanding of God in their lives. We should not panic during these years of doubt, but rather pray for those struggling with this stage in their growth pattern. Hopefully, they will grow toward a greater appreciation of the faith of their roots, with a deeper, more mature relationship with God.

Jesus told a parable about weeds and wheat which reminds us that we cannot always identify those who are good and bad. A farmer had planted some wheat, and an enemy came during the night to plant weeds among the wheat. The farmer decided to allow the weeds and the wheat to grow together, lest in an attempt to root out the weeds, the wheat would also be lost. At harvest time, the wheat would be separated from the weeds. Through this parable, Jesus is telling us that some people, who seem to be the "weeds" of creation, may, at a later time in their lives, prove to be the true wheat and harvest of God's creation. History abounds with the stories of sinners who eventually became saints. The wisdom of Jesus recognized the fact of God's grace and human conversion in creation (see Matthew 13:24–30).

8. Why does God allow suffering?

a. Suffering in life is one of the great mysteries of God's creation.

Why is there disease or sickness in the world? Why do innocent babies die and good, loving people suffer so agonizingly as they near death? Sometimes, the wicked of this world seem to die well or live in luxury. It is a fact of life that the good as well as the bad suffer. Some suffering comes from human selfishness and carelessness. This we can accept as a partial answer for suffering in the world. But why does the innocent baby die at birth when the mother has followed all the rules? Why does the loving, concerned father suddenly die from a heart attack? No matter how many answers we seek for these questions, we must finally admit that they are part of the mysteries of God's creation. If we were to believe that our lives ended here, the answer would be even more difficult. Somewhere, in God's loving plan, lies the answer to suffering in the world.

b. God does not cause suffering in the world.

Suffering reminds us of the incompleteness of our creation. God established the world to move in a certain direction, and God gave the human person free will to share in bringing the world to completion. The striving for this completeness will go on as long as the world exists, and we must never stop working in this direction.

God created the world as though it were on a journey toward perfection. Like any lengthy journey, it will have its joys and fulfillments as well as its tragedies and disappointments. When we stop striving for perfection and the completion of this creation, we will only increase suffering.

When a person suffers, we can never say that God directly caused or planned that particular suffering. In the plan of creation, God allowed suffering, but God did not cause suffering. Suffering and death happen as a normal process of life. God does not decide that on a particular day at a particular time we shall suffer or die. God set up the process of life, and we become part of that process. How we live, the actions we take, the health received from our parents, the carefulness of others, and our continual use of free will often affects the amount and type of suffer-ing and, at times, the moment of our death. God set up a process of life that shares with us health and happiness, sickness and sadness. We continually strive to bring this process to completion by alleviating causes of sickness and sadness and other forms of suffering, but we recognize the fact that suffering and death are part of our incomplete creation.

Paul, the apostle, recognizes the struggle of the world as it reaches toward its fulfillment. He writes, "for the creation was subjected to futility, not of its own will but by the will of the one who subjected it, in hope that the creation itself will be set free from its bondage to decay and will obtain the freedom of the glory of the children of God. We know that the whole creation has been groaning in labor pains until now" (Romans 8:20–22). Despite the suffering found in creation, Paul has a living hope that the end will bring freedom from suffering.

c. God's love calls us to heal suffering.

When we suffer, our faith in God is tested. Without suffering as part of the normal process of life, we might never have a chance to prove just how deeply we love God. In reality, it is not what happens to us that speaks of our love and faithfulness, but rather how we respond to what happens to us. A small pain can cause continual complaining on the part of some, while deep, continuous pain can cause others to reflect on their dependence upon God's strength. A suffering person can often renew the faith of others who see the love of God reflected even in the midst of suffering.

Even though we do not know fully the answer to the mystery of pain, we should still strive to alleviate pain and suffering wherever possible in God's creation. As co-creators with God, we share in the call to bring healing to a broken world. This includes physical as well as spiritual healing. The story of the Good Samaritan, told by Jesus, describes a virtuous Samaritan who helps a battered stranger by dressing his wounds and providing housing for him. Jesus praises the Samaritan for his concern for the physical well-being of the stranger (see Luke 10:25–37).

9. How do we touch God in our daily lives?

a. We can touch God through a continual awareness of God's presence in our lives.

Because God is all-knowing and all-loving, we believe God constantly keeps us in mind. God is always with us, knowing us and loving us. We should strive to return this love by reminding ourselves of God's presence. At times, we become so involved in our day-to-day joys and struggles that we often forget that God is sharing these joys and struggles with us. At any moment of the day, we can say to ourselves, "God is with me and loves me right now." By doing so, we are touching God and growing in consciousness of God's presence with us. The more we grow aware of this presence, the more perfectly we will live our lives.

b. We can touch God by setting aside a quiet time each day for prayer.

We tend to love the people with whom we communicate often throughout our lives. Husbands and wives learn the importance of communication in marriage. As long as they communicate, they continually meet each other and love each other. When communication ceases, loss of love often follows. Prayer is simply communicating with God. What we say to God is not as important as the fact that we spend time in communication. Because we are made for God, our lives will never reach fulfillment unless we spend some time communicating with God. We actually need this communication. This form of communication with God fits the traditional definition of prayer, which is the raising of our minds and hearts to God.

When we neglect to pray, we try to make others fill the gap in our lives that only God can fill. This leads to frustration and unhappiness. We should set aside a quiet time each day to speak with God or simply to sit in silence and let God speak to us. This quiet time can exist when all is quiet around us or even when all is noisy around us. The quiet time is within. On a bus going to work, while preparing lunch, or while jogging, we can withdraw alone into ourselves to speak with God. Through this quiet time for prayer, we reach out to God's presence in our lives.

c. We can touch God through "formal" or "informal" prayer.

In the Bible, the disciples asked Jesus to teach them to pray. Jesus responded with the words and ideas that have shaped the "Lord's Prayer" prayed by Christians today. We pray:

Our Father, Who art in heaven,
Hallowed be Thy name;
Thy kingdom come;
Thy will be done
On earth as it is in heaven.
Give us this day our daily bread;
And forgive us our trespasses
As we forgive those who trespass against us;
And lead us not into temptation,
But deliver us from evil. Amen.

Prayers that have preformulated words, such as the "Lord's Prayer" are called *formal prayer. Informal prayer* refers to those prayers spoken in our own words, expressing our love for God either silently or in sharing with others. Both forms of praying have their place in loving and praising God.

Conclusion

The piece of driftwood has found a home beside the fireplace in the bungalow. The man and woman have long since forgotten the day they brought it home from the beach. Other gifts from the sea have found their way into the bungalow since that piece of driftwood arrived. Although the man and woman are no longer aware of the driftwood, they would notice something missing if it were stolen.

Their bungalow is a creation of their "vacation mind," rustic and reflective of the sea. The piece of driftwood sits clearly in the back of their minds, not drawing attention to itself, but one part of the whole picture.

Like that piece of driftwood, God becomes part of the fabric of our lives. God underlies the whole picture. Every now and then, we must take a steady look at God in our lives so that the presence of God does not fade into the shadows. The world around us, with its children, its gardens, its furnishings, and its painted walls, reflects our part in creation. In the midst of this world, the touch of God, the Creator and lover of creation, must always be felt.

For Scripture reflection and discussion concerning this chapter, see **Journeying in His Light, "In Search of God."**

2 Knowing God Better

Introduction

The man pushed a junk cart through the streets of Brooklyn, and called up to the open windows for old newspapers. One young boy of the neighborhood often joined the other boys in taunting the "junk man" until he would suddenly turn and take a few threatening steps in their direction. At that, the boys would scramble off down the street.

One day, the young boy was picnicking with his family at a neighborhood park. To his amazement, he saw the "junk man," cheaply dressed but clean, playing with some children who were apparently his own. The boy felt ashamed and sad when he saw that the "junk man" was actually someone's father. He realized that his own father could have been a "junk man." Life had treated his father a little more kindly.

The young boy never met the "junk man," but he felt he knew him a little better because he saw him playing with children in a park.

In this chapter, we get to know God a little better. We look not only through our own eyes to understand God, but also through the eyes of the Old Testament people. We try to understand these people, why they wrote, how they wrote, and what they tried to tell us about God. Through their histories, messages, prayers, and poetry, we come to know God better.

1. Where do we learn about God?

a. We first learn about God from people who touch our lives.

Most of us have first learned about God from our families. As we grew, we heard more about God from our teachers, our friends, and our minister or priest in church. The very exceptional person first learns about God through books. Unknowingly, we were developing ideas about God from the world around us and the people who shared in that world. Only later would we turn to books.

b. We deepen our understanding of God by listening to God's message as shared in the Bible.

Although many people are familiar with Bible stories, very few people have read the Bible from beginning to end. Most have heard certain stories drawn from the Bible that teach messages about living life in union with God. When a Bible story or lesson teaches something special, it very often reinforces what we have already learned through our growing process. By reading the Bible, we can begin to understand more about God and how God related to the Chosen People. Through these readings, we learn how we can relate to God in our world today. The Bible challenges us to clarify any false impressions we may have formed about God. We must not only read the Bible, but we must understand how to read it so that we can comprehend the message of the author.

c. We also learn about God from prayers and reflections found in other writings besides the Bible.

Some people have responded to God's presence in their lives by writing down their experiences of God or their innermost prayers and reflections on God's message. Through these writings, we learn how others have responded to God's presence in their lives. Though we do not view their way of approaching God as the only way, we can learn from these people. In their writings, we can learn about God's dealings with others who, in turn, share their gifts with us.

24

We must realize, however, that God deals with each of us in a slightly different manner according to our own personalities.

2. Is the Bible a single book?

a. The Bible consists of a collection of many writings composed or compiled at different stages of history.

Long before the messages of the Bible were committed to writing, they were shared through the spoken word. Eventually, the stories and preaching that the people shared concerning the action of God in their midst were written down for further generations. Certain writings took a central position in the lives of the people of God. In time, these writings were gathered together into the one book of the Bible.

b. Some books of the Bible had several different authors.

Throughout the Bible, we find that some books are collections from several different sources. On close inspection, for example, biblical scholars found different styles and emphases in the Book of Genesis. They even found different words used for *God.* They concluded that the Book of Genesis was a collection of four different writings (called Traditions) brought together by an editor at a later date. The editor was able to fit these stories into their proper place, thus giving later generations the impression that the Book of Genesis was the work of a single author.

c. The Bible consists of the Old Testament and the New Testament.

The word *Testament* means a covenant or agreement —in this case, between God and God's Chosen People. The Old Testament records the events from the creation of the world to the coming of Jesus. It describes the formation, development, and hopes of God's Chosen People. The New Testament treats the events of Jesus' life, his message, and the effect of that message on the early Church.

3. Why is the revelation in the Bible considered an important source of knowing God?

a. Divine revelation comes to us from God.

Human beings can know God to some degree through human knowledge alone, but there are some things we cannot know about God unless God reveals them. The Jewish faith and the Christian faith unfold throughout history. God's revelation comes to us through God's dealing with the Chosen People in the Old Testament and through the life and message of Jesus Christ in the New Testament. Under God's special guidance, the people of the Old Testament era drew conclusions about God that would provide insight into the power, love, mercy, and other unique attributes of God. This message of God, which became the source of Israelite worship, was preached and finally written in the Old Testament.

The New Testament has its source in Jesus Christ and the lived faith of the early apostles and the Christian community. The apostles of Jesus Christ, under the guidance of the Holy Spirit, handed on to us what they received from Jesus' life and teaching. The Christian message, given by Jesus Christ, was preached and practiced by the members of the early Church before a significant portion of it was written down in the New Testament. This lived faith comes down to us under the name of *tradition.* Both Scripture and tradition form a unified source of revelation and have the same goal. On the one hand, the New Testament writings do not contain the total revelation found in the Church's tradition, but on the other hand, tradition can never contradict the Scriptures. Since they both have the same source and goal, they must be in agreement .

b. God inspired certain people who compiled these revelations.

Throughout their history, the community shared among themselves stories and messages about God's presence in their midst. At certain points in history, these ideas were committed to writing under the guidance of God. As mentioned above, not all the preaching and teaching of the people found its way to the written page, but only those parts of the message that the writer, under the guidance of the Holy Spirit, chose from the oral traditions of God's people. We call this guidance *inspiration*. God did not dictate the message to these writers. The writers wrote according to their own worldview and their own style. The writers did not know they were committing the inspired word to writing. They simply reflected the revelation shared by the community in the language and style of the age in which they wrote. Occasionally, the writer might become the receiver and sharer of a new revelation to the community.

c. The Bible, taken as a whole, reflects the true message of God's revelation.

In order to decide the truth of any individual passage of the Bible, we must test that passage against the overall, constant teaching of the Bible. This constant teaching of the Bible is the inspired, revealed truth that the Bible teaches, free from error.

For example, in some Old Testament writings, the authors expressed ignorance or doubt about life after death. They believed not in their own life after death, but that their immortality continued in their children and their children's children. In the Book of Job, we read how death ends all: "But mortals die, and are laid low; humans expire, and where are they? As waters fail from a lake, and a river wastes away and dries up, so mortals lie down and do not rise again; until the heavens are no more, they will not awake or be roused out of their sleep" (Job 14:10–12). In the New Testament, we read clear statements of life after death. To quote the Book of Job as a proof that we have no life after death is to miss the gradual unfolding message of the Bible. This particular teaching of the Book of Job does not stand the test of the more consistent teaching of the Bible, which speaks of life after death.

d. The Church does not expect any new public revelation from God.

The Church teaches that public revelation ended with Jesus, who bears within himself God's definitive Word. The Church looks back to the unified source of Scripture and tradition as its only source of revelation and has no expectations of a new revelation from God.

This does not mean that we cannot have a new understanding of the deep mysteries already revealed by God. As our understanding and experience of the world changes, so can our understanding of God's revelation change and develop.

Private revelation refers to those experiences on the part of saintly people who claim to have heard God's message spoken to them. These private revelations, however, cannot contradict, improve, or complete Christ's revelation, since all public revelation has ended. Although Church authority may accept some private revelations as authentic, Christians have no obligation to follow any specific directions which have their source in these private revelations alone.

4. What is literary form?

a. The Bible consists of many different types of writings.

The Bible consists of hymns, prayers, poems, stories, historical narratives, prophecies, exhortations, and letters. To understand its message more fully, we should attempt to understand the type of writing chosen to convey the message. We should not read a story as though it were history, nor should we read a hymn as though it were a prophetic message. Besides trying to understand the type of writing, we should strive to understand the people who wrote the Bible. For example, our conception of historical writing differs vastly from that of the people who wrote history more than two thousand years ago, in a culture that had its birth almost halfway around the world from our own.

b. These different types of writing or forms of literature are called literary forms.

As we read a newspaper, we encounter several different forms of writing, or literary forms. On the first page, we may read about a bombing somewhere in the world, and we are saddened that a killing has taken place. The front page gives us factual news of the world. On the second page, we might read a small section that tells us of a certain pill that will cure arthritis. We recognize that this is an advertisement for the pill, so we pay little attention. Somewhere in the middle of the paper, certain writers express their opinion of world events. We listen to what they have to say, but we know that what they say is only opinion. On the sports page, we read that one baseball team has bombed another. If our team has taken the "bombing," we feel sad because our team lost the game. The word "bombing" has a different meaning on the sports page than it does on the first page of a newspaper. As we turn from page to page and read a different literary form, we do not have to be reminded to change our mindset. We have lived with these different literary forms, and we automatically accept them.

Unfortunately, when we pick up the Bible, we often expect that the people of ancient Israel are writing in the same literary forms used within our own history books. This is rarely the case. The people of ancient Israel were a more poetic people, interested in expressing the experience of the event and message, rather than the event itself. If they had a message to share, they would package that message neatly in a story that the people could listen to and repeat. In our century and past centuries, we often misunderstood the literary form of many biblical writings and read these stories as though they expressed historical events exactly as they happened. This led to many problems in trying unnecessarily to defend the scientific accuracy and historical truth of the Bible.

5. What is an example of literary form in the Bible?

a. In its early chapters, the Book of Genesis, the first book of the Bible, shows a good example of literary form.

Several centuries before Christ, while the Israelites were in exile from the Promised Land, they needed to keep alive the message of God's relationship to the world. Stories of the creation of the world originated during this period and were later joined with other creation stories to form the first chapters of Genesis. Many of the ideas for these stories could be found in even more ancient stories of other countries—for example, in the Egyptian stories about the tree

29

of life. By reading the creation stories closely, we can conclude that God used the genius of the people to share God's message of creation.

b. The story of creation is a literary form in which the message, not the history nor the science, is inspired by God.

In the first story of creation, the author makes use of the people's knowledge of a seven-day week with the special day of rest, namely, the Sabbath. He draws a poetic balance between the first three days of creation and the next three days. He uses a common poetic device that portrays the first three days as days of separation and the next three days as days of decoration. What God separates on the first day, God decorates on the fourth; what God separates on the second day, God decorates on the fifth, and what God separates on the third day, God decorates on the sixth. In diagram, the days line up as follows:

Separation / Decoration

1—Light from darkness	4—Sun, moon, stars
2—Sky from water	5—Birds and fish
3—Land from water	6—Animal and human life

7—God rests (Sabbath rest)

In describing the second day of creation, the author reveals an ignorance of the shape of the earth and the universe. The author has God creating a world that fits in perfectly with the worldview of ancient times, but does not correspond to our current knowledge of the world and universe.

We read in the Bible, "And God said, 'Let there be a dome in the midst of the waters, and let it separate the waters from the waters.' And God said, 'Let the waters under the sky be gathered together into one place, and let the dry land appear'" (Genesis 1:6, 9). The ancient view described here and accepted by people of biblical times could be drawn as follows:

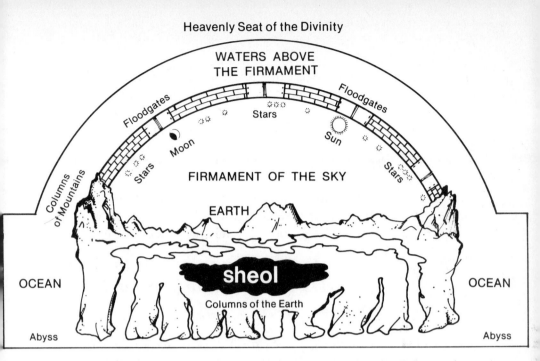

From these observations, we conclude that the "biblical days of creation" were not intended to be scientific explanations of the order of creation. Instead, through a poetic literary device, the writer conveys God's message: that God created the world out of chaos and that God put order into the world. God is greater than the "elements" and "the gods" that ride upon the dome of heaven. Indeed, these are not gods, but simply creations of the one true God. As God rested on the Sabbath, so every good Israelite should rest on the Sabbath. The story moves from the lesser creations to the greater, from light to the peak of creation, the human person.

c. In the second chapter of the Book of Genesis (2:4ff), the author contradicts chapter one by telling us that human life was created first, then animal life.

Chapter 2 tells its own story of creation as though chapter 1 does not exist. Apparently, the editor found another creation story and simply placed it where he felt it belonged in the Book of Genesis. It differs in style from chapter 1 and contradicts chapter 1 by having God create human life before animal life. Chapter 2 tells the story of Adam and Eve, who were placed in a Garden of Paradise, and there failed a great test given by God. Because they failed, they must work the land by the sweat of their brow and bear the pain of childbirth. This chapter suggests that human life is higher than animal life by moving from the greater form of life to the lower. It also conveys the message that marriage is God's idea, ". . . the two of them become one body," and that human beings, not God, are responsible for sin in the world. Again, the message, not the history or the science, is the essential point conveyed by this story told about our first parents. The Garden of Paradise, the first man and woman placed in that garden, and the events that led to the fall are simply literary devices in story form used to convey a message to God's people.

d. The use of this literary form continues to chapter eleven (Genesis 11:9) to show how sin is gripping the world.

Genesis 1 to 11:9 conveys in story form the creation of the world and its subsequent fall into the grip of sinfulness. These chapters are termed *prehistory*. The Bible does not intend to give a history of the world from creation to Abraham, but rather a religious explanation or interpretation of the origin of sin and suffering in creation. In these chapters, we read about Cain killing his brother Abel, and the continued growth of sin in the world. When the world becomes filled with sin, God destroys it with a flood, saving only Noah and his family. Ham, a son of Noah and the father of the nation of Canaan, commits a sin shortly after the flood ends, and he is cursed by Noah. The final sin of these chapters occurs when the people of the world decide to share their knowledge and build their own tower to heaven. The author pictures God as one who is concerned about the ability of these people to do whatever they want, even if it is contrary to God's will. God "confuses their tongues" so that they begin to speak different languages and can no longer work together. Abraham is the first truly historical person of the Bible.

6. What does the Book of Genesis tell us?

a. The message of the first eleven chapters of the Book of Genesis introduces us to God and human beings.

The first story of creation portrays a God of order who has the power and freedom to create the world out of nothing. God resides above all and has power over all. Creation, which comes from God's goodness, shares in God's goodness. The messenger tells us that "God saw it was good." In the message of the second story of creation, God enters the lives of human beings, sharing in their enjoyment of paradise. In this story, God resides outside of creation, but is also present within creation.

The biblical creation stories place human beings at the center of the creation. In the first creation story, the days of creation move from the lesser to the greater, from the creation of light to the final creation of human beings as the pinnacle of creation. In the second creation story, God plants a garden for human beings, creates human beings first and then animals, and finally delights to walk with human beings. God creates everything for the sake of human beings and gives them mastery over the earth.

The ultimate gift to human beings is a share in the image and likeness of God. This means that human beings share in God's own life through their knowledge and love. Like God, they possess the uniqueness and dignity of being more than an animal. Each human being is a person called to respond to God in faith and love. God called human beings to continue human creation through childbearing and to care for all creation. God made human beings male and female, both equal before God, yet both with specific and complimentary roles in creation. God breathed into them a soul which would give them a higher calling, beyond living for the world alone.

When human beings sought to become more powerful, to become in some way like God, they misused their free will and sinned. They brought evil and sin into the world. With sin came mistrust and a breakdown of the harmony which existed in the beginning. Human beings attempted to hide themselves from God and had difficulty communicating openly with each other. They recognized their nakedness. They blamed each other and experienced other consequences of their sin. Life became more difficult, more prone toward sinfulness, yet God did not abandon them. Near the end of the first eleven chapters of Genesis, we see the power of evil in the world. In the end, creation, despite its sinfulness, is still good, and God will remain with this good creation until the end of time.

b. The Book of Genesis continues with the era of the patriarchs.

God chose Abraham as the father of the Israelite nation. While reading the portion of the Bible which speaks of him, we should keep in mind that the story of Abraham was passed on from generation to generation before being written down. Within that time, legend grew. Although Abraham is apparently the first historical person in the Bible, we cannot say the narration about him is history in the modern sense. We are reading the epic of Abraham and his sons, bits of history embellished as the story passed from generation to generation. Again, we look to the message and find that Abraham's gift is his great faith and trust in God. In this narrative, God promises Abraham that he will be the father of a great nation and grants Abraham and his wife, Sarah, a child in their old age. The faith of Abraham is challenged when an angel of the Lord directs him to sacrifice his son Isaac, and Abraham's trust in God is shown as he prepares to kill Isaac. God, pleased with Abraham's faith, stops him from sacrificing Isaac. The faith of Abraham will become an example of perfect faith in the writings of the New Testament.

c. Genesis continues with the story of Isaac, Jacob, and the twelve sons of Jacob.

Short sections of the book of Genesis tell of Isaac and Jacob and their special duty in carrying on the tradition of Abraham. Isaac, the son of Abraham, has two sons, Esau and Jacob. Although Esau is the firstborn, God chooses Jacob to carry on the traditions of Abraham. Jacob has twelve sons, whose names will play an important role in establishing the families of Israel centuries later.

d. A large portion of Genesis deals with one of Jacob's sons, Joseph, who becomes responsible for the family of Jacob settling in Egypt.

Of Jacob's sons, Joseph becomes a favorite, and the other sons of Jacob become jealous of Joseph. Joseph is a dreamer who sees his brothers symbolically bowing down to him in his dreams. When he relates his dreams to his brothers, they become angry with him and eventually sell him into slavery to some merchants. They tell Jacob that Joseph was killed by a wild animal.

In Egypt, the pharaoh's wife, rejected by Joseph, accuses him of trying to seduce her, and the pharaoh has him cast into prison. Years later, the pharaoh has a dream and has Joseph, the interpreter of dreams, brought to him. Joseph interprets the dream, telling the pharaoh that there will be seven years of plenty and seven years of famine over the land. The pharaoh places Joseph second to him in charge of the land. For the first seven years, Joseph leads the people in storing up enough food to feed the people for the seven years of famine. During these last seven years, the family of Joseph come to Egypt for food. Joseph recognizes them, and, after causing them some difficulty, has them all brought to Egypt to settle.

The story of Joseph takes up a large portion of the Book of Genesis, and its purpose is to relate how the Hebrew people came to settle in Egypt. This sets the scene for the next book of the Bible, the Book of Exodus.

7. How did the Israelites come to settle in Palestine?

a. The Book of Exodus records the journey of the Israelites out of slavery in Egypt, through the wandering in the desert, to the borders of the Promised Land, Palestine.

Four hundred years elapse between the end of the book of Genesis and the beginning of the Book of Exodus. During that time, Egyptian rulers, called pharaohs, came into power. Before this, Egypt was ruled by Semitic pharaohs of the same background as the Hebrews (who were later called Israelites). The new Egyptian pharaohs, fearing that the rapid growth of the Hebrew tribes would threaten their hold on the kingdom, forced the Hebrews into slavery. When the Book of Exodus begins, they had struggled and suffered under slavery for some time.

When Moses was a child, the pharaoh ordered that all male children be killed. But Moses escaped death when the pharaoh's daughter found him in a basket among the reeds and eventually adopted him. When Moses grew up, he killed an Egyptian who was striking one of his Hebrew kin. Moses fled into the desert lest the Egyptians discover his crime and kill him. In the desert, he married, had a son, and lived as a shepherd.

After some years, an angel of the Lord appeared to him in a burning bush, and God spoke from the bush, directing Moses to free the Hebrew people from the slavery of Egypt. Since the people were not allowed to use the name of "God," Moses was told to say to the people that "I AM" sent him. In this title, the people would recognize that the source of all creation sent him to lead them from slavery.

On the night they fled Egypt, the Hebrews first celebrated the most significant event of their history. Each household killed a lamb, painted its blood on the doorposts, and ate the lamb as people ready for a journey. The author of the Book of Exodus tells how the angel of death passed over the doors painted with the blood but killed the firstborn children and animals of the Egyptians. Each year, the Hebrew nation would celebrate this feast of the Passover, and it would play a central role in the passion of Jesus. Because of the slaughter of this evening, the pharaoh called Moses and ordered him to take his people and leave.

b. In the desert of Mount Sinai, God delivers to Moses the Ten Commandments.

The most famous and best known moral teachings of many western religions center in some way around the Ten Commandments. As Moses received these (in the story of Sinai), the number was not so clearly given. However, down through the years, the Church has numbered these commandments as ten and listed them as follows:

36

1. "I am the Lord your God, who brought you out of the land of Egypt, out of the house of slavery; you shall have no other gods before me."
2. "You shall not make wrongful use of the name of the Lord your God, for the Lord will not acquit anyone who misuses his name."
3. "Remember the sabbath day and keep it holy."
4. "Honor your father and your mother. . . ."
5. "You shall not murder."
6. "You shall not commit adultery."
7. "You shall not steal."
8. "You shall not bear false witness against your neighbor."
9. "You shall not covet your neighbor's wife."
10. "You shall not covet your neighbor's house. . ." (Exodus 20:2–3, 7–8, 12–17).

The Book of Exodus goes on to explain these laws and others more at length.

The Ten Commandments became the central law of the people of Israel, and Jesus emphasized their importance by quoting some of them to the people of his own day. In the Gospel of Matthew, when a rich man asked Jesus what he must do to possess eternal life, Jesus tells him, "If you wish to enter into life, keep the commandments." "Which ones?" he asked. Jesus answered, "You shall not murder; You shall not commit adultery; You shall not steal; You shall not bear false witness; Honor your father and mother; also, (Jesus adds) You shall love your neighbor as yourself" (see Matthew 19:17–19). Jesus, however, invites the man to live beyond the commandments and to come to perfection. He tells him, "If you wish to be perfect, go, sell your possessions, and give the money to the poor, and you will have treasure in heaven; then come, follow me" (Matthew 19:21). Although Jesus honored the commandments, he asked his followers to do even more than was demanded by the commandments.

c. After the death of Moses, Joshua led the people into the Promised Land.

The next three books following upon the Book of Exodus— Leviticus, Numbers, and Deuteronomy— tell of the extensive laws governing the people of God in their daily lives and in worship. They also describe how the Promised Land is parcelled out among the twelve tribes of Israel. The Book of Joshua tells of the Israelites' entry into the Promised Land and their battles with the inhabitants of that land. The years of struggle continue during which certain great military leaders, called *judges,* play a major role in the conquest of the Promised Land. Many legends surround the stories of these judges.

8. What happened to the people of God in the Promised Land?

a. After the days of the judges, Israel was ruled by kings.

God allows the Israelites to have a king and set up a kingdom similar to those of their surrounding neighbors. Saul, the first king, gradually goes insane, turns his back upon God, and is killed in battle. Samuel, the prophet of the Lord, anoints David the new king of the Israelites. The Scripture stories tell of God's great love for David, but because David is a warrior and a man of blood, God will not allow David to build the temple. David establishes the great city of God, Jerusalem. Solomon, David's son, follows David as king of Israel. He builds a magnificent temple, but eventually succumbs to the pleasures and soft life of the pagan religions. Solomon is the most powerful of the first three kings of Israel, and he is the last king to rule the whole nation as one.

b. At the death of Solomon, his kingdom was broken into the northern kingdom (Israel) and the southern kingdom (Judah).

Under the heavy hand of Solomon's son, the northern kingdom rebelled and chose one of Solomon's generals as its king. Solomon's son was left with only two tribes to rule in the southern kingdom. A line of kings followed in both the northern and southern kingdoms until the Assyrians invaded the northern kingdom in the eighth century before Christ and led most of the inhabitants into exile. At the beginning of the sixth century before Christ, the Babylonians invaded the southern kingdom and led its inhabitants into exile. Eventually, some of the tribes of Judah returned from exile to re-build the temple. From this point onward, the Israelite nation is referred to as the Jewish nation, an allusion to the only known people to return to the Promised Land from exile.

c. The Book of Maccabees tells of the Jewish nation's heroic attempt to overthrow foreign domination.

About the second century before Christ, an attempt was made to suppress Judaism in Palestine. The title of the Book of Maccabees refers to the heroic leader, Judas Maccabee, who led the revolt of the Jewish people. This book stands as an important link between the Old Testament and the New Testament since it gives some insights into conditions only a few centuries before Christ. The Book of Maccabees ends the line of historical books of the Old Testament.

9. What is a covenant?

a. A covenant consists of an agreement between people by which they bind or commit themselves to each other at their deepest level.

A contract and a covenant are both agreements made between people by which they bind themselves in some way. In a building contract, for example, a builder promises to build a house within a certain period of time for a certain amount of money. When the building is finished, the builder receives his pay and the terms of the contract have ended. In a covenant, people bind or commit their whole person to each other, not just for a short period of time, but permanently. When a man and woman enter marriage, they enter a covenant that binds them to each other for life. If they place a period of time on their agreement or a condition that must be fulfilled, then they are simply sharing in a contract, not a covenant, and they would not truly be sharing in marriage.

b. God made a covenant with the people of Israel through Abraham, the father of the nation.

Abraham and God committed themselves to each other through a covenant. God would be the special God of the Israelites and they would be God's special people. We read in the Scriptures, "Then Abram fell on his face; and God said to him, 'As for me, this is my covenant with you: You shall be the ancestor of a multitude of nations' " (Genesis 17:3–4). God then reminded Abraham of his duty toward the covenant. "God said to Abraham, 'As for you, you shall keep my covenant, you and your offspring after you throughout their generations' " (Genesis 17:9). God renewed this covenant with Abraham's son, Isaac, and Isaac's son, Jacob. Abraham and his descendants promised to serve the Lord God and to live with faith in God's promises. In return, God promised Abraham that he would be the father of a great nation, and that God would guide this nation to a fruitful land. As a sign of this covenant between God and the Israelite nation, all male children would be circumcised.

c. A familiar word also used for covenant is the word testament.

When we speak of the Old Testament and the New Testament, we are speaking of the specific covenants God made with the people. The first covenant consists of the covenant made between God and the people before the coming of Jesus Christ. The second covenant consists in a covenant made between God and God's people in the person of Jesus Christ.

10. How does the Bible refer to prophets?

a. A prophet was a person who spoke or acted in the name of God.

Under God's guidance, certain men and women of the Old Testament would remind the people of the covenant that bound their nation to God. They reminded the family of God that God would always keep God's part of the covenant, but they cautioned the people that God would punish them if they broke their part of the covenant. These prophets would share insights into God's work among the people, and on rare occasions, would share a message about some future event. The prophets were not always popular, since they were telling the people (including kings) when God was not pleased with them and that they would soon experience God's wrath. They often predicted such catastrophes as the destruction of the northern kingdom of Israel and the tragic exile in Babylon of the people of Judah.

b. We meet some of the prophets of the Old Testament through their writings, while we meet others through the historical books of the Old Testament.

In the Old Testament, we find seventeen books of prophecy. Among the names of these "writing prophets" are prophets such as Ezekiel, Jeremiah, Amos, and Isaiah. Others come to life in the historical narratives of the Old Testament through stories steeped in messages and legend. Elijah confronts King Ahab of the northern kingdom in an effort to save Israel from the grip of the treacherous Jezebel. Elisha, a follower of Elijah, is called by God from his poverty to eventually destroy Jezebel. The call of these prophets stands upon the need to draw the people back to God's love and message in their lives and to save the nation from the threat that seeks to seize Israel from God's hands.

c. A book of prophecy may also portray a prophet who may never have existed.

The Book of Jonah tells of a man seeking to hide from God to avoid his call to spread the word of God to the nation of Nineveh. A whale brings Jonah to the land of Nineveh, where Jonah preaches and converts the lives of the people of that land. The Book of Jonah is a prophetic book, even though the events most likely never occurred. The message of the book concerns God's care for a sinning nation. God sends whom God wills to send, even against that person's wishes. Several books of prophecy use stories to share their great prophetic message.

41

11. What is wisdom literature?

a. Wisdom literature deals with the question of living successfully in God's world.

Wisdom literature, for the most part, has its roots in the wisdom writings of other ancient countries, especially Egypt. The Wisdom Books have a good deal of natural secular wisdom. What makes the wisdom literature of Israel different from that of other cultures lies in its view of the world as God's world and the theme of fear of the Lord. Through poetry, wise sayings, prayers, or love songs, the different wisdom writers portray a successful response to life in God's world.

b. Wisdom literature faces some of the difficult questions of life.

Wisdom literature includes the Books of Job, Proverbs, Ecclesiastes, Sirach, and the Wisdom of Solomon. Some include Psalms and the Song of Songs under this heading, but others would deny that these properly belong to wisdom literature. Whether we speak of suffering or joy, love or hatred, we find these moments touched upon by the Books of Wisdom. The Book of Job faces the question of evil and suffering in life. Through short, pointed proverbs, the Books of Wisdom speak to living daily life with a knowledge of the sacredness of God in ordinary life. The Song of Songs touches the intimate love that exists in the very nature of creation. The Book of Psalms stands out as a collection of prayerful responses to every condition of life in relation to God.

12. What do the Scriptures tell us about angels?

a. Although the Scriptures speak clearly about angels, they presume rather than prove the existence of angels.

To the people of biblical times, God had a visible hand in everything that happened. Nothing happened by chance. Goodness came at the inspiration or hand of God or angels, while evil occurred at the hands of the devil or Satan. One means used to show God's concern and guidance of the people of God was through special messengers, commonly referred to as *angels*. The word *angel* really means "messenger." Angels appear in the writings of the Scriptures beginning with the story of creation, and they continue to operate throughout much of the Old Testament and the earlier writings of the New Testament. According to the storyteller in the Book of Genesis, an angel stands at the east end of the Garden of Paradise, guarding the way to the tree of life. Angels appear in the story of Abraham and play an important part in the guidance of the people of Israel down through the ages. An angel announces the birth of John the Baptizer and the birth of Jesus. They appear at the time of Jesus' resurrection and at the ascension of Jesus into heaven. For some, to be in touch with the messenger from God is to be in touch with God. Jacob wrestles with an angel all night long and speaks of the event by proclaiming that he has seen God face to face and has lived.

Although the Scriptures speak of the existence of angels, they presume rather than prove the existence of angels. Nowhere in the Scriptures do we read of angels as spiritual beings. Later philosophers and theologians, attempting to explain the difference between angels and human beings, identified them as spiritual beings. They classified them as personal beings with intelligence and free will who were created by God. Just as the human spirit will exist forever once it is created, so angels have this eternal call. Scripture writers, however, did not speak of the angels as spirits, but spoke in a more picturesque manner, showing that God was always present in everything taking place in creation. Angels appear in the oldest writings of the Scriptures, while later writers rarely refer to angels. They appear most frequently in the highly symbolic, mythical, and poetic writings of the Scriptures.

b. In the same fashion, the Scriptures presume but never prove the existence of devils.

In light of the New Testament words of Christ, it seems difficult to deny the existence of the devil. When the disciples returned from their mission full of enthusiasm with their new spiritual powers, Jesus told them, "I watched Satan fall from heaven like a flash of lightning" (Luke 10:18). In referring to evil, Jesus would speak the language of his own culture and tradition.

In the Old Testament story of Job, Satan is not an evil person, but one who is actually visiting with the Lord. Satan appears more as a tester or a type of prosecuting attorney rather than an evil spirit.

c. The tradition of the Church supports the existence of angels.

The Church has taught the existence of angels throughout history. Along with the Scriptures, the Church presumes but never proves angels. This presumption of the existence of angels has been a constant teaching of the Church. In its prayer life, the Church joins its voice with that of the angels in praising God, and the Church sets aside certain feast days to honor the angels. As we behold the universe, we face the real possibility that God has created life on other planets, perhaps in other galaxies. Within this same possibility lies the creation of angelic creatures. God's power and love is certainly open to the possibility of many types of creation.

d. We must accept a presence of good and evil in the world.

Whether God's messenger be an angel or an act of direct inspiration through the Spirit of God, we know that we are guided to good actions. We also recognize that evil exists in the world and takes root within the human person. Some claim that the sinner is a person who accepts evil suggestions in the world, allows them to grow and develop, and tries to draw others into this evil. Evil becomes personified as the devil. Some claim that all evil is the work of the devil. Whatever the cause of evil in the world, we must still act against evil in the same way, namely through avoiding sinful situations and through prayer.

13. What does the Old Testament reveal about prayer?

a. The beginning of the Book of Genesis provides early examples of the intimate relationship between God and human beings.

The early chapters of Genesis provide a foundation for prayer in their portrait of God's familial friendship with human beings. The author offers a personal and human picture of God. God walks in the garden, enjoying the evening breeze and looking for Adam. When Adam finally appears, he speaks with God as though he were speaking with another human being. Unfortunately, Adam must admit to God that he and Eve have sinned, but the relationship between God and human beings, although strained by shame and guilt, continues.

After her expulsion from the garden with Adam, Eve gives birth to a son. She notes her relationship with God when she exclaims that she has borne a child with the help of the Lord. When Adam and Eve's two sons become adults, they continue to maintain a relationship with God by making an offering of first fruits and animals to God. Cain's offering, however, is imperfect, while Abel's is acceptable. When Cain kills Abel, he expresses his fear to God that he will be killed by others for what he has done, but God promises to protect Cain. God still continues to guide human creation.

After the death of Abel, Eve gives birth to another son. She chooses the name Seth for her new child, a name which expresses praise for God's goodness. This again shows a consciousness of the intimate relationship between God and human beings. Several generations later, a descendant of Seth named Enoch is born, and the author tells us that he "walked with God." In a later story, when the author speaks about the great flood, he declares that Noah also "walked with God."

These first chapters of the Book of Genesis not only present a story of sin, but they also present a story of mutual companionship between God and human beings.

b. Abraham proves himself to be a person of prayer.

During his life, Abraham enters into conversation with God. God takes the initiative in the relationship when God directs Abraham to leave his homeland and promises he will become the father of a great nation. When Abraham arrives in the land of the Canaanites, he builds an altar to honor the Lord. God enters into an intimate covenant with Abraham, promising him blessings and offspring as numerous as the stars, while Abraham promises that he and his descendants will serve the one true God alone. Later, Abraham boldly complains to God that he has not yet produced any offspring. Abraham's complaint underlines the strength of his faith. He complains, but does not abandon God. Abraham's prayer leads him to bargain with God concerning the destruction of Sodom. Despite Abraham's bargaining with God, few righteous people are found in Sodom and God destroys the city.

The greatest act of faith and prayerfulness on the part of Abraham comes when God directs Abraham to sacrifice his only son Isaac. When the time for sacrifice comes, an angel of the Lord directs Abraham to sacrifice a ram caught in a nearby thicket. Through his deeds, his faith, and his conversation with God, Abraham proves himself to be a person of prayer. Abraham trusts God, Abraham's constant companion.

Jacob, the grandson of Abraham, also walks with God. In one episode, Jacob wrestles all night with an angel. He captures the essence of all those who strive to serve God when he declares that he has wrestled with the human and the divine.

God remains faithful to the family of Abraham, even when they sin. When Joseph's brothers sell him into slavery, God does not abandon the journey, but draws good out of evil. Through Joseph, the Israelites eventually settle in Egypt, thus preparing the scene for God's later intervention in freeing them from slavery in Egypt.

c. Moses prays on behalf of the people.

God again takes the initiative. The living God of Abraham, Isaac, and Jacob calls out to Moses from the burning bush. In this exchange, Moses tries to shirk his call, to offer questions and excuses, but he finally accepts the mission. Moses learns a new way of addressing God, which is through the name "I Am." This discussion becomes only the first of many conversations Moses has with God.

Moses calls the families of the Hebrews to a new passover prayer on the evening before the Exodus begins. Throughout the Exodus journey, Moses climbs the mountain to spend hours in conversation with God. He does not pray for himself, but for the Chosen People as they journey through the desert and in their battles against superior forces. Moses stands before God with the boldness of an intimate friend when the Chosen People sin. In his efforts to appease God, Moses speaks of God's love, goodness, faithfulness, and promises. He proclaims that God cannot forsake a people who bears God's name.

d. Kings and prophets offer us examples of prayer.

Samuel, the great prophet of the early kingdom of Israel, calls out to God, " 'Speak, Lord, for your servant is listening' " (1 Samuel 3:9–10). David is a king "after God's own heart," the shepherd who loves and trusts God and who prays for his people and prays in their name. Solomon sets the stage for the nation's praise of God in the construction of the temple. Elijah calls the people to faith in prayer and himself experiences God's presence in his life. All the prophets speak in God's name to the people of Israel and Judah. Jeremiah complains to God on the one hand, yet willingly offers his life to God on the other. In the psalms, the people of Israel offer prayers to celebrate God's relationship to the nation in good times and in bad. The psalms express personal and communal prayer, recalling past events, which leads to hope for the future.

Conclusion

The young boy in the introduction to this chapter never again joined the other boys on the street in taunting the "junk man." He tried to explain to the others how he felt, but no one seemed to understand. Perhaps they had to see the man playing with his children to really understand the boy's feelings.

In this chapter, we studied how people of Old Testament days experienced God. Through their writers and prophets, they tried to explain to us their understanding of God as God related to their lives. Throughout their history, they strove to reveal to future generations an image of their loving God. Some would share their feelings and respond to the goodness and love of God, and others would know their history and ignore God. Still others would never take time out of their daily routine to listen to their experience of God.

What happened to the young boy in trying to share his experience of the "junk man" could happen to the writers and prophets trying to share their experience of God. People very often do not listen. But some people do listen, and many people have listened to the message of God's dealing with the people. Our world has grown closer to an understanding of God because of these people who have listened and understood.

For Scripture reflection and discussion concerning this chapter, see **Journeying in His Light, "Knowing God Better: Parts 1 and 2."**

3 Jesus Is Lord

Introduction

The newspapers told of a man who had fallen through ice while fishing. While he struggled and screamed from the water, he saw a man rushing across the ice with a rope over his shoulder. In a few moments, that man had the fisherman out of the water and on his way to the nearest hospital. The man left the half-frozen and frightened fisherman in the emergency room of the hospital, shook his hand and said, "Someday you may find someone in need, and help that person because of this." Only after the man left did the fisherman realize that he did not even know his rescuer's name.

The fisherman told the newspaper reporter that encountering this man had changed his life. As he lay in the hospital nervously realizing that he could have been a frozen corpse at the bottom of a lake, he wondered what he would have done if someone else needed his help. "Never get involved if you don't have to" was his life's slogan. He thanked God that his rescuer did not have the same slogan to guide his life. This fisherman now determined to erase that attitude from his life and to reach out and share with people. He marvelled at how the kindness and courage of one man, who passed through his life for a little more than an hour, had changed his life.

In this chapter, we meet Jesus Christ. Within the course of a few short years, he drastically changed the direction of history. We shall study this person, Jesus, and see how his "stopping to help" has affected the lives of billions of people from his time to ours.

1. Where do we learn about Jesus?

a. A major source of information about Jesus is the New Testament.

The New Testament is a collection of twenty-seven books or writings compiled by early Christian believers. These Christians listened to the preaching concerning the life and message of Jesus and eventually committed this preaching to four books called the *Gospels.* The preaching surrounding the early days of the Christian community after Christ's physical departure from this earth was eventually gathered into a book called the *Acts of the Apostles.* During these early days, missioners would send letters to the people they had brought into belief in Christ to correct, guide, and encourage them to hold to their new beliefs. There are twenty-one such letters, and the majority are attributed to Paul, the apostle. Other letters are attributed to Peter, James, and John. Finally, a highly symbolic book concerning Christianity's final conquest during the last days became known as the *Book of Revelation* or the *Apocalypse.* The twenty-seven books make up the New Testament.

b. We understand these writings more clearly by understanding the literary form used, as we did in the Old Testament.

At the beginning of the last chapter on the Bible, we spoke of the literary form used in the early part of the Old Testament. In reading the New Testament, we should become aware of the culture in which the books were written and the types of writing used. Almost two thousand years have passed since the writing of the New Testament. Cultures and styles of writing have changed in that time. Recent studies and discoveries have provided a new and deeper insight into the writings of the New Testament. We should respect these insights. They should help us understand the message of the New Testament more fully.

c. We understand these writings by understanding the world in which Jesus lived.

Jesus was a true Jew, filled with a love for the Law and the traditions of the Israelite nation. Although we often see Jesus challenging the leaders of the people in their interpretation of the Law, he is always faithful to the spirit of the Law. He often went to the synagogue for worship, and he challenged his listeners to live up to the Law of Moses. In time, he built his new law upon the Law of Moses, explaining that it was the spirit of the person and not just the living of external precepts which led to the fulfillment of the Law.

During the time of Jesus, the land of Israel and its inhabitants belonged to the Roman Empire. The land was ruled by such men as Herod and Pilate, who acted on behalf of Rome. Despite the Roman rule, the leaders who seemed to have the greatest influence upon the daily lives of the Jewish people were the religious leaders, consisting of men from several groups.

The Sadducees were the rich, priestly caste, liberal in politics and conservative in religion. They accepted only the first five books of the Bible as the inspired Scriptures.

The Pharisees were more liberal in religious developments, but conservative politically. They accepted the writings of the prophets and other writings as part of the inspired Scriptures. Being an educated class, they were accepted as the interpreters of the Scriptures. Some of the Pharisees are portrayed as the leading opponents of Christ in the Gospels.

The scribes consisted of the judges, writers, and interpreters of the Law. All the scribes belonged to the Pharisee party, but not all Pharisees were scribes.

The Sanhedrin was the official ruling body of religious leaders within Judaism, and it had in its ranks members from both the Pharisees and the Sadducees. It also had the high priest at its head. The Sanhedrin play a significant role in the passion of Jesus.

The Zealots were a war-like faction within Judaism who believed that they had a divine call to free the nation from its foreign oppression.

A group considered by the Jewish people of the day to be sinful were the tax collectors and others who worked for the foreign rulers. Jesus often mixed with these tax collectors and sinners, much to the unhappiness of the religious leaders.

2. How were the Gospels written?

a. The Gospels came from the good news as preached by the early Christians.

In the early Church, the events and message of Jesus' life, death, and resurrection were preserved through the preaching of the early disciples of Jesus. People listened to their preaching, reflected on its message, and passed the reflections of the community on to other members of the early Christian community. Only after many years of reflecting and preaching the message did writers gather the result of this preaching into written form.

The Gospel of Mark, the first Gospel, appeared sometime between 65 and 70 C.E. The Gospels of Matthew and Luke appeared sometime after the year 70 C.E., but before the year 90. Scholars believe that Matthew and Luke used Mark as part of the outline of their Gospels, and that they both used another common source (called *Q)* which was unknown to Mark. They each also had their own private source, known to none of the others. For Matthew, this is called the *M* source, and for Luke it is called the *L* source. If we were to put this into a formula, we would have the following:

Mark + Q + M = Matthew

Mark + Q + L = Luke

Writers have given the name, "Synoptic Gospels" to the Gospels of Mark, Matthew, and Luke. The word *synoptic* comes from a Greek word which means "seeing together." These three Gospels have so much in common that we find ourselves seeing many of the same events and messages (with slight changes) from one Gospel to the next.

At least thirty years elapsed between the resurrection of Jesus and the writing of the first Gospel. The Gospel of John, the last of the Gospels, appeared between 90 and 100 C.E. This Gospel expresses many of the developments in understanding the divinity of Jesus which took place over the sixty or seventy years between the resurrection of Jesus and the writing of the Gospel.

b. The Gospels are not biographies of Jesus, but reflections of the early Christian community about the person of Jesus as they understood him after his resurrection.

The Gospels were written by followers of Jesus who knew the end of the story. After the resurrection of Jesus, his followers looked back on the events of Jesus' life and saw them in a different light. In preaching about the life of Jesus, the early Christians wanted to share the message that "Jesus is Lord." With a style proper to their own culture, they could portray events of Jesus' life in ways that proclaimed that Jesus was God. The Gospels are more than a simple biography of the life of Jesus. They are a reflection of the faith of the early community who knew Jesus and who knew that he was the Lord who was raised from the dead.

c. The events of Jesus' life greatly influenced the writing of the Gospels.

Although we cannot call the Gospels biographies of Jesus, we must also be careful not to give the impression that the events of Jesus' life had no influence on the writing of the Gospels. The writers did not simply fashion a false image of Christ to emphasize their message. The Jesus they spoke about had a definite history, and this history is portrayed in the Gospels. The early community reflected upon this history and saw it in a new light after the resurrection of Jesus. They understood a great deal more about the person of Jesus and the life of Jesus as they saw his life through the resurrection. In the Gospel of Mark, we read of a centurion at the cross of Jesus. When Jesus expired, the centurion exclaimed, " 'Truly this man was God's Son!' " (Mark 15:39). As the early community looked back over the life of Jesus and reflected in faith on the events of this life, they too wanted to share this message with us . . . "**Clearly** this man was the son of God!" The events of Jesus' life greatly influenced this reflection in faith.

d. The condition of the Church at the time of the writing and the audience for whom the Gospels were written also influenced the authors of the Gospels.

The authors at times arranged the events of Jesus' life and his message for a particular audience or to emphasize a particular point needed at the time of the writing. Matthew, for example, wrote for Jewish converts to Christianity. He wanted to show Jesus as the new Moses and the new Israel. As Moses went up the mountain to receive God's Law for his Chosen People, Christ went up the mountain to give the new law to his followers. To show that Jesus is the fulfillment of the Old Testament prophecies, Matthew often makes reference to the words of the prophets fulfilled in Christ. Concerning the journey of the Holy Family to Egypt, for instance, Matthew writes, "This was to fulfill what had been spoken by the Lord through the prophet, 'Out of Egypt I have called my son' " (Matthew 2:15). These Old Testament references are found throughout the Gospel of Matthew.

Luke, who had no need to portray Jesus as the new Moses, describes Jesus, in the same scene, as coming *down* from the mountain. Both authors describe a similar message from Jesus, but the backdrop for that message changes according to the audience and the more subtle message intended by the inspired author.

3. What do the Gospels tell us about the birth of Jesus?

a. The Gospels tell us little that is historical about the birth of Jesus.

The infancy narratives, which tell of the birth of Jesus and the events surrounding that birth, are found only in the Gospels of Matthew and Luke. The narratives were written long after the resurrection of Jesus; the authors already knew that Jesus had been raised from the dead. The writers wanted to explain the person of Jesus and the message of his life. Unlike the forms of writing today, the literary forms used during the early years of Christianity enabled the writers to present historical facts through events that may not have been historical. They knew that Jesus was the son of Mary, that he was the confirmation of Old Testament hopes, that he was rejected by his own people, and that he would be accepted by many others throughout the world. With these ideas in mind, the writers set out to share the message through a style of writing acceptable in their own day.

b. Matthew and Luke both give a family line for Jesus.

When we look at the family trees presented by both Matthew and Luke, we discover how the authors' purpose in writing affected what they wrote. In recording the family tree of Jesus, Matthew, who wrote for converts from the Jewish belief, wanted to portray Jesus as the hope of the Israelite nation. For this reason, Matthew begins with Abraham, the father of the Israelite nation, and traces the family tree from Abraham to Jesus. Luke, wishing to show that Jesus came for all people, begins with Adam and traces the family tree of Jesus from Adam to Jesus. As we compare the two Gospels, we discover that Matthew and Luke do not always agree on the names contained in the family tree. The fact that the family lines do not match each other would scarcely have disturbed the writers. They were not writing an exact history, but rather sharing a message about the mission of Jesus.

c. Both Gospels show Jesus as the fulfillment of the Old Testament expectation.

Matthew shows that Jesus is the new Israel and the new Moses. He draws events from the life of Moses and applies them to Jesus. At the birth of Moses, all male children two years old and under were put to death. Only Moses was spared. At the birth of Jesus, all male children two years old and under were also put to death. Only Jesus was spared. In the Gospel of Matthew, Jesus is taken to Egypt by Mary and Joseph. He later comes out of Egypt, as the Israelite nation came from the land of Egypt centuries before under the leadership of Moses.

Luke shows that Jesus is "the prophet." In the Old Testament, Hannah begged God for a child, and God heard her prayer. Hannah gave birth to a son named Samuel, who became the great prophet chosen to anoint the first kings of Israel. When Hannah came to worship the Lord in thanksgiving for Samuel, she proclaimed a song of praise to God that closely resembles the prayer that Mary recited at the home of Elizabeth: "Hannah prayed and said, 'My heart exults in the Lord; my strength is exalted in my God . . .' " (1 Samuel 2:1). By structuring the infancy narratives around certain events, both Matthew and Luke portray the message they wish to emphasize in developing these narratives. Their purpose, as stated earlier, is not primarily history, but rather the sharing of a message about Jesus.

d. Both Gospels use stories to portray historical facts.

At the time the Gospel of Matthew was committed to writing, others besides Judeans had joined the early Christians in their belief that Christ was the Messiah. Matthew realized this historical fact as he recounted the story of the astrologers who came from a pagan land. These wise astrologers followed a star which led to Jesus while his own people did not recognize him. Pagans, out of a pagan land (the East), came to pay homage to Christ. The story may not be true, but the historical fact, namely the pagan recognition and acceptance of Christ, was true.

When Luke wrote his Gospel, a surprising number of sinners were flocking to Christianity. In the Judean mind, the shepherds who tended their flocks on the Sabbath day of rest and who took their sheep to graze on foreign soil clearly defied the Judean laws. Luke, through the story of the shepherds called to worship the Christ Child, portrays the historical fact that sinners recognized Christ. Luke also recognizes that Jesus was rejected by his own people, so he narrates the story of the rejection of Jesus' parents as they sought lodging at the inn at Bethlehem. Just as there was no room at the inn, so Jesus would find no room among his own people. The fact that Mary and Joseph found no room at the inn is used by Luke to portray the historical fact of the rejection of Jesus by his own people throughout his life.

Both Matthew and Luke use the literary forms of their own day to share a deep insight into the life and message of Jesus. Through their stories, they are able to summarize historical facts that surrounded Jesus and his message.

e. Both infancy narratives speak of the birth of Jesus as a special event.

The birth of Jesus was no ordinary birth. Jesus, the Messiah and Christ, came into the world. In the Gospel of Matthew, an angel tells Joseph in a dream that Mary has conceived a child by the power of the Holy Spirit. In the Gospel of Luke, an angel appears to Mary to announce that she will conceive a child who will be called "Son of the Most High" (Luke 1:32). Without doubt, a virgin birth is no ordinary birth, and it does point to the fact that a great event has taken place in history.

Some writers feel that the virgin birth of Jesus contains more message than fact. The wide use of symbol and story in the infancy narratives points to the fact that these narratives are more concerned with message than with history. The message simply tells us that a great event has taken place, namely a miraculous birth of the Child Jesus. God has joined our human condition.

Other writers agree that we cannot use the infancy narratives to prove the virgin birth of Jesus, but we also cannot lightly discard the common teaching of the Church that Mary remained a virgin in the conception of Jesus. For them, the fact of the virgin birth cannot easily be denied, even if it cannot be proven from the Scriptures.

One of the merits of this difference of opinion is the fact that the central message becomes more dominant. The message is not merely the virgin birth, but rather the special call of Mary to become the mother of Jesus, who is the Christ. Mary was the highly favored person chosen to give birth to the savior of the world. What more could be said?

At Christmas time, we should continue to use the nativity scene as a portrait of the birth of Christ. Just as the infancy narratives tell a message surrounding the birth of Christ, so the nativity scene reminds us of that message. As in the infancy narratives, if the historical events are not accurate, the historical fact is still there. The **message** of Christmas is far more important than the **events** of Christmas.

4. What do the Gospels tell us about the public life of Jesus?

a. The public life of Jesus began with his baptism at the Jordan by John the Baptizer.

John the Baptizer, a cousin of Jesus, lived in the desert and preached repentance along the shores of the Jordan River. He invited those who wished to commit themselves to God by a change of life to enter the waters of the Jordan and seal their commitment with baptism. The baptism of John consisted in a public commitment, much as we might witness at a revival when some come forward to commit themselves to God. Jesus entered the waters to commit himself to his mission of preaching and sharing the reign of God. At this point, when Jesus was about thirty years of age, he left the obscurity of his private life to begin his public life, which would last two or three years.

The custom of being bathed in water as a sign of some spiritual change in a person's life was a practice used by many religions of Jesus' day, including Judaism. Although this custom offers some insight into the meaning of the Sacrament of Baptism used in Christianity today, we should not confuse the two. The baptism by John was not the same as our Sacrament of Baptism. The people who accepted the baptism of John recognized their own sinfulness and responded to John's call to change their way of life. Their going down into the water was an external sign of an internal change which had already taken place.

Some of the people of the early Church thought that John the Baptizer was the awaited Messiah. The Gospels remind us that Jesus is greater than John as we read the words of the Baptist himself who tells us in the Gospel of Luke, " 'I baptize you with water; but one who is more powerful than I is coming; I am not worthy to untie the thong of his sandals. He will baptize you with the Holy Spirit and fire' " (Luke 3:16).

b. Jesus chose special followers.

When a great rabbi appeared in Palestine, people sought to become his followers to learn from him. Jesus changed this tradition as he changed so many. Jesus chose his own followers. In the Gospel of Mark, we read that Jesus approached some fishermen and said, "Follow me and I will make you fish for people" (Mark 1:17). Jesus gathered around himself fishermen, tax collectors, and known sinners as his followers. Of these, Jesus chose twelve to serve as special companions whom he would instruct throughout the years of his public life. These twelve, called *apostles*, would pass on the message of Jesus to the early Christian community (with Matthias replacing Judas).

Besides choosing his own followers, Jesus invited them to spend some time with him, learning about him and his message. In the Gospel of John, two disciples of the Baptist decide to become followers of Jesus, and they ask Jesus where he is staying. He tells them, "Come and see" (John 1:39). Instead of a short instruction, the disciples must travel with Jesus, listen to him, and "see" as witnesses to his mission and message. Unlike other rabbis of the day who merely teach their disciples, Jesus calls his followers to learn his life and message and to share it with others. This understanding of discipleship is important, since we today, as followers of Jesus, are called to the same mission. During this time of study and reflection, we are called "to come and see" so that we might share with others the true message of Christ.

c. Jesus performed miracles.

In the Gospels, we read of miraculous powers of Jesus extending from calming the seas to healing a paralytic. Nature miracles, such as calming the storms, were certainly acts of God, and only God could control the elements at will. Some writers proposed that these nature miracles were post-resurrection stories intended to teach that Jesus is God. Perhaps we will never definitely know the extent of Jesus' miraculous powers, but we do know that Jesus had a clear reputation as a miracle worker. Miracles are central to the Gospels, and miracles are also part of the message. They point to something more than themselves. When the followers of John asked Jesus if he were the one whom they were awaiting, Jesus responded on the authority of his message and miracles. " 'Go and tell John what you hear and see: the blind receive their sight, the lame walk, the lepers are cleansed, the deaf hear, the dead are raised, and the poor have good news brought to them' " (Matthew 11:4–5). Matthew chooses these words of Jesus to answer, "Yes," he is the one who is to come. In reading the miracles of Jesus, we should strive to understand the truth they point to in the message of the Gospels.

Many writers see the miracles of Jesus as a living sign of the presence of God and a sign pointing to the presence of the reign of God on earth. Jesus came preaching that the reign of God is here among us, and the miracles are signs of this presence. Not only do we see the healing and caring gifts of God in the miracles, but we also see the dawn of a new era ushered into God's creation with the coming of Jesus.

d. Jesus proclaimed a new message for the people.

The central message taught by Jesus concerned the reign of God which entered the world in a dramatic way with the coming of Jesus. This reign of God, preached by Jesus, is not a reign or kingdom which has a specific boundary in this world, but an invisible reign whereby God is properly recognized as the One reigning over all. But Jesus' message had some surprising elements. The reign of God is now present with Jesus and the world in a new way. As people united with Jesus, we can call out to God in an intimate manner, using the title *Abba*, which comes from the Hebrew and means "Daddy" or some intimate equivalent. The call of the reign of God is a call of love—love for God, our neighbor, and ourselves. The reign of God, although existing in the world in a special way now, is yet to reach its fulfillment in our eternal call to glory and happiness in Christ. The reign of God becomes visible not just in our individual response to God, but primarily in our community response to God in Christ. Because the message of the reign of God is so important, we are called not only to hear, but also to spread the message.

In preaching his message, Jesus used an approach not easily accepted by the people of his own day. Rabbis based their conclusions upon rabbis of the past. Jesus drew his conclusions on his own authority, and this disturbed the chief priests and elders of the Israelite nation. "Again they came to Jerusalem. As he was walking in the temple, the chief priests, the scribes, and the elders came to him and said, 'By what authority are you doing these things? Who gave you this authority to do them?' " (Mark 11:27–29). His message condemned the hypocrisy of the leaders of the people, called sinners to repentance, and promised eternal happiness to those who suffer and die for justice's sake. Jesus came with the intention of fulfilling the Law, not doing away with the Law.

After a public life lasting about two or three years, Jesus entered the period of his passion. Within the context of this narrative, we find a description of Jesus celebrating the Last Supper with his disciples. The authors of the synoptic Gospels place this supper within the framework of the Passover meal, although some commentators on the Scriptures wonder whether or not the meal actually took place at the time of Passover. By placing it in the framework of the Passover meal, the writers are telling us that Jesus is the new Lamb of God and the event is the new covenant between God and all people.

e. Jesus suffered and died on the cross.

After the meal, Jesus went to the ordinary place of rest used whenever he and the disciples came to Jerusalem. Judas led the temple guards to the spot and betrayed Jesus with some sign of affection. The pain of the passion not only includes the physical pain Jesus endured, but the pain of being betrayed by one he loved and trusted.

Jesus was brought to trial before the Sanhedrin, and they accepted the testimony of false witnesses in condemning Jesus to death. Because they did not have the authority to put Jesus to death, they brought him before Pilate, the Roman procurator, and demanded that Jesus be crucified. Although Pilate showed little reluctance in the past when it came to condemning someone to death, he is presented by the Gospels as a sympathetic ruler, trying to free Jesus. The leaders of the people accused Jesus of plotting against Rome, and Pilate, afraid that the people would riot, condemned Jesus to death by crucifixion. Before Jesus was led out to his death, he was flogged according to custom, and some of the soldiers mocked him by putting a crown of thorns on his head.

The Gospels tell us simply that when they came to the place of crucifixion outside the city of Jerusalem, "they crucified him." The common place for crucifixion was near a main road where people passing by would witness the punishment and, where necessary, would hesitate to commit any crimes against the laws of the land. After the death of Jesus, a centurion pierced his side, and blood and water flowed forth.

f. Jesus was raised from the dead.

The Gospels tell the story of some women coming to the tomb on the morning of the third day and finding it empty. Through the resurrection stories of the Gospels, we learn that Jesus has been raised from the dead, and that he has appeared to many. The fear and confusion of the followers of Jesus turned to amazement as the word spread, "He is raised." With the resurrection of Jesus, the real beginnings of Christianity began to take root. Because Jesus was truly raised, the Church could now preach of Jesus, the living Messiah. Now they could say with the apostle Paul, "and every tongue should confess that Jesus Christ is Lord, to the glory of God the Father" (Philippians 2:11).

5. Was Jesus human like us?

a. The Son of God is one with the Father and existed with the Father from all eternity.

Although God is neither male nor female, the people of the ancient Jewish culture ordinarily used the male image in referring to God. For this reason, many of our words used for God in the Scriptures present God as our Father and Jesus as the eternal Son of God. This Son of God is one with the Father, that is, equal to the Father. The Son became human in the person of Jesus, the son of Mary.

John's Gospel refers to the Son as the "Word" of God, and he tells us that the Word existed with God the Creator from all eternity. John writes, "In the beginning was the Word, and the Word was with God, and the Word was God. He was in the beginning with God. All things came into being through him, and without him not one thing came into being" (John 1:1–3). Later in the same Gospel, Jesus gives himself the same eternal title given by God as God spoke to Moses from the burning bush. Jesus said to the Jewish leaders, "Very truly,

I tell you, before Abraham was, **I am"** (John 8:58). Christians believe that "... the Word became flesh and lived among us, and we have seen his glory, the glory as of a father's only son, full of grace and truth" (John 1:14). Our faith tells us that the Word is eternal, one and equal with the Father.

b. *An ancient hymn proclaims that Jesus was human like us.*

In a letter to the Christians at Philippi, Paul includes a hymn that predates the letter and apparently was used shortly after Christ's resurrection. This hymn spoke of Jesus during his life as emptying himself and becoming like us. He became fully human.

Who, though he was in the form of God,
did not regard equality with God something to be grasped.
Rather, he emptied himself,
taking the form of a slave,
coming in human likeness;
and found human in appearance,
he humbled himself,
becoming obedient to death,
even death on a cross (Philippians 2:6–8 NAB).

How Jesus emptied himself is hard to understand. Somehow, he became like us in all ways, with the exception of sin. We must admit that we are facing a mystery when we declare that Jesus became fully human and that he emptied himself of the powers and gifts of his Godhood while still being God. This hymn does not tell us how it happened, but simply tells us that it did happen. The passage would imply that Jesus had to go to school to learn as we do; that he grew tired, hungry, and weak as we do; that he had to live with the insecurity of searching for the correct words to share a message as perfectly as possible or the insecurity of wondering what tomorrow would bring, as we do; and that he lived by faith and feared suffering and death, as we do. In simplest terms, Jesus was human like us, yet still God.

c. Some parts of the Gospels show the humanness of Jesus.

In a Gospel story taken from Luke, we read of Jesus around the age of twelve. Although he was God, Jesus still had to grow in wisdom. Jesus had been lost for three days when Mary and Joseph found him and took him home. Luke tells us, "And Jesus increased in wisdom and in years, and in divine and human favor" (Luke 2:52).

The Gospels tell about Jesus sleeping, eating, weeping, and experiencing fear—all human qualities. At one point, Jesus professed a lack of knowledge about the end of the world: "But about that day or hour no one knows, neither the angels in heaven, nor the Son, but only the Father" (Mark 13:32).

In the past, we often spoke of Jesus as having the full and continual experience of God's presence. With this experience, suffering becomes impossible due to the extreme joy of the experience. As humans, we can experience this presence only in a partial way. We must wait for our resurrection in order to experience the fullness of this presence. The fact that Jesus feared and suffered implies that Jesus "emptied himself" of this full experience of God's presence. Otherwise Jesus would have been acting as he cried out in pain from the cross. This, of course, would contradict the complete openness and honesty of Jesus.

d. Knowledge of the human condition of Jesus helps us to understand why the followers of Jesus continually misunderstood him.

Jesus' own townspeople, who grew up with him and saw him in a very human light, wanted to put him to death because of his message. Despite Jesus' miracles and his debates with some of the Pharisees, the apostles still saw him as a human person. They thought Jesus foolish to head for certain death in Jerusalem, and they tried to persuade him to avoid the trip to that city. Through many of the reactions of the followers of Jesus, we see them in the Gospels as viewing Jesus in a fully human way.

e. In becoming human, Jesus showed his great love for all people.

That the Son of God would take upon himself a human nature and join us in the struggles of life could never have been imagined by anyone except God. The act of love shown through this entry into our human existence tells us more about the loving God. The fact that Jesus "emptied himself" and became like us in all ways but sin shows the degree of his love. If Jesus had kept the powers of his God-hood, we would still marvel at his love. The fact that he emptied himself of these powers makes his sign of love more astounding.

Another message we receive from the "new Adam" (as Jesus is called in the writings of Paul) reminds us of the wonders of our human calling. Although sin has a deep effect upon our human condition, we remember that God created human beings and saw that the act was good. God's creation is a good creation. In the story of the first sin, we read that Adam and Eve sinned because they wanted to be like God. In the story, the serpent tells Eve that she will be like God if she grasps the forbidden fruit and eats it. The Son of God, on the other hand, totally one with God, "though he was in the form of God, did not regard equality with God as something to be exploited" (Philippians 2:6). Instead, he empties himself and becomes one with our human condition. In this way, the new Adam overwhelms us with a great act of love and, at the same time, lifts our humanness to a new dignity.

6. Did Jesus come to die?

a. Jesus came to give life.

Past theologies drew an image of God the Father as experiencing a deep hurt at the sin of Adam and Eve. In order to appease this God, the people of the Old Testament offered animal sacrifices, fasts, and long hours of worship. But these were never enough. Finally, this God's innocent Son became man, suffered, and died. Now God the Father was appeased, and God showed His pleasure by raising His Son from the dead and bringing redemption to all people. This was an unfortunate image of God not drawn in the Scriptures but from a misunderstanding of certain Scripture texts. We can say that Jesus did not come to die to appease a hurt God the Father, but rather that Jesus came to give life.

In the Gospel of John, we read that Jesus is the Good Shepherd who is willing to lay down his life for his sheep. A shepherd protects the sheep and shares his life with them. Jesus himself says, "The thief comes only to steal and kill and destroy. I came that they may have life, and have it abundantly" (John 10:10). In protecting the sheep, Jesus, the Good Shepherd, would remain faithful to protecting them to the end, even with his life.

b. Jesus came to give life by confronting the power of evil and sin in the world.

Jesus came into a world controlled by evil and sin. Throughout the Old Testament, we read how people tried to overcome evil but often found themselves caught up in its power. Even if someone was able to live a good life, the final weapon of evil, namely death, would have its day. Jesus came to confront evil head-on. Evil attempted to have Jesus join with it. The temptations in the desert portray in story form the weapons evil used. If Jesus would kneel to evil and worship its existence, he would control the whole world. Jesus rejected in his life this temptation to join with evil. Evil then tried to embarrass Jesus or frustrate him in striving to share his message. Still Jesus did not give in to evil. Finally, evil moved the hearts of the people to bring Jesus to suffering and ultimately to death. When Jesus was raised from the dead by God the Father, evil had no weapons left and for the first time in history had to admit defeat. Jesus did not come to die, but to give life. The fact that he confronted evil head-on inevitably led to his death.

c. By confronting death in obedience to God the Father, Jesus brought redemption to the world.

Jesus' mission of bringing redemption to the world came not simply because he confronted evil, but because he committed himself, in his human condition, to confronting evil on behalf of God. He showed a great love of God the Father by obediently living out his commitment in confronting evil, even when he saw that this confrontation would lead to a horrible death. Jesus did not seek suffering, but suffering came to Jesus. In the same way, Jesus did not seek death on the cross, but his obedience led him to accept this death in carrying out his mission. St. Paul writes in the Letter to the Philippians, ". . . he humbled himself and became obedient to the point of death—even death on a cross" (Philippians 2:8). Through this obedience to God the Father, Jesus was raised up and brought redemption to the world.

In the garden on the Mount of Olives, Jesus prays to the Father to take the cup of suffering away from him, but, if it be the Father's will, Jesus willingly accepts the cup. Jesus prays, "Father, if you are willing, remove this cup from me; yet, not my will but yours be done" (Luke 22:42). The mission of Jesus asks that he be obedient to his commitment to the end, even if that commitment demands suffering and death. When Jesus began his passion, the power of evil had reached its peak. Jesus tells those who come out to take him, "When I was with you day after day in the temple, you did not lay hands on me. But this is your hour, and the power of darkness!" (Luke 22:53). In the death of Jesus, evil would triumph, but, in his resurrection, evil would be overcome.

d. To understand our part as Christians in the world, we must imitate the love and commitment of Jesus.

Like Jesus, we too are called to confront evil head-on. We have the special gifts of Jesus' resurrection to help in this mission. Because suffering shows the grip of evil in the world, we should strive to alleviate suffering wherever possible. If Jesus came only to die and if suffering alone had a redemptive power, then we should seek to keep suffering in the world. If love and commitment are the acts that make suffering redemptive, then we should strive for love and commitment in all we do rather than strive for suffering. Love leads us to overcome the grip of suffering and evil in the world.

When Mark wrote his Gospel, Christians were facing persecution in Rome, and they wondered why they were called to suffer. If Jesus had overcome the power of evil and suffering in the world, why did suffering still exist? Mark wrote his Gospel to tell the disciples of Jesus that they must not expect anything to be easier for the follower than it was for the master. In Mark's Gospel, Jesus tells us, "If any want to become my followers, let them deny themselves and take up their cross and follow me. For those who want to save their life will lose it, and those who lose their life for my sake, and for the sake of the gospel, will save it" (Mark 8:34–35). Although we should not seek suffering, we must realize that the message of the life of Jesus will often demand sacrifice and suffering on our part. Like Jesus, we, the disciples, must be willing to travel the same road.

7. What were the effects of the resurrection?

a. Through his resurrection, Jesus Christ could properly be called Lord.

The word *Lord* was used in many different ways in the Scriptures. Here, however, we use the term as referring to the divine nature of God. At the resurrection of Jesus, his human nature entered fully into union with his divine nature. He now received into his human nature the fullness of his Godhood with all its powers. Now the name of Jesus became sacred and the power and knowledge of Jesus was fully that of the Son of God. Again we tread on mystery. In the same early hymn we quoted under the humanness of Jesus, we find the reward of Jesus' human obedience:

> *Therefore God also highly exalted him and gave him the name that is above every name, so that at the name of Jesus every knee should bend, in heaven and on earth and under the earth, and every tongue should confess that Jesus Christ is Lord, to the glory of God the Father (Philippians 2:9–11).*

Because of the exaltation of Jesus, we can now say for the first time "Jesus Christ is Lord!" How it happened, we do not know. That it did happen in the resurrection, we learn from the Scriptures.

b. Through the resurrection, Jesus could properly be called the Christ or the Messiah.

The Jewish tradition expected a kingly ruler to rise up and bring the Jewish nation to victory over its enemies. By the time Jesus came upon earth, this tradition was not as strong as it had been in the past. Throughout the Gospels, we often find Jesus rejecting the title given to this ruler, namely, the *Messiah.* Jesus thought as the rest of the people of his own age, and he knew he would not lead an uprising against the Roman authorities.

Only after the resurrection did the early Christians see the title of *messiah* as referring to a savior in the spiritual sense rather than the earthly ruler mistakenly sought after by the Israelites. Once the idea of messiah was properly understood as referring to this spiritual savior, the title could be applied to Jesus. Although Jesus, at times, denied that he was the Messiah, (especially in the Gospel of Mark), at other times he accepted the title where it was fully understood.

When Jesus asks his disciples who people said he was, Peter answers, "You are the messiah, the Son of the living God" (Matthew 16:16). Immediately after Peter's profession of faith found in Matthew's Gospel, the author of the Gospel offers us the true meaning of Messiah through the words of Jesus who states that he must suffer, die, and then rise. When Peter tries to deny that Jesus, the Messiah, must pass through his death to his resurrection, Jesus answers him sharply, saying, "Get behind me, Satan! You are a stumbling block to me; for you are setting your mind not on divine things but on human things" (Matthew 16:23). Despite his profession of faith, Peter would not understand the meaning of the title *Messiah* until after the resurrection of Jesus. Through his death and resurrection, Jesus properly became the Messiah or the Christ. The word *Christ* is the Greek equivalent of the Hebrew *Messiah.*

c. Through his resurrection, Jesus could properly be seen as one with God the Father, that is, as God.

After the resurrection, the early Christians recognized Jesus as the *Lord.* In calling him Lord, they were professing a faith in his Godhood, using the same term for Jesus that was used for God the Father in other Scripture writings. By the time the Gospel of John was written (c. 90–100 c.e.), the early Church clearly accepted Jesus as one with God the Father. When Philip approached Jesus and asked to see the Father, Jesus replied, "Have I been with you all this time, Philip, and you still do not know me? Whoever has seen the Father. How can you say, 'Show us the Father'? Do you not believe that I am in the Father and the Father is in me? The words that I say to you I do not speak on my own; but the Father who dwells in me does his works" (John 14:9–10). Jesus declares flatly in another section of the Gospel of John, "The Father and I are one" (John 10:30). The Gospel of John shows a belief in Christ that has developed to a point of fully accepting his Godhood.

d. Through the resurrection, a new hope and new life were brought to all of God's people.

The resurrection confirms all Christ's works and teachings. Paul the apostle based his preaching on the message of Jesus Christ, and he finds support for his preaching in the resurrection of Christ. He writes, ". . . and if Christ has not been raised, then our proclamation has been in vain and your faith has been in vain" (1 Corinthians 15:14). Through the resurrection of Christ, God affirms all that Jesus says and did. Paul writes, "Therefore we have been buried with him by baptism into death, so that, just as Christ was raised from the dead by the glory of the Father, so we too might walk in newness of life" (Romans 6:4). If Jesus had not been raised from the dead, we would still be in our sins. Death was the last weapon of evil, and by the resurrection of Jesus, death and evil were overcome. A new life came into the world through the resurrection. As Jesus' humanness was raised up on the day of his resurrection, so our humanness was lifted up. We are now capable of entering into a special union with Christ. Our belief that sin has been overcome likewise flows from Jesus' resurrection, and we now have hope for a similar resurrection. Paul writes, ". . . for as all die in Adam, so all will be made alive in Christ" (1 Corinthians 15:22).

8. What is the meaning of the ascension of Jesus?

a. The death, resurrection, and ascension of Jesus are all the same one act of redemption.

In our world, we live in time. Eternity is timeless, with no past and no future. We are faced with a mystery outside our experience, and we have no way to explain timelessness. In speaking of the ascension of Jesus, the Scriptures follow a time sequence. In reality, at the moment of Jesus' death, he was raised and exalted at the right hand of the Father. Christ ascended at the same time he died and was raised. In St. Paul's Letter to the Philippians, Paul actually skips the resurrection of Jesus and reports that the exaltation, or ascension, took place immediately upon the death of Jesus. Paul writes,

> . . . he humbled himself and became obedient to the point of death— even death on a cross. Therefore, God also highly exalted him and gave him the name that is above every name (Philippians 2:8–9).

In the resurrection of Jesus, we see his glory. This glory belongs to his heavenly glory which actually comes through his place at the right hand of the Father. This presupposes that an ascension had already taken place.

b. The Scriptures portray a visible ascension of Jesus into heaven forty days after his resurrection.

We read in the Acts of the Apostles, "When he had said this, as they were watching, he was lifted up, and a cloud took him out of their sight. While he was going and they were gazing up toward heaven, suddenly two men in white robes stood by them. They said, 'Men of Galilee, why do you stand looking up toward heaven? This Jesus, who has been taken up from you into heaven, will come in the same way as you saw him go into heaven' " (Acts 1:9–11). In this reading, Luke speaks of the ancient view of the world. Jesus ascends to heaven upon a cloud and will pass through the dome into the heavenly realm. In this picturesque narrative, The Acts of the Apostles is telling us that the apostles had the mission of continuing the mission of Jesus. In the early preaching, a definite point in time was chosen to portray the end of Jesus' sojourn on earth and the beginning of the new era of the early Church.

9. Was Jesus really raised from the dead?

a. The effect of this belief in the resurrection of Jesus was too dramatic to deny that he was raised from the dead.

The early followers of Jesus changed so drastically from fear to courage and from doubt to belief that it would be impossible to presume that Jesus' resurrection was a hoax. We must remember, however, that when we speak of the resurrection of Jesus, we are speaking of a new form of life. Unlike Lazarus, who was raised from the dead and who would die again, Jesus would no longer face death. He now lived in his new, eternal, and glorious life.

In one of the resurrection stories, two men are walking along a road to a town called Emmaus. Jesus joins them in this walk, but they do not recognize him. In speaking of resurrection in general, St. Paul writes, "So it is with the resurrection of the dead. What is sown is perishable, what is raised is imperishable. It is sown in dishonor, it is raised in glory. It is sown in weakness, it is raised in power. It is sown a physical body, it is raised a spiritual body. If there is a physical body, there is also a spiritual body" (1 Corinthians 15:42–44). Because Christ was present in his resurrected, glorious body, the friends of Jesus on the road to Emmaus did not recognize him. However, they recognized him as he broke bread with them and disappeared from their midst. When they ran to tell the other apostles, they were greeted with " 'The Lord has risen indeed, and he has appeared to Simon!' " (Luke 24:34).

b. We do not know exactly what took place, since each Gospel tells a slightly different story.

Although each of the Gospels speaks of the empty tomb, no one actually saw Jesus raised from the dead. They report the evidence only after the resurrection. Even this evidence varies from Gospel to Gospel. In Matthew's Gospel, Mary Magdalene and the other Mary are at the tomb as the stone is rolled back by an angel in dazzling garments. Jesus is not in the tomb when the stone is rolled back. In Mark, Mary Magdalene, Mary, the mother of James, and Salome come to the tomb to find the stone already rolled back and find a young man inside dressed in a white robe. Jesus is not there. In Luke, Mary Magdalene, Joanna, and Mary, the mother of James, come to the tomb and find the stone rolled back and the tomb empty. Suddenly, two men in dazzling garments are beside them. In John's Gospel, Mary Magdalene comes to the tomb and finds the stone rolled back. Instead of entering, she runs to tell Peter and John that the body has been taken from the tomb, apparently stolen. John and Peter rush to the tomb and find it empty. In John's Gospel, there are no angels, no young man or young men present.

Some today claim that this resurrection story of the empty tomb was the early Christian faith simply saying that Jesus was raised. Some feel that the body of Jesus was placed in an unmarked potter's grave, but this is simply a conclusion drawn from the differences in the stories of the resurrection. All we can say is that Jesus actually was raised from the dead, but we do not know how this happened.

c. The Christian Church centers its belief on the resurrection of Jesus.

What type of experience of the resurrection the apostles had cannot be definitely stated, due mainly to the different literary forms used in the Gospels. The writers could simply be trying to tell us that the apostles knew with certainty that Jesus was raised. The writers expressed this belief by showing through the resurrection narratives that Jesus was alive and living with them . From the reading of the Scriptures, we know that the apostles had more than an inner experience of Christ's resurrection. They had a real experience of a special presence of Christ among them. Whether we accept the stories as written or whether there was another experience of Christ that led the apostles to preach the message in this way is not the center of our faith. Our faith centers on the fact that Jesus Christ was raised, that he is Lord, and that he lives in his resurrection. The resurrection narratives, under the inspiration of God, share this message, and today we celebrate the fact that "Jesus is alive; he has been raised."

10. What is the second coming of Jesus?

a. In the Scriptures, we read of a presence of Christ in creation that is yet to happen.

We know very little about the second coming of Jesus. Christ told us to be on our guard for the end of the world, but he claimed that only the Father knew when this would come. Many of the writings of St. Paul tell us that the early Christians expected this coming shortly after the ascension of Jesus. After some time, when the second coming did not take place, the tone of the letters of Paul changed, and he no longer spoke of the second coming as being near. St. Luke expressed the imagery that told of the second coming of Jesus when he writes, "Then they will see 'the Son of Man coming in a cloud' with power and great glory. Now when these things begin to take place, stand up and raise your heads, because your redemption is drawing near" (Luke 21:27–28). We still await the second coming of Jesus Christ, whatever that second coming may entail.

b. The second coming of Jesus should fill us with hope rather than fear.

A majority of people tend to fear the second coming. They read in the Scriptures that great earthquakes and catastrophes will occur upon the earth just before the end. But even here, the Scriptures do not clearly state exactly what we are to look for. The earth has had earthquakes, war, and catastrophes almost every decade since the beginning of recorded history. We simply must be ready for the great day of the coming of the Lord: "Now when these things begin to take place, stand up and raise your heads, because your redemption is drawing near" (Luke 21:28). On that day, the Son of God will invite the just into the everlasting joy of heaven, and this is a cause for rejoicing.

11. What do the Gospels tell us about Jesus and prayer?

a. The Gospels present Jesus as a man of constant prayer.

Jesus prayed at critical moments in his life. We need mention only a few examples here. The Gospel of Mark describes Jesus as stealing away to pray on a quiet morning. The people, excited by Jesus' healings, want him to remain with them, but, in his prayer, Jesus is able to focus his attention on his mission and his need to move on to other towns and people. Jesus prays before he chooses the twelve apostles, before healings, and during his agony in the garden and on the cross.

The Gospel of Luke reminds us that Jesus also offered public prayer. The author of the Gospel of Luke tells us that "When he came to Nazareth, where he had been brought up, he went to the synagogue on the sabbath day, as was his custom. He stood up to read . . ." (Luke 4:16). His prayer became an example to his disciples. On one occasion, right after he had finished praying, one of his disciples asked him, "Lord, teach us to pray, as John taught his disciples" (Luke 11:1). When his disciples returned from their missionary journey, Jesus attempted to lead them off to a place of solitude for prayer.

b. Jesus taught his disciples to pray.

Jesus taught his disciples to call out to God in intimate terms in their prayer. He used the term "Abba" which can properly be translated "Dad" or "Daddy." He taught them to begin their prayers with words of praise to God and to lay their petitions before God in faith. He tells them to ask and they shall receive, to seek and they shall find, to knock and it will be opened to them. He urges them to pray with persistence, and not to become discouraged in their prayer. He stresses that God already knows their needs and wants to help them. They should trust that God will provide for their needs as

God provides for the needs of the lilies of the field and the birds of the air. He advises them to pray in groups and to find a quiet place for private prayer.

c. Jesus taught the underlying attitude for prayer.

Jesus teaches that it is the faith of one's prayer and not a multitude of prayers that is important. Jesus tells his disciples to believe that they will receive whatever they ask of God in prayer. Jesus can say to the blind man, "Go, your faith has made you well" (Mark 10:48 NAB).

Not only does Jesus desire faith on the part of the one who prays, but he demands a forgiving attitude in the one who prays. Jesus tells his disciples to pray that God will "forgive us our trespasses as we forgive those who trespass against us." Forgiveness must reside in the heart of the one who prays. Before offering one's gift on the altar, one should seek forgiveness for faults against others. Prayer demands more than mouthing words. It is not the person who prays "Lord, Lord," who will pray correctly, but those who do God's will in their lives and live with the proper attitude. Jesus urges his disciples to love their enemies, pray for their persecutors, and seek God before all else.

d. Jesus responded to prayer during his ministry.

Jesus responds when a leper asks to be cured, a blind man asks for sight, a foreign woman asks for healing, and a centurion asks for a cure for his servant. The stories of Jesus' many acts of healing in the Gospels begin with pleading on the part of those seeking a cure. The physical healings Jesus performs in response to prayer are meant to offer a message of God's spiritual healing for those who pray. Jesus forgives the sins of the paralytic who obviously is hoping for a physical cure. In Jesus' day, the sign of a spiritual healing took place when the physical healing took place. Jesus makes use of this attitude of his day to show that the paralytic receives not only a physical cure, but the more important spiritual cure as well.

e. Mary's prayer is one of trust in God.

When Mary accepts her role as the mother of Jesus, she prays, "Here am I, the servant of the Lord; let it be with me according to your word" (Luke 1:38). When she comes before Elizabeth, the mother of John the Baptizer, Mary proclaims the greatness of the Lord in a prayer similar to that on the lips of Hannah, the mother of an Old Testament prophet Samuel. She not only proclaims the greatness of the Lord on her behalf, but the greatness of the Lord in preparing for the coming of Christ throughout the history of Israel. The Gospel of John portrays Mary, at a wedding feast in Cana, interceding with Jesus to change water into wine. She prayerfully ponders in her heart all that she learns of Jesus. Although we hear very little from Mary throughout the Gospels, her willingness to respond to God's will echoes throughout the whole gospel message. Jesus himself repeats this message in the garden, when he accepts his death with the words, "Father, if you are willing, remove this cup from me; yet, not my will but yours be done" (Luke 22:42).

Conclusion

As the fisherman in the introduction to this chapter grew to a wise old age, he often told his grandchildren about the stranger who saved his life. The story had grown over the years, but the kindness of the stranger was always there. The more the fisherman thought of the stranger, the more he realized his goodness. This realization found its way into his story. When he told the children about this adventure, he embellished by adding that the stranger had a great appointment he missed because of this encounter. The parents of the children who heard the story and actually knew what had happened just shook their heads and smiled that the fisherman could add these details with such enthusiasm. But the parents had to admit that perhaps the fisherman had captured the real personality of the stranger. After all, he was a definite part of the experience, and he had to have the deeper insight.

For Scripture reflection and discussion concerning this chapter, see Journeying in His Light, "Jesus Is Lord: Parts 1 and 2."

4 The Holy Spirit in Our Lives

Introduction

The newspaper told of a skydiver whose parachute did not open and who fell two-thousand feet to the ground. Miraculously, the man did not die, although he broke almost every bone in his body. After twelve months in the hospital, he was able to limp back into the world. The doctors predicted that he would always have that limp. The man began to walk every day and finally to jog. Gradually, the limp disappeared, and the man was able to run in a marathon in a major city. He did not win the marathon, but he celebrated the fact that he could jog respectfully along with hundreds of others in that marathon.

In the last chapter, we looked at Jesus' resurrection and ascension. We are specially chosen to share the message of Christ through our lives, but in many ways we are a broken, weak people. We need strength to carry out this task, and God gives us this strength through the presence of the Holy Spirit in our lives. We take faltering steps in the faith, but, with the help of the Holy Spirit, we can begin to move more firmly, trusting in the Spirit's guidance and continual presence.

1. Where do we hear of the Holy Spirit?

a. The Gospels speak of the Holy Spirit as possessing or being in Jesus.

The Holy Spirit is mentioned often in relationship to Jesus during his earthly life. In the Gospel of Luke, the author uses a dramatic story to show the Holy Spirit entering Jesus' life. "Now when all the people were baptized, and when Jesus also had been baptized and was praying, the heaven was opened, and the Holy Spirit descended upon him in bodily form like a dove. And a voice came from heaven, 'You are my Son, the beloved; with you I am well pleased' " (Luke 3:21–22).

In the following chapter, the author of Luke has the Spirit guiding Jesus and being with Jesus: "Jesus, full of the Holy Spirit, returned from the Jordan and was led by the Spirit in the wilderness, where for forty days he was tempted by the devil. He ate nothing at all during those days, and when they were over, he was famished" (Luke 4:1–2). The Gospels proclaim the presence of the Holy Spirit in Jesus from the lips of Jesus himself: ". . . and the scroll of the prophet Isaiah was given to him. He unrolled the scroll and found the place where it was written: 'The Spirit of the Lord is upon me, because he has anointed me to bring good news to the poor. He has sent me to proclaim release to the captives and recovery of sight to the blind, to let the oppressed go free.' . . . Then he began to say to them, 'Today this scripture has been fulfilled in your hearing' " (Luke 4:17–18, 21).

As we read these and other similar declarations throughout the Gospels, we conclude that the Holy Spirit worked in, with, and through Jesus throughout his life. The Holy Spirit filled him, guided him, inspired him, and worked through him.

b. The New Testament proclaims that Jesus would send the Holy Spirit upon the world.

In the Gospel of John, we read that the work of the Holy Spirit will take place in the followers of Jesus after his resurrection. Jesus tells his apostles, "Nevertheless I tell you the truth: it is to your advantage that I go away, for if I do not go away, the Advocate will not come to you; but if I go, I will send him to you" (John 16:7). Only through his death and resurrection will the early followers of Jesus receive this Holy Spirit. He must go before he can send the Spirit.

On a special festival day, Jesus talks about the living waters that would flow forth from him. John makes a commentary here when he writes, "Now he said this about the Spirit, which believers in him were to receive; for as yet there was no Spirit, because Jesus was not yet glorified" (John 7:39). Through the glorification of Jesus will the waters of the Spirit flow forth. As we read through the writings of John, we realize that the later community understood the Spirit as being in Jesus while he lived on this earth, and as being sent by Jesus into the world after his glorification.

c. Jesus speaks of the Holy Spirit as an independent person.

In the Gospels, Jesus speaks of the Holy Spirit as a person separate from himself: "And I will ask the Father, and he will give you another Advocate, to be with you forever. This is the Spirit of truth, whom the world cannot receive, because it neither sees him nor knows him. You know him, because he abides with you, and he will be in you" (John 14:16–17). In another section of the same discourse, Jesus speaks of the Paraclete as a separate person, "But the Advocate, the Holy Spirit, whom the Father will send in my name, will teach you everything, and remind you of all that I have said to you" (John 14:26). Although the Holy Spirit guided Jesus on earth, he is still independent of Jesus, a separate person.

d. The Old Testament speaks of the Spirit of God as an action of God rather than as a separate person.

In the story of creation, the Spirit of God sweeps across the waters and brings order into creation. This action of God refers more to a wind or a breath that moves across the waters. When Isaiah the prophet first used the expression of the Spirit's presence, he was probably speaking of the guidance of God rather than the action of another person: "The Spirit of the Lord God is upon me, because the Lord has anointed me; he has sent me to bring good news to the oppressed, to bind up the brokenhearted, to proclaim liberty to the captives, and release to the prisoners . . ." (Isaiah 61:1). This action of God fully possesses a person and enables the person to live out the word of God. In this case as in other cases in the Old Testament, God's Spirit affects people for a short time, to preach the word or to perform some action. At certain prophetic moments in their lives, the prophets feel the Spirit of the Lord upon them.

In these and other uses of "the Spirit" in the Old Testament, we can hardly refer to the Holy Spirit as we understand the Spirit through the New Testament. But the Old Testament can easily pave the way for a deeper New Testament understanding of the action of the Spirit. As we look back today from our understanding of the Holy Spirit as a person separate from the Father, we can see a far more significant message than even the prophets saw.

2. Is the Holy Spirit God?

a. The Gospel of John tells of the Holy Spirit as coming from both the Father and the Son.

The Holy Spirit is described as coming directly from the Father and being sent by the Son. Implied here is an equality of mission in sharing the truth: "When the Advocate comes, whom I will send to you from the Father, the Spirit of truth who comes from the Father, he will testify on my behalf" (John 15:26). When Jesus speaks of the Holy Spirit, he says that the Spirit will not speak on his own, but only what he receives from the Son, who in turn will always be reflecting the Father. This shows the independence of each person, yet the unity of the three persons.

b. In giving the apostles the power and mission to baptize, Jesus also proclaims the oneness of the Father, the Son, and the Holy Spirit.

In the Gospel of Matthew, Jesus speaks of the three separate persons, the Father, the Son, and the Holy Spirit, yet he places these three under a single "name." "And Jesus came and said to them, 'All authority in heaven and on earth has been given to me. Go therefore and make disciples of all nations, baptizing them in the name of the

Father and of the Son and of the Holy Spirit' " (Matthew 28:18–19). Just as Jesus proclaimed that he and the Father were one, he here proclaims that the Father, Son, and Holy Spirit are one. We are again enveloped in the mystery of God.

c. In its early centuries, the Church struggled with this mystery of three persons in one God, calling this mystery the Blessed Trinity.

The Scriptures clearly speak of only one God, yet they also speak of the Father as God, the Son as God, and the Holy Spirit as God. All are equal, all are one, yet all are independent of each other. If God had not revealed this mystery to us through the Scriptures, we would never have known it. We are at a loss fully to understand this mystery, because we have nothing in our experience to compare with this idea of three persons having only one nature. Each of us is an individual person having an individual human nature. God is three persons having a common divine nature.

A common picture of the Trinity (which means "three-in-one") is the three-leaf clover. But three leaves on one stem still do not portray the Trinity. Each leaf does not act independently, nor can we look upon God as having one stem. A legend is told of St. Augustine in the fifth century walking along a beach trying to understand the Trinity. He met a little boy on the beach who had dug a hole in the sand and was running back and forth from the water to the hole with a pail, continuously putting water into the hole. Augustine asked the boy what he was doing, and the boy told Augustine that he was going to put the ocean into this hole. Augustine laughed and told the boy that this was impossible. The boy answered, "It is more possible for me to put all the water from the ocean into this hole than it is for you to understand the Trinity." Although this story most likely never happened, the message it teaches is a good one. We can never understand how there can be three persons in the one God, since this is one of the mysteries of God. We simply accept this revelation on faith.

3. Why did God reveal the Trinity?

a. We could never say with full certainty why God revealed the Trinity.

The ways of God will always remain a mystery, and perhaps we can never really know why God does anything. We can guess, but only God truly knows God's own inner thinking. In the case of the Trinity, God did not have to tell us about the three persons in one God. God could have left us with the revelation that the one true God became man and the one true God is sharing personal guidance with us in life. But God revealed that each of these works was the work of an individual person who is also the one true God. God revealed this mystery, and, instead of asking "why," we should ask ourselves what the revelation teaches us.

b. The three-persons-in-one God tells us of the value of unity.

In the Book of Genesis, we read under the sixth day of creation, "Let us make humankind in our image, according to our likeness; and let them have dominion over the fish of the sea, and over the birds of the air, and over the cattle, and over all the wild animals of the earth, and over every creeping thing that creeps upon the earth" (Genesis 1:26). Besides the ability to think, judge, will, and act as sharing in the image of God, we should see as our goal another image in God through revelation, namely the unity of three distinct persons. Our aim as God's human family and as an image of God is not to destroy our individuality, but rather to make our own personhood work toward unity. By remaining different, yet working with a unity of concern and love, we are more truly reflecting the image of God.

4. Do the Scriptures reveal when the disciples received the Holy Spirit?

a. The Scriptures reveal that Christ gave the Holy Spirit to his disciples shortly after his resurrection.

In the Gospel of John, the apostles gathered together in fear in the upper room, apparently the room of the Last Supper. Jesus suddenly stood in their midst and said, " 'Peace be with you. As the Father has sent me, so I send you.' When he had said this, he breathed on them and said to them, 'Receive the Holy Spirit. If you forgive the sins of any, they are forgiven them; if you retain the sins of any, they are retained' " (John 20:21–23). In the Gospel of John, Jesus promised to send the Holy Spirit upon the disciples after his resurrection, and he fulfilled this promise as one of his first acts after the resurrection.

b. In the Acts of the Apostles, we read that the Holy Spirit came upon the apostles on Pentecost.

On the feast of Pentecost, the apostles were gathered together in one place. The Acts describe a strong, driving wind and "tongues as of fire" that rested upon each of them. The Acts go on to say simply, "All of them were filled with the Holy Spirit and began to speak in other languages, as the Spirit gave them ability" (Acts 2:4). Courage comes with this gift of the Spirit, and Peter goes out to preach to crowds of people from many distant lands, who heard his words in their own languages. Again, the Scriptures present us with a problem. When did the apostles first receive the Holy Spirit, immediately after the resurrection of Jesus or on Pentecost Sunday? We must look to the message and realize that although we too have received the Holy Spirit, the awareness and guidance of the Holy Spirit is not always strongly felt in our lives. At times, however, we can fully experience the guidance of the Holy Spirit that fires us up to share Christ's message in some special way. Exactly what happened on Pentecost must remain a mystery, but the fact that the Holy Spirit shares special gifts with us is the revealed message.

5. What is the mission of the Holy Spirit?

a. The Holy Spirit enables us to understand the message of Jesus.

In the Gospel of John, we read the words of Jesus, " 'I have said these things to you while I am still with you. But the Advocate, the Holy Spirit, whom the Father will send in my name, will teach you everything, and remind you of all that I have said to you' " (John 14:25–26). Just as the Holy Spirit instructed the early disciples, so the work of the Holy Spirit guides us that we too may be better able to understand the message and life of Jesus. The Holy Spirit comes as the Spirit of Truth; "When the Spirit of truth comes, he will guide you into all the truth; for he will not speak on his own, but will speak whatever he hears, and he will declare to you the things that are to come" (John 16:13). The continuing mission of the Holy Spirit is to guide the followers of Jesus in understanding the truth about Jesus.

b. The Holy Spirit guides us in witnessing to Christ.

We again read in the Gospel of John, "When the Advocate comes, whom I will send to you from the Father, the Spirit of Truth who comes from the Father, he will testify on my behalf. You also are to testify because you have been with me from the beginning" (John 15:26–27). The Gospel tells us that just as the Holy Spirit will bear witness on behalf of Jesus, so the disciples, filled with the Holy Spirit, must also, in their turn, bear witness to Jesus. We too, under the guidance of the Holy Spirit, receive our call to witness to Jesus by our words and the way we live.

In the Acts of the Apostles, Jesus reminds the disciples that this witness must reach to the very ends of the earth: "But you will receive power when the Holy Spirit has come upon you; and you will be my witnesses in Jerusalem, in all Judea and Samaria, and to the ends of the earth" (Acts 1:8). The ministry of the Holy Spirit is to guide the followers of Jesus in witnessing to Jesus throughout the whole world.

c. The Holy Spirit shares different gifts for the sake of the ministry.

The Holy Spirit provides different gifts for the sharing of Jesus' message throughout the world. Although there are many gifts shared, they all come from the one and the same Holy Spirit. The Holy Spirit decides on the distribution of these gifts and freely distributes them as the Spirit wills. St. Paul writes:

> Now there are varieties of gifts, but the same Spirit; and there are varieties of services, but the same Lord; and there are varieties of activities, but it is the same God who activates all of them in everyone. To each is given the manifestation of the Spirit for the common good. To one is given through the Spirit the utterance of wisdom, and to another the utterance of knowledge according to the same Spirit, to another faith by the same Spirit, to another gifts of healing by the one Spirit, to another the working of miracles, to another prophecy, to another the discernment of spirits, to another various kinds of tongues, to another the interpretation of tongues. All these are activated by one and the same Spirit, who allots to each one individually just as the Spirit chooses (1 Corinthians 12:4–11).

All of us share in some gifts of the Holy Spirit. In sharing in these gifts, we should never become proud of our accomplishments, but remember the words of Paul in this same letter, "To each is given the manifestation of the Spirit for the common good" (1 Corinthians 12:7). God shares the gifts of the Spirit that the Christian community might grow.

d. The Church identifies certain gifts and fruits of the Holy Spirit.

Church teaching speaks of seven significant *gifts* of the Holy Spirit which bestow on the faithful the capacity to open their hearts and minds to the inspiration and guidance of the Spirit. Through these gifts, the faithful can fulfill the mission entrusted to them. These seven *gifts* of the Holy Spirit are wisdom, understanding, counsel, fortitude, knowledge, piety, and awe in God's presence (known also as fear of the Lord).

Church teaching also lists twelve *fruits* of the Holy Spirit which the Holy Spirit confers on us through the sacraments. The twelve *fruits* of the Spirit include love, joy, peace, patience, kindness, goodness, fidelity, gentleness, self-control, modesty, chastity, and generosity.

The exact number or identification of each individual gift or fruit of the Spirit is not as important as the message expressed, namely that the Holy Spirit fills Christians with an abundance of blessings.

e. The Holy Spirit calls us to holiness.

We cannot achieve holiness on our own, since holiness comes from faith, and faith comes through gifts of the Holy Spirit. In his First Letter to the Corinthians, Paul tells us, "Therefore I want you to understand that no one speaking by the Spirit of God ever says 'Let Jesus be cursed!' and no one can say 'Jesus is Lord' except by the Holy Spirit" (1 Corinthians 12:3). In his Letter to the Galatians, Paul reminds them that those who follow the ways of the world experience every kind of evil, while those who follow the Spirit experience the fruits of the Spirit which lead to holiness. Paul writes, "By contrast, the fruit of the Spirit is love, joy, peace, patience, kindness, generosity, faithfulness, gentleness, and self-control. There is no law against such things" (Galatians 5:22–23). He urges his readers, "If we live by the Spirit, let us also be guided by the Spirit" (Galatians 5:25).

6. How does the Church honor the Holy Spirit and the Trinity?

a. The Church encourages all Christians to seek continually the guidance of the Holy Spirit.

The Church encourages prayer to seek the guidance of the Holy Spirit before any great work or decision in life. Even for the simple decisions of life, the Church encourages this devotion, realizing that nothing is too tedious for God. A prayer often used in invoking the Holy Spirit is the following:

Come, Holy Spirit,
fill the hearts of your faithful
and enkindle in them
the fire of your love.
Send forth your Spirit
and they shall be created,
and you shall renew the face of the earth.

b. The Church honors the Blessed Trinity with the sign of the cross accompanied by the words of faith in the Trinity.

At the beginning of prayer, a Catholic will often make the sign of the cross. The ordinary way of making the sign of the cross is to touch the forehead, the chest, the left shoulder, then the right with the right hand, praying as we do so:

In the name of the Father,
and of the Son,
and of the Holy Spirit, Amen.

c. The Church also proclaims a prayer for glory to the three persons in one God.

The Church has a special prayer which praises God in God's glory and proclaims that the Godhood of the three persons is eternal. We pray:

Glory to the Father,
and to the Son,
and to the Holy Spirit.
As it was in the beginning,
is now, and will be forever. Amen.

Conclusion

As Christians, we believe in sharing in God's presence on earth. We live our days with the conviction that we are filled with the power of the Holy Spirit. Like the marathon runner at the beginning of this chapter, we do not run the race to outrun everyone else, but we celebrate the fact that God has chosen to give us the power to move along with the rest. We have our particular task within the human family, whether the task be rearing a family, studying at school, working in an office or a factory, or simply accepting the inactivity of sickness or aging. Whatever our call at this moment, we are racing along with the rest of the human family, doing our special tasks under the guidance of the Holy Spirit. And like that marathon runner, we must struggle to realize fully the great power and hope of the gifts within us.

For Scripture reflection and discussion concerning this chapter, see **Journeying in His Light,** *"The Holy Spirit in Our Life."*

5 Sin and Life

Introduction

    The counselor listened to the story he had heard so many times before. The mother and father told him how their teenage son had gone on picnics with them in his early years, how he had gone to church each Sunday and even stopped into church for special visits, how he had brought his friends home and played in the yard and how he had hated to see his father smoke. Now he no longer wanted to join the family in outings; he never went to church; they never met his friends; he left home early and came back late; he skipped school, and not only did he smoke, but he also drank. The reason they had come to the counselor was an event that happened just a week ago. The boy had cursed at his mother when she asked where he had been, and the father, when he had heard the boy swear at the mother, had slapped the boy so hard he had stumbled across the room and tripped over a chair. In a tirade of angry words and in tears, the boy had slammed out the door and had not returned till early the next morning. The parents were seeking help in relating to their son.

    The counselor tried to explain to the parents how children often rebel as they grow. In some cases, the rebellion takes form in simple laziness, irritability, and a desire to get their own way, while others make a complete rejection of their younger years. The child has to break away from the nest, and for some this becomes more violent than for others. The counselor advised the parents never to break with the boy no matter what he did, while at the same time they must continue to keep before the boy's eyes the fact that he must learn to live in a mature society which demands that he give as well as receive. Hopefully, the boy would return in some way to the lessons of his youth.

1. What is sin?

a. Sin is a weakening or breaking of a love relationship between a person and God.

Life is filled with relationships. We relate in one way to the person who works at the grocery store; we relate in another way to our friends; and we relate in an even different way to our families. These relationships are based upon some degree of love. We know that God loves us deeply, and so we can claim a deep love relationship between ourselves and God. The parents in the introduction love their teenage son, and they see him weakening or breaking that love relationship. Their son is moving away from them, and they feel his alienation. Because the relationship is growing weaker, they seek the help of a counselor before the relationship breaks completely.

When we sin, we act in a fashion similar to that of the son in the introduction. We either forget about God's love for us and ignore it, or, at times, we might completely reject God's love just to have our own way in life. Whenever we ignore God's love for us or reject that love, we commit sin, because we are weakening or breaking that love relationship between ourselves and God. As the parents in the introduction will never stop loving their son, so God will never stop loving us. We are the ones who choose to break that love relationship or to weaken it, and so we are the ones who commit sin.

In the Gospel of Luke, Jesus speaks of his helplessness as the people of Jerusalem refuse to respond to his love. In the face of this rejection, Jesus tells them, "Jerusalem, Jerusalem, the city that kills the prophets and stones those who are sent to it! How often have I desired to gather your children together as a hen gathers her brood under her wings, and you were not willing" (Luke 13:34). Despite their rejection of him, Jesus will continue to reach out to the Judean leaders until his death.

b. This sin which consists of weakening or breaking a love relationship with God occurs when we hurt our neighbor.

The author of the First Letter of John reminds us that we cannot love God unless we first love our neighbor: "Those who say, 'I love

God,' and hate their brothers or sisters, are liars; for those who do not love a brother or sister whom they have seen, cannot love God whom they have not seen. The commandment we have from him is this: those who love God must love their brothers and sisters also" (1 John 4:20–21).

When someone asked Jesus who his neighbor was, Jesus told the story of the Good Samaritan. " 'A man was beaten by robbers and thrown into a ditch. A priest and a Levite passed the man by, but a Samaritan stopped to help the man. He bound his wounds, took him to an inn for lodging and told the inn-keeper that he would pay whatever he owed on his return.' " Jesus then let the questioner answer his own question: " 'Which of these three, do you think, was a neighbor to the man who fell into the hands of the robbers?' He said, 'The one who showed him mercy.' Jesus said to him, 'Go and do likewise' " (Luke 10:36–37).

Our neighbor is all around us. As we relate to him or her, we relate to God. As we hurt our neighbor, we hurt God, and as we love our neighbor, we love God. Whenever we weaken or break a love relationship with our neighbor, even an unknown neighbor in need, we weaken or break a love relationship with God. In this way, we commit sin.

c. We sin by weakening or breaking a love relationship with God even when we hurt ourselves.

God has made us a most precious part of creation and has even commanded us to love ourselves: " 'You shall love the Lord your God with all your heart, and with all your soul, and with all your strength, and with all your mind: and your neighbor as yourself' " (Luke 10:27). Love of self differs from selfishness which is often destructive of self. When we accept our dignity as special creations of God and strive to develop our gifts in a proper fashion, we show love of self. When we abuse the gifts God gives us or allow them to be destroyed by our own laziness or negligence, then we hurt ourselves and weaken our relationship with God who is deeply and lovingly concerned for us. The parents of the boy in the introduction agonize over their son as they see him drinking into the early hours of the morning. So it is with God. As the parents seek the good of their son, so God seeks our good.

To truly love oneself consists in living with appreciation of the gifts God has given us with the realization that God truly loves us.

We are closest to God when we love, and we are farthest from God when we lack love. In the First Letter of John, we have a summary of the need for love in our lives if we wish to remain aware of God's presence within us. The author writes, "God is love, and those who abide in love abide in God, and God abides in them" (1 John 4:16). Since God is love, we cannot truly know God unless we love.

2. How do we explain sin in the world?

a. We do not know how sin began in the world.

In the story of Adam and Eve, we read that human beings are responsible for sin in the world. God granted them many gifts and only one small precept: " 'You may freely eat of every tree of the garden; but of the tree of the knowledge of good and evil you shall not eat, for in the day that you eat of it you shall die' " (Genesis 2:16–17). A serpent tempted Eve to eat the fruit, and Eve enjoyed the taste so much she ran to share the fruit with Adam who also ate it and sinned. By this action, they broke the love relationship between God and themselves. They covered themselves with leaves in order to hide from each other. They also tried to hide from God. The love that once bound them together in an open, free way was destroyed by the sin of eating the fruit. The message behind the story tells us that human beings, not God, had broken this love relationship and brought sin into the world.

b. The early stories of the Book of Genesis following upon this sin share the message that sin gradually gained a grip on the world.

After Adam and Eve were cast out of the garden of paradise, the story of Cain and Abel, the sons of Adam and Eve, told of another sin being committed. God was pleased with Abel's gift, and Cain, in his anger, killed Abel. In this destruction of his brother, Cain broke his love relationship with God. Shortly after this, the storyteller

94

drew a story from mythology. Just as the gods of mythology married human beings, so the storyteller wrote, "When people began to multiply on the face of the ground, and daughters were born to them, the sons of God saw that they were fair; and they took wives for themselves of all that they chose" (Genesis 6:1–2).

Finally, in a world filled with sin, only Noah and his family were sinless and worthy of salvation. Noah built the ark and saved his family and all the animals from the terrible flood that covered the earth. No sooner had the ark landed than Noah's son, Ham, committed sin by looking upon his father's nakedness and ridiculing his father.

These early stories end with the building of the tower of Babel by which these people attempted to reach God in their own way. The tower would soar to the dome of heaven and give vain glory to its builders. Because of the pride of these people, God mixed up their languages that they could not work together. Instead of using their common gift for good, they sinned through this gift. By the time we come to the end of chapter 11 in Genesis, we have read through the stories that tell of sin gaining a grip on the world. When Abraham comes on the scene, sin already controls the world.

c. The grip of sin in the world is called original sin, since it stands at the origin and base of our creation.

With the sin committed by the first human being, the Scriptures tell us that sin began to inundate the world. This build-up of sin in the world has never ceased, even down to our present day. Whenever we accept sinful attitudes that become part of the thinking of society, we contribute to original sin. The acceptance of racism, excessive profits, abortion, and "taking care of number one first" are all attitudes of sin existing at the very base of our creation. By the "base of our creation," we simply mean those sins that have rooted themselves in a people, a society, or a culture. Nowhere in the Scriptures do we have the expression "original sin." The term seems to have its birth somewhere in the early centuries after Christ.

When we speak of being born in original sin, we not only refer to the sinful attitude of the world that surrounds us, we also refer to our own inability to confront and overcome this sinful attitude that grips the world. Through the resurrection of Jesus, we are able to share in a new strength and new life that enables us to do our share in overcoming the sin of the world. Christ came to confront this grip of sin in the world, and he successfully overcame sin. Now, through the gifts of Christ's resurrection, we too are called to do our part in overcoming these sinful attitudes that surround us. In his Letter to the Romans, Paul reminds us of the power of Christ over sin. He writes, "Therefore just as one man's trespass led to condemnation for all, so one man's act of righteousness leads to justification and life for all" (Romans 5:18).

3. What are some examples of actions that are considered sinful?

a. In the Old Testament, we read of the Commandments given by God to the Israelite community (cf. pages 36–37).

The Ten Commandments still have importance and value and are taught by the Church today. When someone asked Jesus what he must do to merit eternal life, Jesus told him to keep the Commandments. Jesus referred him to the Ten Commandments when he stated, " 'You shall not murder; You shall not commit adultery; You shall not steal; You shall not bear false witness; Honor your father and mother; also, You shall love your neighbor as yourself' " (Matthew 19:18–19). The first three Commandments of the Old Testament Law touch upon our relationship with God, while the rest touch upon our relationship with one another.

The First Commandment calls us to honor and worship the one true God alone, both as individuals and as a community of people. This commandment warns against idolatry or a complete indifference toward God or denial of God.

The Second Commandment calls for honor and respect of God's name and person. This commandments warns against blaspheming God or swearing a false oath in God's name.

The Third Commandment calls us to keep holy the day of the Lord, to set aside a day of public and visible worship of God. This commandment seeks to give proper worship to God, our creator and guide. It calls for a day of rest and worship, that we may grow more aware of God's presence in our lives and respond to that gift.

The Fourth Commandment calls for honoring one's parents. This commandment seeks to strengthen the family and to direct the proper attitude toward one's parents. In our day, when so many elderly must depend on their adult children for support, the commandment has special meaning for those who must care for elderly parents. The commandment also calls for respect of all rightful and morally good authority, and it calls for civil authority to have respect for families.

The Fifth Commandment warns against the killing of another human being. It seeks to develop a deep respect for human life, from the womb to the tomb. This commandment does not exclude a legitimate defense of one's life. But, even in war, this commandment forbids unjust and random killing.

The Sixth Commandment warns against adultery. This commandment seeks to strengthen the true meaning of the proper use of sex within marriage. It seeks to protect the family and fosters the true meaning of sexuality and love within the community.

The Seventh Commandment warns against stealing, which involves taking the property or goods of another without the right to do so. This involves stealing another's possessions, and it also involves stealing another's labor or time without just compensation. It calls for the practice of justice in the administration of the world's goods and for proper and charitable stewardship of the goods of creation.

The Eighth Commandment warns against bearing false witness against a neighbor's good name. It seeks to protect one from rash judgments, slander, lying, or the ruining of one's reputation.

The Ninth Commandment warns against lust or coveting a neighbor's wife. The commandment demands respect for the spouse of another, and the avoidance of all immodest proposals, innuendoes, or actions which would offer an invitation to sin.

The Tenth Commandment warns against coveting a neighbor's goods. This commandment encourages one to avoid greed, injustice, and avarice. It warns against an inordinate attachment to wealth which can hurt the dignity and needs of others in society. It demands an attitude of mind which calls for the sharing of one's gifts with others.

b. Jesus gave a new law to his disciples.

In the Gospel of Matthew, chapters five to seven, we learn of a new law of the reign of God based upon love. When he writes his Gospel, the author of the Gospel of Matthew links the new law of Christ with that of the Commandments of the Old Testament. Just as Moses went up the mountain and received the Ten Commandments from God, so the disciples went up the mountain and received the precepts of the reign of God from Christ. Where the Commandments gave specific laws (mostly in a negative way by telling people what to avoid), the message of Jesus centered more on an attitude of mind or way of thinking. Some writers today use the Ten Commandments as a framework for the moral law, and they apply Christian principles to the law which were never intended in the original Commandments. In this way, they are able to make the Ten Commandments applicable to a Christian audience. The law given by Christ goes far beyond the original precepts of the Ten Commandments.

c. Many of the basic ideas of the new law given by Jesus are found in the Sermon on the Mount as presented in the Gospel of Matthew.

In his famous Sermon on the Mount, Jesus called his disciples to have an attitude of mind which reflected the presence of Christ in the world. He called them and (through them) all his followers, the salt of the earth and the light of the world. The basis of the Christian life is found in these words of Jesus:

Blessed are the poor in spirit . . . .
Blessed are those who mourn . . . .
Blessed are the meek . . . .
Blessed are those who hunger and thirst for righteousness . . . .
Blessed are the merciful . . . .
Blessed are the pure in heart . . . .
Blessed are the peacemakers . . . .
Blessed are those who are persecuted for righteousness' sake . . . .
Blessed are you when people revile you and persecute you and utter all kinds of evil against you falsely on my account . . . (Matthew 5:3–11).

Jesus calls his followers to recognize that this new law builds upon the old and fulfills the old. Where the old law forbade killing, the new law forbids any kind of destruction of the dignity of another, whether by abusive language or words. Reconciliation is central to the message of the reign of God.

Where the old law forbade adultery, the new law forbids any form of sinful or lustful glances or thoughts which destroy the dignity of others and makes them objects. The new law calls for personal sacrifice of some kind to overcome any sinful tendencies.

Where the old law allowed divorce with a written notice of divorce, the new law states that a divorced person commits adultery in a case of divorce and remarriage. This will be explained more at length in the chapter on the Sacrament of Marriage.

Where the old law stated that people should avoid false oaths, the new law states that no one should take an oath lightly. Honesty should be so much a part of a person's life that there should be no need of an oath to convince another of one's truthfulness.

Where the old law allowed equal retribution for an offense, the new law calls for total forgiveness of those who offend us.

Where the old law called for love of the people of one's nation and allowed for hatred of one's enemies, the new law calls for love of all, enemies, persecutors, and those who love us. The central law of Christianity is to love God and our neighbors as we love ourselves.

Jesus warned his followers against seeking earthly rewards or praise for their actions. Almsgiving from one's need is seen as an act of virtue and a great source of blessings from God. But the person who gives for the sake of praise has already received his or her reward. As Christians, we are called to share our goods with those in need.

Christians are also called to pray with simplicity, perseverance, trust, and patience. Prayer should be done not for personal praise, but for the sake of honoring and praising God. Those who constantly ask and seek will be heard.

Christians are called to fast and perform works of penance. For Catholics, Friday becomes a special day of penance in union with Jesus who suffered and died on a Friday. The Lenten season, which recalls the suffering and death of Jesus, is a special season for penance in union with the suffering Christ. In fasting, people should not seek the praise of others, but should fast in such a way that no one knows of the fasting. In this way, God will reward them.

Jesus calls Christians to a total attitude of trust. They should seek the things of God rather than the things of the world, and they should serve God as their true master, and not the needs of the flesh. Jesus, although he encourages people to use their talents, cautions them against being overly concerned about material needs. They should trust God.

The true Christian has no right to judge others. Because we cannot know the motives behind actions, we have no ability to judge. We look only to the surface, and our judgment is often wrong and unfair. There are occasions in our society when we are permitted and even have an obligation to judge the actions of another, such as serving on a jury to judge the guilt or innocence of a person on trial for breaking a just law.

Jesus warns that others will come with new laws and ways of acting, but we should avoid these. They will have an appeal about them, but their call must always be measured against the guidelines of the New Testament message. A person's basic way of thinking (fundamental option) will be betrayed by his or her way of acting. Jesus tells us, " 'In the same way, every good tree bears good fruit, but the bad tree bears bad fruit. Thus you will know them by their fruits' " (Matthew 7:17, 20).

To be a true and firm Christian in the world, we must take these words of Christ and put them into practice in our lives. Our call as a Christian is to be a light to the world, reflecting the presence of Christ through our words and actions.

4. Are some sins more serious than others?

a. The seriousness of a sin depends upon a person's basic attitude or "fundamental option" in life.

By basic attitude or fundamental option, we refer to the basic stance a person continually takes toward life, in other words, a person's common way of thinking. When a person marries and dedicates his or her life to loving and respecting a spouse, that person has a basic attitude of love and respect. If a person marries and still feels free to date other people whenever he or she wishes, the person has a basic attitude of mind that lacks love and respect for his or her spouse. A person who seriously strives to show love and respect for God's presence in life has a continual way of thinking that seeks to live this love and respect. On the other hand, if a person chooses his or her own will over the will of God, that person's basic option is toward oneself and against God.

For the seriousness of a sin, we do not look to the individual actions, but rather to the "fundamental option" that guides a person through life. We must remember, however, that our actions flow from our basic attitude of mind. They are signs of our fundamental option. In speaking of good and bad actions, Jesus said, " 'The good person out of the good treasure of the heart produces good, and the evil person out of evil treasure produces evil; for it is out of the abundance of the heart that the mouth speaks' " (Luke 6:45).

A Vatican document on sexual ethics recognizes the idea of "fundamental option," but it rightly warns that we should not go to the extreme of saying that an individual action, especially if it results from a series of lesser sinful actions, cannot change one's basic stance. The document states, "In reality, it is precisely the fundamental option which in the last resort defines a person's moral disposition. But it can be completely changed by particular acts, especially when . . . these have been prepared for by previous more superficial acts. Whatever the case, it is wrong to say that particular acts are not enough to constitute mortal sin" (*Vatican Declaration on Sexual Ethics,* number 10). In the same way, we can say on some occasions an individual act of love can totally change a person's fundamental way of thinking from one of rejection of God to one of total love of God.

b. A serious or mortal sin is a fundamental option to seek one's own will and to reject a love relationship with God.

When a person consciously decides to follow his or her own will in life, this person rejects God and commits a serious sin. This is a continual way of thinking, a "fundamental option" to choose oneself over God. Just as we cannot say that one act of love always makes a person a loving person (although there are cases where this does happen), we cannot say that one unloving act always makes a person an unloving person. The seriousness of a sin is determined by the fundamental way of thinking of an individual. If one unloving act can change a person's whole direction of thought, then the person has commited a serious or mortal sin.

c. A less serious or venial sin occurs when a person retains an attitude of loving God yet at the same time commits an individual action that weakens or eventually could lead to a breakup of a love relationship with God.

A person could love and respect a marriage partner, yet, at times, have some very hurtful arguments with that partner. If a person continues to prolong these arguments, he or she could be weakening the fundamental attitude of love and respect toward the partner. By seeking an early reconciliation, the partners can admit they have hurt each other while at the same time admitting that their love and respect remain. By delaying the reconciliation, the couple could be seriously hurting their relationship. When we speak of less serious sins, we realize that some of them happen quickly and are reconciled quickly. They do little harm to our fundamental option of loving God. Other less serious sins may seriously hurt this fundamental option as in the case of a person who continuously steals more and more from a neighbor till he or she has completely broken the love relationship and concern for his or her neighbor. The fundamental option that says, "I don't care," gradually takes over and the person is then living with a fundamental option that could be seriously sinful.

All of us must struggle with weaknesses in our lives, and we easily find ourselves performing those very actions which we do not wish to do. Even Paul, the great apostle to the Gentiles, complained about this weakness in himself when he wrote, "For I do not do the good I want, but the evil I do not want is what I do. For I delight in the law of God in my inmost self. . ." (Romans 7:19, 22). Although he recognizes these small faults within himself, Paul eventually proclaims that it is Christ who will save him and us from this power of sin.

5. What is necessary for a person to commit a serious sin?

a. In order for a person to commit serious sin, the offense itself must be serious.

A serious offense against love of God, neighbor or oneself is a serious sin. The Ten Commandments enable us to recognize the gravity of sin by listing those offenses considered serious. Paul reminds Christians of their call to perfection when he lists serious offenses against God in his Letter to the Colossians. We read:

> Put to death, therefore, whatever in you is earthly: fornication, impurity, passion, evil desire, and greed (which is idolatry). On account of these the wrath of God is coming on those who are disobedient. These are the ways you also once followed, when you were living that life. But now you must get rid of all such things—anger, wrath, malice, slander, and abusive language from your mouth. Do not lie to one another, seeing that you have stripped off the old self with its practices and have clothed yourselves with the new self, which is being renewed in knowledge according to the image of its creator (Colossians 3:5–10).

Although these listings cover many sinful actions, they do not cover all sinful actions. They can, however, enable us to understand the types of actions considered seriously sinful.

b. For people to sin, they must freely and consciously choose actions they know to be sinful.

The actions mentioned above are sinful because they are contrary to the good order of God's creation. But if the person performing the action does not know it is wrong, then that person is not guilty of sin before God. If a cannibal believes that the killing and eating of a young warrior is a form of worshiping his gods, the cannibal is not responsible for any personal sin in the eyes of God. In the same way, a person cannot commit a sin if a person does not know right from wrong. There is, however, an obligation to search out what is right.

The Church serves as a guide in this search to understand right and wrong in God's creation.

A person cannot commit a sin if that person does not have the ability to know right from wrong. A person who loses his or her mind is not responsible for his or her actions. Some of the things he or she does may be wrong, but because he or she does not do these actions freely and consciously, they are not sinful actions. The person must also be physically capable of avoiding sin. A person sitting at a beach house with a broken leg cannot go running down the beach into the water to save a drowning child. There is a big difference between "I don't care," and "I am not physically able."

6. What do the Scriptures tell us about God's love and sin?

a. Christ tells us about the love of God for sinners.

In the Gospel of Luke, we read a story about a son who asked his father for his inheritance so he could leave home and spend his time with his friends. The father sadly granted the request, and the boy left home. Eventually, he squandered the inheritance and went to work tending pigs. He would eat the leftovers after the pigs had eaten. Finally, he decided to return to his father's house, not to regain his right to sonship, but rather to work as a hired hand. The story tells of the merciful, forgiving father.

> *"So he set off and went to his father. But while he was still far off, his father saw him and was filled with compassion; he ran and put his arms around him and kissed him. But the father said to his slaves, 'Quickly, bring out a robe—the best one—and put it on him; put a ring on his finger and sandals on his feet. And get the fatted calf and kill it, and let us eat and celebrate; for this son of mine was dead and is alive again; he was lost and is found!' And they began to celebrate"* (Luke 15:20, 22–24).

The forgiving, merciful father is an image of God as a loving parent who rushes out to greet the sinner who returns. Through this parable, Jesus tells of the great love of the Father for sinners. Jesus tells of the joy of God over the sinner who returns to God. He tells of having a hundred sheep and losing one. The sheep herder will leave the ninety-nine to look for that one and will celebrate when that one is found. Jesus goes on to say, " 'Just so, I tell you, there will be more joy in heaven over one sinner who repents than over ninety-nine righteous persons who need no repentance' " (Luke 15:7). Sinners who recognize a need for God's forgiveness have a special place in God's heart.

b. In the infancy narrative, Joseph receives the message, "She will bear a son, and you are to name him Jesus, for he will save his people from their sins" (Matthew 1:21).

The mission of Jesus is to save the people from their sins. The same idea stated in the infancy narrative of Matthew is repeated in the words spoken at the Last Supper: " '. . . for this is my blood of the covenant, which is poured out for many for the forgiveness of sins' " (Matthew 26:28). These texts at the beginning and end of Jesus' life remind us of the mission of Jesus toward sinners.

c. Jesus associated with sinners.

While Jesus dined at the house of a Pharisee, a woman known to be a sinner came to the Pharisee's house to wash Jesus' feet. Jesus knew what his host was thinking concerning the woman, and Jesus responded to his host, " 'You did not anoint my head with oil, but she has anointed my feet with ointment. Therefore, I tell you, her sins, which were many, have been forgiven; hence she has shown great love. But the one to whom little is forgiven, loves little' " (Luke 7:46–47). In the Gospel of Luke, we read, "Now all the tax collectors and sinners were coming near to listen to him. And the Pharisees and the scribes were grumbling and saying, 'This fellow welcomes sinners and eats with them' " (Luke 15:1–2). Throughout his life, Jesus never hesitated to mix with sinners.

d. Jesus overcame sin by his death and resurrection, and he shared this gift with us.

In the Letter to the Romans, Paul tells how Christ overcame sin and shared that gift with us: "The death he died, he died to sin, once for all; but the life he lives, he lives to God. So you also must consider

105

yourselves dead to sin and alive to God in Christ Jesus" (Romans 6:10–11). Through the death and resurrection of Jesus, we have a new life. We now live for God in the name of Christ Jesus, and we now dare to approach God more closely in the name of Jesus who overcame sin and shared the gifts of his conquest with all of us.

In the First Letter of John, we read, ". . . if anyone does sin, we have an advocate with the Father, Jesus Christ the righteous; and he is the atoning sacrifice for our sins, and not for ours only but also for the sins of the whole world" (1 John 2:1–2).

7. What is grace?

a. Grace is a special gift from God consisting of a deeper relationship or union with God.

The word *grace* means gift or favor. Some have falsely pictured grace as a type of spiritual liquid pouring into us and filling us. In simple terms, grace deepens our relationship with God. It is a participation in the life of God. Just as two people who love each other experience a deepening of their love-relationship each time they share in love through their everyday life, so grace is simply a deeper experience of loving as we share with God through our daily lives. Through our prayers, our good works, our loving concern for our neighbor, we are deepening our relationship with God. We say that people grow in grace as they share more deeply in a loving union with God.

In speaking to his disciples, Jesus tells them that they now have a special relationship with him. They are no longer slaves, but they are friends who have the special gift (grace) of knowing him and the Father. In the Gospel of John, Jesus says to his disciples, " 'You are my friends if you do what I command you. I do not call you servants any longer, because the servant does not know what the master is doing; but I have called you friends, because I have made known to you everything that I have heard from my Father' " (John 15:14–15).

b. This gift of a deeper relationship with God is a gift freely given to us by God.

God freely chooses to share this gift with us. Even when we act in a way pleasing to God, we still do not have a right to this grace. God does not have to share this love with us, but out of God's goodness God has freely chosen to do this. The writer of the First Letter of John shows an admiration of God's love when he writes, "In this is love, not that we loved God but that he loved us and sent his Son to be the atoning sacrifice for our sins" (1 John 4:10). True love is recognizing the grace of God, namely that God first loves us. This is freely given. In writing his Letter to the Ephesians, Paul tells us, "For by grace you have been saved through faith, and this is not your own doing; it is the gift of God—not the result of works, so that no one may boast" (Ephesians 2:8–9).

Paul writes, "For once you were darkness, but now in the Lord you are light. Live as children of light—for the fruit of the light is found in all that is good and right and true" (Ephesians 5:8–9).

c. A person sharing in God's grace is often prompted to perform more good works.

A person who deeply loves his or her spouse will often strive for ways to show this love. Since grace is a love relationship with God, a person who shares in this love will also strive to find some way to express this love for God. Each time a person acts out of love, this love relationship deepens and the person grows in grace. Since grace demands love, it must also demand freedom. We are free to accept or reject God's gift of grace. It is the free acceptance or response to grace which makes it a human act of loving God.

8. How does grace affect our ability to pray?

a. Through our share in Christ's life, we dare to pray to God.

When we pray the Lord's Prayer in our liturgy, we introduce it with the words, "We dare to say . . . ." Our boldness arises from our faith in our relationship with Christ. Through no merit of our own, Christ has made us the adopted children of God. We recognize our personal weakness and some unworthiness, but we dare to approach God in prayer. Each form of prayer comes as a result of grace as well as our response to grace.

b. Through the gift of grace, we offer prayers of adoration.

Adoration acknowledges that we are creatures, freely created by an infinite, powerful, and loving God. We praise and adore God simply because God exists. We bless God for the many gifts we have received. We stand in awe before God's love for us, and we proclaim the greatness and glory of God who chose to create us and to save us. Grace fills us with the gift of love and faith necessary to adore the one true God and no one else.

c. Through the gift of grace, we offer prayers of petition.

Like a child who has received many gifts from his or her parent, we do not fear to ask for the needed gifts in our lives. God has blessed us, and we now call upon God for greater blessings. We ask, we knock, we seek, and we expect to find. Our faith, which is a gift of God's grace, leads us to pray for our own needs, the needs of family members, friends, strangers, those who are suffering, the outcast, and all who need our prayers. We should have no hesitation in praying our petitions and interceding for the needs of others. Because we are weak and cannot bring about on our own all the good we desire, we remind God of our weakness and we petition

God, who is strong, to answer our needs. The intimacy which comes from sharing in God's gift of grace enables us to pray with boldness and an expectation of being heard by God.

d. Through the gift of grace, we offer prayers of thanksgiving.

From the moment of our conception, even before we did anything to merit God's love, God loved us. One of the wonders of God's creation is that we can also give God a gift which even God cannot give. We alone can give our love and thanks to God. The freedom and ability to love and thank God comes from God, and we make the best use of these gifts when we offer our love and thanks back to God.

e. Through the gift of grace, we offer prayers of contrition.

When we sin, we dare to approach God to seek forgiveness. In the Gospel stories, we learn of God's steadfast concern for sinners. We learn that there is great rejoicing in heaven over the return of a single sinner to God. God's continual call to repentance and forgiveness found in the Scriptures encourages us to seek forgiveness of God and neighbor, not just once, but "seventy times seven times," or, in other words, a countless number of times. In our prayer of contrition, we admit our guilt and ask God for forgiveness.

Conclusion

To the surprise of the parents, the boy in the introduction graduated, went to work on road construction during the summer, and planned on entering a school of engineering in the early fall. Christ once told a story about the weeds and wheat growing up together. The owner of the wheat fields did not allow his hired hands to pull up the weeds because they looked too much like the wheat in their young growth. In pulling up the weeds, some valuable wheat would be destroyed. On the day of graduation, the parents of the boy could easily understand the meaning of this parable of Jesus. Just when they thought the relationship with their son had been shattered, he grew closer. Their love had gradually won his love. Their relationship with their son had moved from a broken one to a loving one. In reviewing this chapter, we could say the boy's relationship to his parents had moved from one of sin to one of grace.

For Scripture reflection and discussion concerning this chapter, see **Journeying in His Light, "Sin and Life."**

6 Our Christian Family— Church

Introduction

A Catholic presbyter was speaking at an interfaith convention when he turned to two Methodist ministers who happened to be very close friends of his and who were sharing the stage with him. As he looked at them, he told a very surprised audience, "It would be the happiest day of my life if these two Methodist ministers would become Catholic. They mean so much to me. They are so special that I would love to share my faith with them."

An embarrassed silence followed as he looked back to the audience. "And I would hope," he continued, "that their concern for me is so deep that they would wish with all their hearts that I would become Methodist."

He went on to say that all people should see their belief as so precious that they would wish with all their hearts to share that faith with people close to them.

In this chapter, we take a look at the mission and structure of the Catholic Church. In choosing or receiving any gift from God, we should strive to know that gift as well as possible. If we love someone, and wish to share a gift with the one we love, we should know the gift we are sharing. In this chapter, we touch upon the gift of the Catholic Church.

1. How did the Church develop?

a. Jesus chose twelve men from among his disciples who shared and spread his message.

During his earthly life, Jesus gathered a community of twelve apostles. These men would share in a special way in Jesus' everyday actions. He would share with them insights into his messages and parables. Finally, he would send them out to bear witness to his message. "Then Jesus called the twelve together and gave them power and authority over all demons and to cure diseases, and he sent them out to proclaim the kingdom of God and to heal" (Luke 9:1–2). After Judas' betrayal during Jesus' passion, eleven of Jesus' apostles remained faithful. In Matthew's Gospel, we read that Jesus commissioned them in a special way after his resurrection.

Now the eleven disciples went to Galilee, to the mountain to which Jesus had directed them. When they saw him, they worshiped him; but some doubted. And Jesus came and said to them, "All authority in heaven and on earth has been given to me. Go therefore and make disciples of all nations, baptizing them in the name of the Father and of the Son and of the Holy Spirit, and teaching them to obey everything that I have commanded you. And remember, I am with you always, to the end of the age" (Matthew 28:16–20).

In looking back, we see how Jesus, through his public life and under the guidance of the Holy Spirit, shaped this early community. This community, along with other followers of Jesus, began to lay the foundations for the Church after the ascension of Jesus.

b. The Acts of the Apostles describe the development of the early Church after the ascension of Jesus.

On Pentecost Sunday, the Holy Spirit filled the apostles with a new understanding and a new courage. On that day, they converted masses of people to Jesus. The message of Jesus spread first to the Jewish communities, then outside these communities to the Gentile communities. The apostles and followers of Jesus went about preaching the message of the reign of God. Small groups of people joined them and spread the faith along with them. The early Christian Jews had no idea of breaking away from the Jewish traditions of their Jewish faith. They went to the temple daily to pray and to offer sacrifices with the Jewish community. Their habits, customs, language, and religious practices were those of normal Jewish life. Only in the way that they spoke of the man Jesus did they differ from the other people in Jerusalem. Eventually, these Jewish converts to Christianity were rejected by their own people and not permitted to share in temple worship.

A man named Saul, later known to us as Paul, was an early convert to Christianity. From a great persecutor of the faith, he became a great defender of the faith. Paul would be one of the first to see the Christian community as a continuation of Christ's presence here on earth. In the Acts of the Apostles, we read of his conversion: "He fell to the ground and heard a voice saying to him, 'Saul, Saul, why do you persecute me?' He asked, 'Who are you, Lord?' The reply came, 'I am Jesus, whom you are persecuting' " (Acts 9:4–5). In this reading is a vision in which Christ identifies himself with the suffering members of the Church, as though he were these members. After this experience, Paul began to speak and to witness about Christ's presence in his life. He traveled throughout Asia Minor setting up small communities and continually speaking the praises and the message of Jesus.

Because many converts came into the Church from the non-Jewish sector of the world, Paul strongly requested that the Jewish traditions not be imposed upon these converts. At the Council of Jerusalem (54 C.E.), the leaders of the early Church agreed with Paul. This decision would eventually move Christianity even further away from Judaism.

c. The Church struggled from persecution to acceptance.

Around the year 64 C.E., a fire raged through Rome. Rumors spread as quickly as the fire that the Christians were responsible for this burning of Rome. From that year until the year 311 C.E., frequent persecutions were inflicted upon the Christian community. Finally, after three centuries, a Roman Emperor, Constantine the Great, converted to Christianity. The Church now became associated with the worldwide Empire. This changed the Church in many ways and influenced the very structure of the Church. From 311 to our present day, the Church has passed through many kingdoms and many cultures. Through the changing times, the Church has often turned back to its roots, to assure itself that it still carries out the message and commission of Jesus Christ.

2. What do we mean when we say that the Church is a community?

a. A community consists of a group of people working together with a common goal.

We use the word *community* in many different ways. A group of people living and working together in a certain town is called a community. A community could refer to families on one street, or members of a club, or to a family group. Whenever a group of people join together with a common goal, we call this group a community.

b. The Church is a group of baptized people joined together for the common purpose of sharing Christ's redemption.

The Church is not a building nor an organization, but rather a community of people who are joined together through baptism. The people forming this community believe that Jesus Christ is both God and man, that he came upon this earth, suffered, died, and was raised from the dead to glory. They also believe that Jesus shared a message and a life with his people, which in turn must be shared with all people. This community comes together in the one Christ, shares each other's joys, and experiences each other's sorrows. This community, which knows that Christ is God and responds fully to the knowledge, is called the *Christian community* or the *Church.*

c. The Israelites of the Old Testament formed a community called the "People of God."

In the Old Testament, the Israelites were often referred to as the "Chosen People" or the "People of God." The Israelite community responded to their covenant by accepting the true God as the God of the community. In the Old Testament, we saw how God related to a community. God chose the family of Abraham and guided that family as it grew into a nation. That nation was the Chosen People of God, the People of Israel. The Old Testament tells the story of God as God related to the special community of the People of God.

d. The Church community is the new "People of God."

The image of the People of God includes all those who participate in Christ's life through baptism. Unlike the Israelites who saw themselves as members of the People of God through birth, the People of God of the New Testament enter this state by means of a spiritual birth through water and the Holy Spirit. They do not choose this state on their own, but become a Chosen People who must respond to God's blessings in their lives. Speaking of the new People of God, the Scriptures tell us, "But you are a chosen race, a royal priesthood, a holy nation, God's own people . . ." (1 Peter 2:9). God chooses this new People of God with a mission to "proclaim the mighty acts of him who called you out of darkness into his marvelous light" (1 Peter 2:9).

3. What are some other images which enable us to understand the meaning of Church as community?

a. St. Paul used the image the "Body of Christ" to speak about the community of the New Testament.

In speaking of the Church in the New Testament or the community with which Christ has shared his gifts, St. Paul speaks of the image of the "Body of Christ." We read:

> For just as the body is one and has many members, and all the members of the body, though many, are one body, so it is with Christ. For in the one Spirit we were all baptized into one body—Jews or Greeks, slaves or free—and we were all made to drink of one Spirit. Indeed, the body does not consist of one member but of many (1 Corinthians 12:12–14).

115

In speaking of the image of the Body of Christ, St. Paul points out that we, the Church, need one another to truly make Christ present here on earth. Just as the whole body is in pain if one part of the body feels pain, so the whole community feels the loss of any single member. St. Paul writes, "If one member suffers, all suffer together with it; if one member is honored, all rejoice together with it" (1 Corinthians 12:26). The community of the Church is more than a street or a club or a family. It is a community joined to Christ in such a way that Christ and the community become one with each other. Christ brings redemption to the community, and we, by entering the community, share in this redemption.

b. The Church is also called the Temple of the Holy Spirit.

The Holy Spirit gives life and saving power to the Church. In the Church, there are many gifts, just as there are many members constituting the Church, yet there is a unity in these gifts which come from the one Spirit of God. These gifts or graces come from the Holy Spirit with the express purpose of building up the Church. We receive them not for ourselves alone, but for others and for the holiness and growth of the Body of Christ on earth and for the mission of the Church. Saint Augustine once compared the role of the Holy Spirit in the Church to that of the soul or life-giving spirit of the body. In this way, the image of the Church as the Temple of the Spirit helps us to understand another aspect of the Church.

c. The community called Church is a mystery which can never be fully understood.

We often confuse the words *problem* and *mystery*. A problem can be solved. If I owe a friend five dollars, I solve that problem when I pay my friend. A mystery, however, is a continual search to reach into the depths which seem bottomless. Human beings can never be solved. We are mysteries to be continually discovered, continually learned anew but never fully understood. In this sense, the Church is a mystery. Some aspects of the Church are easily identified, while others are not. The more we know about the Church, the more we recognize our inability to fully grasp the total mystery of the Church.

Because the Church is a mystery, images become more helpful than definitions in understanding the Church . Through the images of the People of God, the Body of Christ, and the Temple of the Holy Spirit, we recognize that the Church consists of a visible union of people, but it also possesses invisible attributes. The Church exists and has its mission in this world, yet the Church is not of the world. We can see the people who constitute the Church, but we recognize that the Church is a spiritual reality which brings divine life and salvation to the world. We can continually search more deeply to understand many of the surprises contained in the mystery of Church and the mystery of Christ among us in his Church, but we will never totally know the whole meaning of Church in creation.

4. What sources are used as a basis for Catholic teaching?

a. A written source for the teachings of the Catholic Church is the Bible.

Catholics, along with all Christians, believe that the Bible is the inspired word of God, through which God speaks to all people. As mentioned earlier in this book (page 26), the inspired message of God is called *revelation*. Through this revelation, we not only learn about God, we learn about our manner of relating in love with God. Christians look to the Old and New Testaments as the source of their faith, with special emphasis on the message of the New Testament. The New Testament not only offers us guidelines by which we should conduct our lives as Christians, it also tells us about the love of God for us, shown through Jesus Christ, and it offers us a motive for responding in love to God.

b. A written and lived source for the teachings of the Catholic Church is tradition.

Before any of the New Testament was written, it was lived and preached by the early Church community. After a period of reflection and preaching, writers committed some of the message to written form, while other aspects of the message continued to be lived and practiced in Christian teaching. Tradition refers to the manner in which the Church understood and lived the faith. The New Testament writings actually have their roots in the tradition of the Church, but tradition covers a far wider area than the New Testament alone.

The earliest records (which we call the *apostolic tradition*) consist of writings from authors other than those who wrote the New Testament books and the creeds and prayers found in the early Church. The value of this Christian tradition is that much of it has its origin before the writing of the New Testament, and it reflects the manner in which the early Church **lived** the message of Christ in their daily lives. In later centuries, the teachings of Church councils, the creeds, and the widely accepted teachings of the Church continued to reflect these early traditions in a manner and language familiar to the people of a specific age in history. In this way, although tradition may be expressed in various ways throughout history, its expression always remains faithful to the roots from which it springs.

c. For the sake of common practice and order within the Church, the Church has compiled a summary of laws and guidelines which is called the Code of Canon Law.

In 1917, the first Code of Canon Law was compiled by the Church. Until that time, most of the laws and guidelines for the daily practice and order of the Church could be found in many different documents. To help those who were not able to know or understand all these previous documents, the Church gathered together the laws and guidelines and placed them in one book which was called the *Code of Canon Law*.

Gradually, the 1917 code became outdated as, over the years, many new insights into tradition were expressed through documents from the Church. In 1984, a new Code of Canon Law took the place of the old, gathering together many of the guidelines which have their source in the Second Vatican Council (1962–1965) and other recent Church teachings. As important as it is to the Church, the Code of Canon Law cannot propose any laws which contradict the constant tradition of the Church.

d. In 1992, Pope John Paul II authorized the publication of the Catechism of the Catholic Church.

The *Catechism of the Catholic Church* presents the teachings of the Catholic Church in light of the Second Vatican Council and the whole tradition of the Catholic Church. Over a period of six years, the Catholic bishops of the world worked together with others to compile this Catechism. Their resources consisted of Sacred Scriptures, the tradition of the Catholic Church, the teachings of the college of bishops, and the popes throughout the ages, as well as the spiritual heritage of the early saints and theologians of the Church. A major influence on the Catechism was, of course, the Second Vatican Council.

The primary intent of writing such a Catechism is not to replace current catechisms in use in teaching the faith, but to present a resource for those responsible for teaching the faith, especially for the bishops who have the duty of teaching a unified faith throughout the world. The Catechism also provides a foundation for those writing catechisms for the faithful. The *Catechism of the Catholic Church* offers a guide and norm for other catechisms to use in making their presentations of the living faith of Catholics.

5. What is the mission of the Church?

a. The mission of the Church is to proclaim Jesus Christ and his message.

When we speak of the life of Jesus and his message we should bear in mind that the life of Jesus **is** his message. The message of Jesus and his life, death, resurrection, and ascension flow together as the one proclamation of the whole person, Jesus who became Christ. The mission of the Church is to share this message to the very ends of the earth so that all might be able to proclaim together with the Church. ". . . Jesus Christ is Lord, to the glory of God the Father" (Philippians 2:11). "And Jesus came and said to them, 'All authority in heaven and on earth has been given to me. Go therefore and make disciples of all nations, baptizing them in the name of the Father and of the Son and of the Holy Spirit. . . ' " (Matthew 28:18–

19). The word *catholic* actually means "universal," and it shows the call of the Church to reach out to all people.

b. The mission of the Church is to carry out the mission of Jesus in sharing the gifts of God's reign with all people.

By his life and message, Jesus continually proclaimed that the reign of God had already come into the world. He also proclaimed that the future of this reign is yet to be fulfilled. The Church proclaims the presence of this reign in the world today by pointing to the gifts that God is sharing through Christ's resurrection and ascension. At the same time, the Church shares these gifts with all people so that the fullness of the reign may more easily be attained. Christ shares gifts with all people through his Church, and these gifts enable people to reach the eternal fullness of the reign of God's presence for all eternity. Through these gifts, the Church announces the present reign and, through these gifts, we will be able to attain the fullness of that reign in the future.

c. All the baptized are called to share in the mission of the Church.

From the moment of their baptism, all people share in the mission of living and sharing the message and gifts of Jesus Christ. The mission of the People of God is to be the salt of the earth and the light of the world, and the destiny of the People of God is the reign of God which has already begun in Christ and which will reach its perfection and completion at the end of time. To help fulfill this mission of the Church in an orderly fashion, there exists in the Catholic Church a structure of service which includes the laity, the ordained, the bishops, and the pope. Instead of viewing this image as a type of pyramid with the pope at the top, the bishops next, the ordained under the bishops, and laypeople at the bottom of the pyramid, we should see it more as a circle, with all working together for the mission of the Church, yet with each one having a particular function of service to the world and to each other. In diagram form, it would look like this:

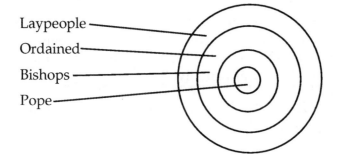

Laypeople
Ordained
Bishops
Pope

6. What do we mean by the term *laity?*

a. *The Church includes among the laity all the baptized who are not ordained or who do not belong to the religious state in the Church.*

The official application of the term *laity* found in the Second Vatican Council refers to all baptized men and women except the ordained and those who belong to an approved religious state in the Church. When speaking of the religious state, Church teaching here excludes from the "laity" those commonly known as Sisters and Brothers. When speaking of the "People of God," we should remember that in includes all the baptized. The laity, the ordained, and religious belong to the People of God.

b. *The laity have their own special role in the mission of the Church.*

At one time, the apostolate of the laity was seen as a share in the ministry of the ordained, but the reality is that the laity have their own vocation and role in the mission of the Church. At one time, a vocation implied a call to the ordained priesthood or a call to become a Sister or Brother. Now, however, Church teaching recognizes that the state of the laity is also a specific vocation and calling.

The laity have the closest contact with the temporal affairs of the world. Although Church leaders strive to share the message of Christ with all people of the world, the laity are the ones who come into closest contact with people of other beliefs or no belief at all.

They constantly find themselves in the midst of people who live for this world alone and who have no idea of the importance of God in their lives. Since the role of the laity is central to the social, political, and economic elements of the world, it is here that the laity must make the message of Christ heard and lived.

c. The voice of the laity is important in the daily life of the Church.

The laity serve in other areas of Church activities, such as participating in the liturgy, teaching religion, parish or diocesan administration, planning and directing youth groups, retreats, workshops, organizing activities for the Church community, etc. They also have the duty to speak to Church leaders on behalf of the needs of the people with whom they work, recreate, and worship. Because of the unique position of the laity in the world, some leaders of the Church seek their input in making important decisions which affect pastoral decisions for the Church community. As members of the People of God, the laity have a right to speak and be heard within Church structures.

7. What is a bishop?

a. In carrying out its mission, the early Church established a set order in its ministry.

The apostles held a special position of honor and respect among the Christians of the early Church. Even before Pentecost, there was established a set order in the ministry of Christ's message. Peter announced that Judas had betrayed his right to apostleship, and they elected a new member to replace Judas. This member had to be a person who had witnessed Christ from the time of his baptism by John the Baptizer to his resurrection. Two men were chosen, Joseph and Matthias, and they drew lots to see who would become the new apostle. "And they cast lots for them, and the lot fell on Matthias; and he was added to the eleven apostles" (Acts 1:26). The apostles exercised leadership within the Church and within their own particular communities. Eventually, others joined them in this leadership. From the earliest centuries, men were chosen to succeed the apostles and to act as bishops in the Church. The ceremony for passing on this power became the symbol of "laying on of hands."

b. Bishops, with the ordained priests as their co-workers, have as their primary mission the duty of preaching the gospel to all people.

The Catholic Church teaches that the bishops are the official teachers of the faith. The teaching of the Church has as its source the one Spirit. Christ endowed certain leaders with a special call and gift to preserve the traditional teaching. These leaders are today seen as the bishops and the pope. The general title for those who hold these offices in the Church is the *magisterium.* The faithful, under the guidance of the teachings of the bishops and the pope, are able to hear and live the faith of the Church. Besides being the major teachers in the faith in the Church, the bishops also are the stewards of God's blessings upon the Church, and they serve the Church through their office of governing and guiding the Church in its daily endeavors. In performing these duties, the bishops share in the teaching, sanctifying, and governing office of the Church.

c. A bishop often serves as pastor of a large area called a diocese in which there are many parishes.

Bishops may serve the Church in various ways. Today we are familiar with bishops who serve over a large area called a diocese. Within this diocese, there are usually many parishes which are served by ordained priests. Other bishops may assist him within that diocese. Those who assist in this way are called "auxiliary bishops" or "coadjutor bishops," which mean co-helpers.

d. Every bishop is ordained for the whole Church.

The visible head of the Catholic Church, the pope, appoints a bishop. Although a bishop receives his appointment from the pope, he does not receive his power from the pope but rather from God.

He is ordained a bishop in the Catholic or universal Church. He might serve one area of the world and one diocese of that area, but a bishop still has a great responsibility in sharing the message of Christ throughout the whole world. He must be concerned not only for his own diocese but for every person on God's earth.

e. We refer to the entire community of bishops as the college of bishops.

The group or college of apostles received a call from Christ himself. The *college of bishops* is the successor of this group or college of apostles, and as a member of this college of bishops, a bishop shares in its apostolic power. When the bishops meet together in Rome, as a council, the college of bishops becomes much more visible to the world. Through the college of bishops, individual bishops have the opportunity to bring the teaching of the universal Church to the local community, and the voice of the local community to the attention of the universal Church.

f. Some bishops are given the honorary title of cardinal.

During the Middle Ages, the Church established the title of *cardinal* as an honorary title for bishops who served the Church in a significant way. It is a title of honor that adds no new spiritual powers to the one who receives this title. Cardinals are usually bishops of a large diocese or bishops who serve in some central position in the Church. By Church law, cardinals are responsible for electing the pope. If a pope decides for the good of the Church to open future elections to others besides cardinals, he may change the law. Throughout the centuries, the cardinals have elected one of their number to the papacy, although they may choose for pope someone who is not a cardinal.

8. How did the office of pope develop?

a. Tradition in the Catholic Church honors Peter as the first pope (leader of the first disciples) and believes that Peter died in Rome under Nero between 64 and 67 C.E.

An early tradition in the Church claims that Peter went to Rome and served there as bishop for several years. He was put to death under Nero. The early Church saw this as referring to the words of Christ which said of Peter:

> *"Very truly, I tell you, when you were younger, you used to fasten your own belt and to go wherever you wished. But when you grow old, you will stretch out your hands, and someone else will fasten a belt around you and take you where you do not wish to go."*
>
> *What he said indicated the sort of death by which Peter was to glorify God. (John 21:18–19)*

b. Throughout the Gospels, the authors portray Peter as having a special role among the apostles.

The Gospel of Matthew reflects this special role as seen by the early Church in an episode between Jesus and Peter. Jesus had just asked his followers who people say that the Son of Man is.

> *Simon Peter answered, "You are the Messiah, the Son of the living God." And Jesus answered him, "Blessed are you, Simon son of Jonah! For flesh and blood has not revealed this to you, but my Father in heaven. And I tell you, you are Peter, and on this rock I will build my church, and the gates of Hades will not prevail against it. I will give you the keys of the kingdom of heaven, and whatever you bind on earth will be bound in heaven, and whatever you loose on earth will be loosed in heaven" (Matthew 16:16–19).*

In the Gospel of John written much later, we see a special honor and commission given to Simon Peter by Jesus after his resurrection.

> *When they had finished breakfast, Jesus said to Simon Peter, "Simon son of John, do you love me more than these?" He said to him, "Yes, Lord; you know that I love you." Jesus said to him, "Feed my lambs." A*

second time he said to him, "Simon son of John, do you love me?" He said to him, "Yes, Lord; you know that I love you." Jesus said to him, "Tend my sheep." He said to him the third time, "Simon son of John, do you love me?" Peter felt hurt because he said to him the third time, "Do you love me?" And he said to him, "Lord, you know everything; you know that I love you." Jesus said to him, "Feed my sheep" (John 21:15–17).

To say something three times in Scripture writing is to say it in a most emphatic way. The Gospel of John is emphatically proclaiming Peter as the new shepherd, the visible shepherd of his flock.

c. In the Acts of the Apostles we read how the other apostles accepted the leadership of Peter.

When the time came to choose a member to replace Judas, Peter stood up before one hundred twenty people and announced an election. They accepted Peter's leadership in this. On Pentecost Sunday as the Holy Spirit in the narrative comes upon the apostles, it is Peter who gives the discourse under the influence of the Spirit. Peter became the first to work miracles in the name of Christ, and the first real missionary. When the time came to exempt the Gentiles from the traditions of the Jewish religion, Paul faced Peter in order to convince him that the Gentiles should not be bound by these laws. By choosing Peter as the one to convince in this case, Paul showed the position of leadership given to Peter in the eyes of the early Church.

d. From later letters of the early Church, we find that the bishops of Rome, Peter's successors, retain an honored position.

About the year 100, letters already existed suggesting that the bishop of Rome was held in high esteem. No special organization decreed this, nor did Christ himself decree this. However, bishops of other areas would often consult with the bishop of Rome before important decisions were made. The reason seemed to be based on the belief that an ancient apostolic community in Rome went back to Peter. The bishops of the early Church were carrying out a custom seemingly established during the time of the apostles. At a very early date, unity with the succession of Peter became a sign of being in unity with the whole Church.

e. The Catholic Church today accepts the bishop of Rome as a true successor of the apostle Peter and as the visible head of the Roman Catholic Church.

Jesus Christ himself is considered the invisible head of the Church, the true shepherd and leader. The pope, as the visible head of the Church, should reflect the leadership of Christ which was a leadership of servanthood. The pope is at the service of the entire Church and, as such, holds a privileged position within the Church. Being pope does not guarantee holiness. A pope, as other members of the Church, must work toward holiness, even though he is the visible head of the Church. Although the Church has been blessed throughout history with many holy men to serve as popes, the Church must also admit that some were far from the ideal of holiness the visible Church would hope to find in its leaders.

9. Is the pope infallible?

a. The Catholic Church teaches that the pope may speak infallibly in matters that pertain to faith and morals.

If the pope were to announce to the world that it would rain all over the earth tomorrow, Catholics need not believe this. They need only respond to those matters which refer to faith or morals. Infallibility does not mean that the pope has knowledge of all truths. There are some matters of faith and morals which the pope does not know. However, when he proclaims as infallible matters of faith and morals and follows the required steps for infallibility, the pope is making an infallible statement.

b. Catholics believe that the pope is infallible in matters proposed for the universal Church.

A pope cannot make a statement on faith and morals that pertains to only one area of the world. It must pertain to the whole universal Church. What is infallible for one area must be infallible for all areas.

c. Catholics believe that the pope is infallible when he is acting from his special office as shepherd and teacher of all Christians.

When the pope speaks officially as pope on matters of faith and morals and declares his statement as infallible, Catholics accept this infallible statement of faith. Only when he officially, from his position as pope, declares a statement to be infallible, need Catholics accept his position as infallible. If he were expressing an individual theological opinion to another person in a private conversation, Catholics would not have to accept this as an infallible statement.

d. The infallibility of the pope is the same infallibility possessed by the Church.

The pope is infallible to the degree that he reflects the infallible faith of the whole Church. He does not decide one day to make an infallible statement out of thin air, but rather listens to the Church as it is reflecting its faith. He enunciates the expression of this faith as well as possible. He and the Church proclaim that faith to the world as the faith of the infallible Church.

e. The college of bishops in union with the pope possesses this infallibility.

The college of bishops along with the pope also shares in reflecting the faith of a community. By coming together and sharing the reflection of the Catholic community at large and drawing up statements flowing from that faith experience, the college of bishops along with the pope, but not without him, can proclaim in an infallible way matters of faith and morals which must be accepted by the entire Church.

10. Can the Church ever change its teaching?

a. The Church may never change its basic infallible teachings about faith or morals.

As we look back through history, we note that the Church has always been guided in stating its infallible teaching either through councils or through papal statements. When Christ called upon the apostles to teach this message with authority, he promised ". . . I am with you always, to the end of the age" (Matthew 28:20). Being under the guidance of the Holy Spirit, the Church has never had to change any of its basic teachings.

b. The explanation of these basic teachings may change, since their explanations are limited by the languages and worldview which surrounds them.

As language changes and as we gain deeper insights into science and human nature, we can sometimes explain things in a much better way than we could in the past. As we begin to understand more clearly God's hand in nature, we are able to more clearly explain basic teachings of the Church in such a way that they could seem different from previous explanations, but which in reality explains the basic teaching more clearly. For example, in trying to explain the fact that God is the Creator of the world and that God created the world out of nothing, we could confuse the issue by trying to retain stubbornly the idea that God created the world in six days. The message has to do with God's power of creation out of nothing, not the fact that God created it in six days. As we understand the writings of the Scriptures in a clearer manner, we are more able to explain the basic doctrine that God is the Creator of the world.

11. How often do the pope and the college of bishops meet together?

a. The pope and the college of bishops meet together as the need arises.

The Church has no set law for a time when the pope and the college of bishops must meet together. Throughout history, popes have called all the bishops of the world together in order to determine how the Church can best serve in a particular age.

b. In the Church today, the pope meets with a synod of bishops every three years.

This synod of bishops consists of representatives from different countries throughout the world. These representative bishops speak on behalf of their own national conferences. In this way, the Church is able to continually meet the needs of the present day without calling all the bishops of the world together to answer this need.

c. A gathering of the bishops of the world in union with the pope is called an ecumenical council.

The most noted council in our present age is the Second Vatican Council (1962–1965), called by Pope John XXIII. The council prior to this one was held one hundred years before and was called the First Vatican Council. In the early days of the Church, some of these councils were called by emperors, but, throughout most of Church history, popes have called these councils together under the guidance of the Holy Spirit. The Second Vatican Council in the Roman Catholic Church has ushered in many changes which we are experiencing in the Church today. Any document or decree that comes from such councils must be approved by the pope.

12. What names do we give to meetings among members of different beliefs?

a. Ecumenism *refers to those activities among Christian communities whereby they come together for the sake of understanding, sharing, and praying toward unity.*

There are many different Christian communities in the world today. Ecumenism is an attempt on the part of all members of these Christian communities to come together to share their understanding of the Christian message. Their hope and prayer is unity. Ecumenism is the challenge of sharing one another's belief in the Christian message and attempting to discuss that belief at an honest level. It does not mean "giving in," nor does it mean "giving up," but rather it means coming together, trying to listen, trying to understand, and trying to share, in the Spirit of Christ, the message of Christ as each one understands and lives this message.

b. Interfaith *refers to those activities among Christian communities and communities who profess belief in God but who do not accept that Jesus is God.*

Christians meet in a spirit of love, understanding, and prayer with those who accept belief in God, but who do not accept the belief that Jesus is God. The Jewish faith, as well as other world religions, accepts God as we do, but they do not accept the Godhood of Jesus. This difference should not drive us apart, but should make us open to a deeper understanding of and sensitivity to one another. In this openness, we hold firmly to the truths taught by the Church and strive to understand the faith of our brothers and sisters who do not accept the Godhood of Jesus.

c. In the spirit of ecumenism and interfaith we should respect the faith of our neighbor.

At the Second Vatican Council, the bishops sought to identify the "sole Church of Christ which in the creed we profess to be one, holy, catholic and apostolic . . ." ("Constitution of the Church," number 8). But in proclaiming this Church of Christ as the Catholic Church, the bishops also realized that other Churches had certain elements which flowed from the true Church of Christ. They write:

This Church, constituted and organized as a society in the present world, subsists in the Catholic Church, which is governed by the successor of Peter and by the bishops in communion with him. Nevertheless, many elements of sanctification and of truth are found outside its visible confines ("Constitution on the Church," number 8).

Although they see the Catholic Church as the sole Church of Christ professed in the Creed, they are quick to point to the beauty of Christ's Church found "outside its visible limits." Because of this statement, we could never allow ourselves to look down upon any other Church.

13. What does the Catholic Church believe about Mary, the Mother of Jesus?

a. Mary has been named the Mother of the Church.

In calling Mary the *Mother of the Church,* the Church proclaims her spiritual motherhood over all the Church. In being the mother of Jesus, Mary was accepting the motherhood of all that Jesus stood for. She was accepting the spiritual motherhood of the Mystical Body of Christ here on earth. The Gospel of John portrays this acceptance on the part of Mary of this motherhood of the Church by the words of Jesus from the cross: "When Jesus saw his mother and the disciple whom he loved standing beside her, he said to his mother, 'Woman, here is your son.' Then he said to the disciple, 'Here is your mother.' And from that hour the disciple took her into his own home" (John 19:26–27). Many see in these words a special call of Mary to become the mother of all people, symbolized in the person of John. It is not simply that Jesus is telling

John to take care of his mother after his death, but even more that Jesus is concerned for all people and is making Mary the mother of all people. Because of this, the Church addresses Mary by this title, "The Mother of the Church."

b. *Mary is also called the* Mother of God.

The Church teaches that Jesus is one person, even though he is human as well as divine. This is one of those mysteries that stand outside our experience. Because the Church proclaims that Jesus is one person and not two, the Church also recognizes that the mother of Jesus cannot be mother of the human Jesus alone. To accept this would be to accept two persons in Jesus instead of one person. The Church, in the early centuries, proclaimed that Mary is the Mother of Jesus and as such must also be called the Mother of God. We again speak of a mystery outside our experience. What the title *Mother of God* fully entails, we will never know until we reach eternity. In the meanwhile, we can safely say that this is the greatest title that could be given to Mary. With the Church, we give Mary the highest honor when we call her "The Mother of God."

c. *The Church declared in an infallible statement that Mary was assumed body and soul into heaven.*

When we speak of body and soul, we simply mean that Mary's whole person was taken into eternal happiness. When we use the expression *assumed into heaven,* we are simply using a scriptural sense of being taken up. What the doctrine of the assumption of Mary really means is that Mary has been taken fully into eternal happiness. Her whole person now shares in Christ's resurrection and ascension. The meaning of this can never be fully understood in this life. The fact that Mary's whole person has entered into eternal happiness is meant as a sign for the rest of us that we too, like Mary, are called to this eternal happiness and that, if we respond, we shall be taken with our whole person into eternity. In this way, Mary, as Mother of the Church, becomes the model for all people within the Church. Mary's assumption is one of the few official infallible statements made by a pope. We celebrate the feast of the Assumption of Mary on August 15.

133

d. The Church has proclaimed in an infallible statement that Mary is the Immaculate Conception.

Since Mary was chosen to be the Mother of God, God freed her from all the chains of sin within her life. From the moment of her conception, Mary already shared, by God's special plan, in the gift of redemption. One of the inspired messages from the infancy narrative comes through the mouth of an angel, " 'Greetings, favored one! The Lord is with you' " (Luke 1:28). In these words, the author tells us that Mary is most blessed among all women, in fact, most blessed among all people. "O highly favored one" is not just a title, but actually a name given to Mary. We celebrate the feast of the Immaculate Conception on December 8.

14. How do Catholics honor Mary?

a. Catholics honor Mary by praying to her, but never by worshiping her.

Only God may be worshiped. Whenever we pray in Mary's honor, we are actually praising God through the person of Mary and thanking God for allowing one of God's creatures to be so highly favored. We honor God as we pray in Mary's name. By proclaiming our love and honor for one of God's favored creatures, we are thanking God for the gift of Jesus' mother, Mary. Mary does not have power equal to God, nor is she divine. Mary is created just as we are. She is a model of what holiness can be in a human person on earth and a model of God's love for all people.

b. We honor Mary by a special form of prayer called "The Hail Mary."

A popular Catholic prayer in honor of Mary is a prayer that has its roots in the infancy narratives. After the angel greets Mary and tells her that she is favored by God, Mary goes to visit her cousin Elizabeth who is with child. As Mary comes into the home of Elizabeth, the Scriptures tell us, "When Elizabeth heard Mary's greeting, the child leaped in her womb. And Elizabeth was filled with the Holy Spirit and exclaimed with a loud cry, 'Blessed are you among women, and blessed is the fruit of your womb' " (Luke 1:41–42). The Church has added the second part of the prayer of the Hail Mary, asking Mary's special help in this life and at our death. The prayer is as follows:

Hail, Mary, full of grace!
The Lord is with you.
Blessed are you among women,
And blessed is the fruit of your womb, Jesus.
Holy Mary, Mother of God,
Pray for us sinners,
Now and at the hour of our death. Amen.

c. Catholics honor Mary in a special way by a prayer called "The Rosary."

The Rosary consists of prayers which are prayed while meditating upon a mystery of Christ's life. Catholics keep account of the prayers by following them upon beads called the *rosary beads.* The prayer begins with the Apostles' Creed, followed by the Lord's Prayer, three Hail Marys for the virtues of faith, hope, and charity, and the Trinity Prayer. The person prays one Lord's Prayer, ten Hail Marys, and one Trinity Prayer, while meditating upon a mystery (an event) in the lives of Jesus and Mary. This is repeated four more times, each time meditating on a new mystery. (See Prayers, Practices, and Precepts at the end of this book for the mysteries of the rosary.)

d. The Church honors Mary in a special way through the prayers of the Church.

The Church honors Mary when it joins together in worship and sets aside certain days in her honor. These days point to some special mystery in the life of Mary. For example, we celebrate the feast of the Immaculate Conception on December 8, the Assumption of Mary on August 15, the Birth of Mary on September 8, and the Solemnity of Mary as the Mother of God on January 1. In these and other feasts which honor Mary, we are worshiping God in a special way for the blessings God has shown to Mary. In this way, we thank God for God's goodness in giving us Mary.

Conclusion

In the introduction to this chapter, we spoke of a presbyter who shocked his audience by inviting his Methodist friends to become Catholic. After his talk, one of the Methodist ministers told the audience that this presbyter would make a fine Methodist minister, since he liked to talk so long. The audience laughed, enjoying the friendly exchange between the minister and the presbyter that would have seemed almost impossible forty years ago.

The minister became more serious as he continued, "With all my heart I would like to share in faith with this wonderful man. But even more! I would like to know about a faith that nourishes such people as my friend here. But before we share as one faith, we must pray, enjoy, and study together. We must share our insights and discoveries. And we must do it carefully and slowly. It would be a shame if we lost the gifts we all have to share because of our impatience to be one faith. The seed is in the ground. Now we must give it time to take root and grow."

In these few words, the audience caught a glimpse of the difficult road to unity. The love and desire for unity was present, but the need for understanding and discovery that come only in time will be its foundation.

For Scripture reflection and discussion concerning this chapter, see **Journeying in His Light, "Our Christian Family—Church."**

7 The Sacraments and Love

Introduction

As they drove home from the ball park, Tom and his fourteen-year-old son talked excitedly about the game that day. A car sped suddenly from a side street and rammed the side of Tom's car where Billy sat. The ambulance attendants found Billy slumped lifelessly in a bundle on the floor and his father breathing heavily with blood pouring from his nose and ears. The ambulance attendants put Tom and the two passengers from the other car into two ambulances and covered Billy's lifeless body. At the hospital, a doctor friend of the family worked on the three survivors, while Billy was left alone, presumably dead. A short time after, Billy's mother, along with some friends, came in quietly to the hospital, sat down next to Billy's body, and wept. As they sat there, his mother suddenly noticed an almost imperceptible twitch in Billy's face. A scream rang down the corridor, "He's still alive!" Attendants came running, hurrying, pushing back Billy's eyelids, and rushed him off behind a curtain, the family doctor following them. After some time, the family doctor came downstairs to Billy's mother and sat next to her. He whispered, "Billy is going to be all right," and he burst into tears. For a moment, all the tension, all the fears, all the love came pouring out in those tears of the family doctor and friend. He patted Billy's mother on the hand and walked back into the emergency room.

1. Why is the Church concerned about signs and symbols?

a. Signs tell us something is happening or something should be happening, or they may simply give information.

A sign on a door could tell us that Joseph Smith is an "Attorney at Law," or a sign on the highway could warn us that the "Right lane ends 1000 ft."

In the story in the introduction, we have a series of signs at work. The stop sign told the driver of one car that he should have stopped rather than run through an intersection. The stop sign could not make him stop. It simply informed him that he should stop. A twitch was a sign that Billy was still alive. The sign showed life. When the doctor came down to share the good news, his weeping was a sign of his love for Billy and his family. In all of these cases, nothing is said, nothing need be said. The sign told us that a stop should have taken place, that life was still going on, that love was in the doctor's heart. A central part of being human consists in the fact that a great deal of our day is spent sharing and responding to signs.

b. A symbol points beyond itself and has a deeper meaning.

As human beings, we have an ability to look beyond the immediate sign to its deeper meaning. When we are able to do this, we refer to such a sign as a symbol. For example, the tears of the doctor in the opening story tell us more than the external sign of drops of water staining his face. We can look beyond the tears and see in them an expression of the doctor's love for the child and the family. This ability to look beyond the signs to their deeper meaning is important to our understanding of the sacraments.

Because symbols have a far deeper meaning than signs, we can never use the expression that something is "just a symbol." In reality, a symbol has the power to move beyond a sign and to make present a far deeper meaning than any external sign.

One of our insights into the personality of Jesus comes through our human ability to look beyond signs. In one of the miracle stories found in the Gospel of Luke, Jesus raises a widow's son from the dead (Luke 7:11–17). We can marvel at the wonderful powers of Jesus, but we also read the deeper meaning of the healing—the compassion of Jesus (Luke 7:13). Because the author was able to look beyond the external signs of touching and healing, he was able to see the action as a symbol of Jesus' loving compassion.

c. Jesus is a symbol of God's presence among us.

The life of Jesus tells us not only about himself, but it also tells us about an aspect of God's love and concern for all people. Jesus is God, and when he became flesh, he gave us an opportunity to truly meet and understand the presence of God in our midst. Revelation in the Scriptures not only tells us some deep mysteries about the nature of God, but it also tells us about the personal love and compassion of God for all people.

In the Gospel of John, Philip comes before Jesus and says to Jesus, "Lord, show us the Father, and we will be satisfied" (John 14:8). Jesus' reply shows that he is a symbol of God's presence here on earth. Jesus tells Philip, "Have I been with you all this time, Philip, and you still do not know me? Whoever has seen me has seen the Father. How can you say, 'Show us the Father'?" (John 14:9). As we look back through the Scriptures we see the love of God reflected in the life of God's Son, Jesus. We see the power and compassion of God, we see the forgiveness of God, we see the concern of God. In the Gospel portrayal of Jesus, we see a symbol of God's presence in the world.

d. The Church is a symbol of Christ's continued presence in the world.

The New Testament book of the Acts of the Apostles tells us about the ascension of Jesus and the message given to his followers on that occasion. We read, "While he was going and they were gazing up toward heaven, suddenly two men in white robes stood by them. They said, 'Men of Galilee, why do you stand looking up toward heaven? This Jesus, who has been taken up from you into heaven, will come in the same way as you saw him go into heaven.' " (Acts 1:10–11). The episode marks the end of Jesus' appearance in visible form on earth, and it looks forward to the day of the second coming of Christ. In the meanwhile, the Church must continue to make the world realize that Jesus still lives in the world through its members.

The New Testament continues to remind us of this presence of Christ in the Church. St. Paul, speaking of the Church as the Body of Christ, wrote, "Now you are the body of Christ and individually members of it" (1 Corinthians 12:27). As we read earlier, when Paul was persecuting the Church, Jesus appeared to Paul. "He fell to the ground and heard a voice saying to him, 'Saul, Saul, why do you persecute me?' He asked, 'Who are you, Lord?' The reply came, 'I am Jesus, whom you are persecuting' " (Acts 9:4–5). The Church has the mission to proclaim, live, and share the gifts of Jesus Christ. In this way the Church is a symbol of Christ's presence here on earth.

e. The Church uses signs to bring about a deeper relationship between God and all people.

By using water, oil, bread, and other familiar items from life, and by prayers, the Church, a visible channel for God's blessings, establishes a relationship with the individual, the community, and God. Because the Church gives these signs a meaning which extends far beyond their external appearances, we can properly call them symbols.

2. What is a sacrament?

a. One characteristic of a sacrament is that it is a sacred and symbolic action.

In the introductory story of this chapter, the tears of the doctor, because of his close relationship with the family, expressed a feeling that already existed within him. His tears did not make him love the child; they simply expressed a love that already existed. For the mother of the child, the tears conveyed a deep message. Through them, she knew of the doctor's love for the child.

In the sacraments, Christ uses symbolic actions which not only tell us of the love God has for us, but actually bring about a change in the relationship between ourselves and God. God loves us, and through the external symbolic actions, such as, flowing water and the prayers prayed at baptism, we know of this love. In the very expression of this love, a change takes place. The symbolic actions not only express what is happening; they are making it happen. This is one aspect of a sacrament.

b. Another characteristic of a sacrament is that it consists in an intimate encounter with Christ.

Our lives are filled with intimate encounters. Whenever we meet someone whom we have come to love, we experience an intimate encounter. As we draw closer to a person, we become more informal and free in our expressions. We call that person by his or her first name (or nickname), and we tell that person details of our lives which we would not share with others. In time, a man and woman may decide to join together in marriage, and the intimacy which they have enjoyed now becomes a deeper intimacy. They share a life as husband and wife.

Our life is filled with encounters, but most of them lack the intimacy found in loving friendships. Even among friends, the depth of the encounter differs because the intimacy differs. A married couple share a deeper encounter (because of their intimacy) than two friends working at the same place. With Jesus, our encounter can become most intimate; we can actually become one with him.

A true encounter moves in two directions. It expresses a gift and a response. In a sacrament, God's care and concern come to us through Christ, and this brings us closer to Christ and to one another in Christ. This intimate encounter with Christ is a second characteristic of a sacrament.

c. An additional characteristic of a sacrament is that it is an action which comes to us from Christ and is celebrated through the Church.

In the past, some viewed sacraments as "things." Sacraments are not things, but living, symbolic "actions" by which Christ touches us in a most intimate manner. The sacraments come from Christ and are celebrated by the Church. These actions which make up the intimate encounter are truly celebrations of God's love given to us through Christ. In stating that the sacraments are symbols of God's love and care for us, we should not reduce sacraments to a single moment. Because they are actions, they touch every aspect of our lives. The time during which we celebrate this special encounter with Christ, that is, the period of celebrating the sacrament, is not a passing moment, but a new beginning whereby we deepen our relationship with God through Christ.

d. A sacrament has the threefold effect of recalling the past, bringing it into the present, and giving us hope for the future.

The sacraments have their roots in the death, resurrection, and ascension of Jesus. Each of the sacraments recalls what Jesus has done for us, and they bring this gift of Jesus' life into the present. Because this gift is always present and living, sacraments give us hope for a life lived in union with Christ. Although centuries have passed since Jesus' public ministry, the sacraments continually remind us that his ministry is still active and living in every one of us who shares in these gifts of the sacraments. Each sacramental celebration brings the past, the present, and the future together in Christ.

e. A sacrament can be defined as an intimate encounter with Christ, which comes to us through living symbols of God's loving care, and which is celebrated by the Church.

A sacrament is a mystery, and we will never fully understand its meaning. Any attempt to define a sacrament will always fall far short of the true mystery, but we must always strive to express the mystery in our limited way so that we can have some understanding of this great gift which comes from Christ.

3. Why do we refer to the presence of Jesus Christ and the Church as sacraments?

a. Jesus Christ is considered a sacrament in the broader sense because he gives us an image of the living God.

When Jesus told Philip that the one who sees him sees the Father, he was speaking of a visible presence of God the Father as shown through the presence of the Son, Jesus, here on earth. The life of Jesus not only pointed to the living God, it also brought about an intimate encounter with God for all people. Since there is only one God, and since Jesus is God, we conclude that Jesus not only tells us about God's presence here on earth, but that Jesus **is** God's presence. Just as a sacrament not only tells us about a presence, but actually brings about that active presence, so Jesus is not merely telling us that God is present; he is God's living presence among us. As human beings, we are able to look beyond the external, physical appearance of Jesus and understand his true meaning in our lives and in all of creation.

In the Gospel of John, we read the words of Jesus who proclaims this oneness with God. Jesus says, " 'Whoever believes in me believes not in me but in him who sent me. And whoever sees me sees him who sent me' " (John 12:44–45). With our human ability to look beyond the external signs, we recognize in the presence of Jesus the one who sent him.

b. The Church is considered a sacrament in the broader sense because it gives us a living image of Christ's presence among us.

In the Church, we have Christ's living presence within the world. In a letter to the Corinthian community, Paul speaks of all members of the Church being united with one another as the one body of Christ. He tells them that they become one in Christ through the gift of baptism. Paul writes, "For just as the body is one and has many

143

members, and all the members of the body, though many, are one body, so it is with Christ. For in the one Spirit we were all baptized into one body—Jews or Greeks, slaves or free—and we were all made to drink of one Spirit" (1 Corinthians 12:12–13).

4. Where does a sacrament take place?

a. A sacrament takes place within the Christian community called Church.

To fully understand the sacraments, we must understand the idea of community as mentioned in the previous chapter on Church. The Church is the living symbol of the continued presence of Christ here on earth. Through this living community, Christ is able to reach out and touch each person by certain symbols. A community called *Church* shares Christ's gifts though the sacraments and grows closer to Christ as each member shares in the sacraments. Each sacrament becomes a community event, a community celebration, and no sacrament is a private encounter between an individual and God. Since the sacraments come from Christ through the power of the Spirit and the activity of the community, the sacraments take effect even if the minister of the sacrament is in a state of sin or lacks personal holiness.

b. A sacrament takes place within a community worship service which is called liturgy.

As members of the Church, through symbols and ceremonies, we join with Christ in worshiping the First Person of the Trinity. These symbols and ceremonies by which we join with Christ in the Church are called *sacred liturgy.* The word *liturgy* originally referred to "work of the people." The word *liturgy* has many connotations which flow from the idea that it is a work of the People of God. Some understand it in the sense of a shared energy in the worship of God. Through the liturgy, it is Christ who is acting on our behalf through the prayer of the community. Liturgy refers to Christ acting in, with, and through the Church's official prayer. The liturgy is the peak toward which all the activity of the Church directs itself and is the font from which all its power flows.

The whole liturgical life of the Church revolves around the celebration of the sacraments. Through the sacraments, we join more fully with Christ in worshiping God the Father. Even when celebrated in the absence of the assembly, the celebration is still an act of the total Church and, as such, it is still liturgy. Unfortunately, the valuable symbol and experience of community becomes lost when the assembly is not present.

c. Because a sacrament is a community event, Catholics should strive to share in the sacrament at a time when the community is present.

A sacrament should bring joy, not only to the one celebrating the sacrament, but to the whole community. As each new member shares in a deeper relationship with God, the whole community shares in some way in that deeper relationship. The image of the body of Christ emphasizes this, as Paul writes "If one member suffers, all suffer together with it; if one member is honored, all rejoice together with it" (1 Corinthians 12:26). Proper liturgy demands that internal and spiritual joys should be expressed in some external form. If the community rejoices and grows through the celebration of sacraments by individual members, then the whole community should gather together to live the symbol of this sharing. Whenever possible, a sacrament is celebrated when the greatest number of the community can come together to celebrate the sacrament.

5. How many sacraments are there?

a. There are seven sacraments through which we recognize God's continuous concern for our lives.

Although each one of us is a unique and individual person, we have much in common. We are born; we eat to live; we age, passing through different crises or phases of life as we do so; we face anxiety in life, sometimes guilt and failure; we are challenged to act in a responsible manner; we choose to marry or remain single; we choose to relate to God in our lives in many different ways; we suffer physical or mental pain; we face the inevitable fact that someday we will die, and we live in a large human family made up of relatives, friends, and people of other neighborhoods and countries whom we will never meet. God knows that we must face these and other aspects of life as we journey from birth to resurrection. The sacraments remind us that we are not making this journey alone.

b. The sacraments, by touching us at significant points in our lives, remind us that Jesus is always present to our lives.

Through the Sacraments of Baptism, Confirmation, and Eucharist, we are initiated into the family of Christ. In these sacraments we are reminded of Christ's continual activity in our everyday life. Through the celebration of baptism, confirmation, and Eucharist, a person becomes one of the faithful. For that reason, we call these sacraments by the name, *Sacraments of Initiation.*

The Sacraments of Reconciliation and Anointing of the Sick point to physical and spiritual healing. In the Sacrament of Reconciliation, we recognize that we can hurt our relationship with God, our neighbor, and ourselves, and we seek to reconcile ourselves to God and the community through this sacrament. In the Sacrament of the Anointing of the Sick, we recognize that some of us will experience the pain of sickness or disease in our lives and that we need the special help of God and the community in this time of anxiety.

The Sacraments of Marriage and Holy Orders are sacraments at the service of community. In the Sacrament of Marriage, we acknowledge the joys as well as the difficulties of family life, and we call upon Christ to be present in an active way within the family, the basic foundation of the community. In the Sacrament of Holy Orders, we recognize our call to be a worshiping community and our need for order and leadership in worship and building up the Church.

c. Through these significant moments in our lives, God shows concern.

The power and help of the sacraments flow from these special moments into our daily lives. They affect everything we do. They tell us that God does not leave us alone on the earth, but that God is continually working in, with, and through us. They remind us that we continually share in the power and gifts of Jesus Christ. Through these sacred symbols, the sacraments, Christ shares with us in a visible way, symbols of his continual, living presence.

d. The Sacraments of Baptism, Confirmation, and Holy Orders bring about a permanent effect known as a sacramental character.

The Sacraments of Baptism, Confirmation, and Holy Orders may be celebrated only once, since they have a lifelong effect on those sharing in these sacraments and on the community. These sacraments establish a unique and enduring relationship with Christ and the Church, known as a sacramental character. A person may celebrate the other sacraments more than once. A married person may marry again when a spouse dies.

6. What is the "Rite of Christian Initiation of Adults"?

a. The Rite of Christian Initiation of Adults, known by many as the RCIA, refers to the process by which unbaptized persons become one with the Christian community.

In question five of this chapter, we mentioned that the Sacraments of Baptism, Confirmation, and Eucharist are called the *Sacraments of Initiation.* When a person has shared in these three sacraments, that person is one of the faithful in the Catholic Church. Before adults share in these sacraments, however, they begin a journey or a process whereby they gradually enter into the understanding of Christ and his Church. This journey consists of a series of ritual actions and sacred celebrations whereby a person becomes one with the Catholic family. During this journey, the unbaptized share their own experiences, and reflect upon the Scriptures (with special emphasis on the Gospels) and the teachings of the Church.

b. In the Christian initiation process, there are four periods and three steps.

In the early Church, the Christians used a Greek word meaning "to teach" to refer to the process used for those seeking to become members of the faithful. They used the name *catechumenate,* and those who were going through the process were called *catechumens.* A short description of the periods and steps used in the initiation process follows:

Period 1: Evangelization and Precatechumenate
The journey actually begins long before the participants come together to share in any formal process. By the time they enter this period, the participants may already be aware of some activity of the Holy Spirit in their lives. This is a period of evangelization, a time when the participants share their experiences and ask questions about the Catholic faith. This period has no formal reception or prayer of welcome. After a period of time, when the catechists and the participants recognize that it is time to enter a new phase of the process, they are ready to take the first formal step.

First Step: Rite of Acceptance into the Order of Catechumens
The participants now arrive at their first step on the journey as they declare their intentions before the Church, and the Church in turn accepts them as persons who have the intention of becoming members. This is the first time the participants gather publicly, and through this step they officially become *catechumens.* This is the first liturgical rite of the process.

Period 2: Catechumenate
The catechumens now begin a journey which takes them through a time of sharing and reflecting upon the Scriptures, the teachings of the Church, and their own faith stories. It is a time for the maturing and growth of the faith of the catechumens, a time of gradual conversion.

Second Step: Rite of Election or Enrollment of Names
When the Church is satisfied that the candidates have shown a sincere desire to become one with the community and have undergone a long period of instruction and reflection, it calls them to a new step designed for a more intensive spiritual preparation. In this liturgical rite, the Church acknowledges that the candidates are now

ready for their final spiritual preparation for the Sacraments of Initiation, and the catechumens express their desire to celebrate the sacraments. During this celebration, the catechumens become the *elect*.

Period 3: Purification and Enlightenment

The elect now enter a time of more intensive spiritual preparation and conversion. During this period, the elect celebrate several rites within the community which are aimed at protecting the elect from the power of evil and at publicly presenting the elect with the faith and prayer life of the community.

Third Step: Celebration of the Sacraments of Initiation

In this step, the candidates enter the community of the faithful through the Sacraments of Initiation (Baptism, Confirmation, and Eucharist). This rite is ordinarily celebrated during the Easter Vigil.

Period 4: Postbaptismal Catechesis or Mystagogy

Throughout the weeks which follow initiation, the newly initiated Christians meet together to share their experiences of the sacraments and their life as members of the Church community. During this period, they may also select a ministry within the community.

Baptized candidates go through a similar process, especially if they are uncatechized. However, the baptized candidates seeking full communion in the Catholic Church experience different Rites.

I. Rite of Welcoming the Candidates

II. Rite of Calling the Candidates to Continuing Conversion

III. Reception of Baptized Christians into the Full Communion of the Catholic Church.

The periods and steps of the process of Christian initiation often appear too lengthy to some who believe that becoming a member of the Church should be a simple matter taking only a few months. When we understand the great gifts and responsibilities involved in being a Christian, we can easily understand why any preparation should be long. Some of these gifts were named by Peter on the morning of the first Pentecost when he spoke to a large crowd of people gathered together in Jerusalem for the feast. Peter quotes from the Old Testament prophet Joel, who tells of the changes that take place in those guided by the Spirit. Peter tells us:

". . . this is what was spoken through the prophet Joel: 'In the last days it will be, God declares, that I will pour out my Spirit upon all flesh, and your sons and your daughters shall prophesy, and your young men shall see visions, and your old men shall dream dreams. Even upon my slaves, both men and women, in those days I will pour out my Spirit; and they shall prophesy. And I will show portents in the heaven above and signs on the earth below, blood, and fire, and smoky mist' " (Acts 2:16–19).*

c. This process is an adaptation of a process used in the early Church for those who wished to become members of the faithful.

In the early Church, a candidate, seeking entrance into the community of the Church, would pass through several stages of preparation before entering fully into the community. The Church today has reached back to it roots in its desire to prepare properly adults seeking to share in the community of the Church. In planning the ritual for the various steps on the journey into full communion with the Church, the Church also looks for a renewal within the community, preparing itself to receive this new member. While the candidate is making his or her spiritual journey into the community, the community is urged to renew its commitment in faith and love to Christ and his gospel.

7. What are sacramentals?

a. Sacramentals are blessings, prayers, or blessed objects designated as sacred in a unique way by the Church.

Catholics perform many actions that are unknown in other faiths. As they enter the Church, they bless themselves with holy water. Some wear blessed medals around their necks, keep blessed statues in their homes, and finger rosary beads as they pray. The presbyter makes a motion of the symbol of the cross over a person who requests a blessing. On Ash Wednesday, Catholics stroll the avenues with a dab of black ash on their foreheads. On Palm Sunday, they come from church with palm branches for their homes. Their celebration of sacraments is surrounded with anointings and prayers that do not directly affect the celebration of the sacrament. The Church calls these actions, blessings, prayers, and blessed objects *sacramentals*. These include only a few of the many sacramentals in the Church.

The purpose of a sacramental is to show, in a visible way, the continued action of Christ among us. They differ from sacraments insofar as they flow from the Church rather than from Christ. The sacraments come down to us from the life and message of Jesus Christ. In its holiness, the Church places certain merit upon other visible actions to share the same message of Christ's continued presence and gifts among us. The sacraments are far more important than the sacramentals, but the sacramentals should serve to make the sacraments more meaningful to all of us.

b. Sacramentals must not be used in a superstitious way.

Because a person wears a blessed medal around his or her neck does not mean that he or she will be able to take risks with a hope of never being hurt. Sacramentals are ways of honoring the saints or sharing in special blessings from the Church. To use them in a superstitious way is to use them in a way never intended by the Church. For example, to feel that sacramentals would miraculously keep a reckless driver from having an accident is a false, superstitious use of a sacramental. We should treat sacramentals with respect, realizing that they have been set aside in a special way by the Church to bring about Christ's blessings through the Church.

8. What is the liturgical year?

a. The liturgical year is the Church's celebrating of and entering into the major events of Christ's life through a twelve-month cycle.

In our own day, we are familiar with the calendar year that begins on the first of January and continues to the end of December. The Church also has a type of calendar year. The first day of the Church's calendar year begins four Sundays before the celebration of Christmas. This is late November or early December. The Church year also follows a twelve-month cycle, and, during this time, we move from a period that prepares for the birth of Christ to a period that celebrates Christ's continued presence in the Church. The central feast of the liturgical year is the feast of Easter. The Church believes that Easter is the major feast of the Church's life, since it is the culmination of the Christ's passover into glory and the celebration of the gift of salvation which flow from Christ into the world. It is the Paschal Mystery of the New Testament, the feast of feasts in the Church. The Church year moves toward this feast and continues on after this feast.

b. The period of preparation for the feast of Christmas is called Advent.

Four Sundays before the celebration of the feast of Christmas, we begin the Church year and the season of Advent. During this season, we look forward in three ways: we look forward to a memorial of the birthday of Christ; we look forward to a new spiritual birth of Christ in our lives on Christmas Day; and we also look forward to the second coming of Christ. During Advent, we place ourselves in union with the people of the Old Testament by longing for the coming of the Messiah. We remember that there was a time when people did not fully understand Christ and the meaning of Christ in their lives. With the people of the Old Testament, we share their spirit of hoping and longing for the coming of salvation into the lives of God's people. During the season of Advent, we try to improve our lives so that we might be fully prepared to celebrate the birth of Jesus. During this season, the presider will wear violet vestments during the Eucharistic liturgy as a sign of anticipation and hopeful preparation.

c. After Advent, we celebrate the feast of Christmas and the events that flow from this feast.

After the four weeks of Advent have been celebrated, we joyfully come to the feast of the birth of Jesus on December 25. The Church celebrates the joy of this season by directing the presider to wear white vestments in the celebration of the major feasts of this season. During the Christmas season, we celebrate a solemn feast in honor of Mary, the Mother of God. The feast of the manifestation of Jesus to the world as shown through the visit by the magi in the infancy narrative is also celebrated during this season. The number of Sundays celebrated in the Christmas season depends upon the date of Easter, which changes each year. This season leads us to the doorstep of Lent.

d. On Ash Wednesday, six and a half weeks before Easter, the season for preparing for the celebration of Easter begins with Lent.

The season of Lent is a strongly penitential season. Christians put themselves in union with the suffering Jesus, remembering his passion and death, but always looking forward to a joyful resurrection. During this season, the catechumens prepare themselves through the process of initiation to celebrate the Paschal Mystery of Jesus' death and resurrection. For them, it is a period of spiritual preparation. The faithful prepare for the celebration of the Paschal Mystery by being reminded of their own baptism and by their call to penitential practice. During this season, Catholics enter more fully into the preparation period by making certain sacrifices. These sacrifices aim toward living the Christian life more fully, such as praying better or more consciously reaching out in love to others in their need. They also consist in staying away from certain permitted pleasures. For instance, during this time, many Catholics will fast from certain food or drink. Whatever penance one might choose, he or she should recognize that the purpose for the penance is not to burden one with useless pain, but to place oneself in union with the suffering and death of Jesus Christ. Its main purpose is to prepare one for the celebration of the joyful coming of Jesus through the celebration of his resurrection. The vestments worn during the Eucharistic liturgy in Lent are violet to remind us that this is a penitential season.

The Church obliges Catholics to fast from food and abstain from meat on Ash Wednesday (the first day of Lent) and Good Friday. The general norm for fasting is that the two small meals eaten on that day should not equal the normal big meal of a person's day. The one big meal may also be eaten on that day, but no food should be taken between meals. On Fridays during Lent and on Good Friday, the Church obliges Catholics to abstain from meat. The obligation for fasting with the Church involves everyone from eighteen to the beginning of their sixtieth year. The obligation for abstaining from meat involves those who are fourteen years of age and older. If a person has a good reason for not following these obligations, the person is excused.

e. The Season of Lent ends with the "Sacred Triduum," the three sacred days which include Holy Thursday, Good Friday, and the Easter Vigil.

Lent properly ends with the beginning of the celebration of the Liturgy of the "Lord's Supper" on Holy Thursday. On Holy Thursday, the Lord's Supper liturgy begins with the opening prayer, but the liturgy has no ending. When it is over, the people simply leave the church quietly or remain for further adoration of the Eucharist. The Good Friday liturgy has no beginning and no ending. The Easter Vigil liturgy has no beginning, but it does have an ending. These three sacred days, known as the *Sacred Triduum*, actually form a single liturgy which begins on Thursday and ends with the Easter Vigil. During these days, the Church celebrates the central Passover Mystery of the death and resurrection of Christ.

At the Easter Vigil, the Church rejoices that Christ, who has died, has now been raised, and has brought us into a new life. On this feast, we celebrate Christ's Paschal Mystery as the beginning of our salvation. The presider wears white vestments to symbolize the joy of the great gift shared with all people through the resurrection and exaltation of Jesus Christ. At the Easter Vigil and throughout the Season of Easter, the Easter candle, a symbol of the light of Christ in the world, burns brightly at all liturgical celebrations.

A major feast that occurs during the Easter season is the feast of the Ascension which celebrates Christ's ascension and complete union with the Father and the Spirit. The feast underlines our mission to follow in Christ's footsteps in bringing his message to every corner of the world.

f. The Easter Season ends with the celebration of the feast of Pentecost.

Since Pentecost is the feast of the Holy Spirit, the Church uses red vestments to symbolize the flame of God's love, which is the work of the Holy Spirit. The Church celebrates the feast of Pentecost as the day when the Holy Spirit began to move the apostles to go out and share Christ's message and to draw all people into the community called *Church.*

g. After Pentecost, we continue to celebrate the guidance of the Holy Spirit in the Church.

After Pentecost, we celebrate the presence of Christ in the Church as the Church carries out its mission under the guidance of the Holy Spirit. These Sundays after Pentecost will take us to the final Sunday before the beginning of the new liturgical year. On the last Sunday of the liturgical year, the Church will again look to the final coming of Jesus and remind us that Jesus is our final and eternal hope. Throughout these Sundays, the Church celebrates its journey, a pilgrimage toward God. During this season, the presider will wear green vestments, a color symbolizing hope. Since the Spirit is continually working in the Church as Christ promised, there is always hope for a better world and for eternal joy for all people.

Conclusion

When Bill grew to adulthood, he entered an overseas medical program to help the poor receive medical attention. The doctor who saved Billy's life proudly commented on his part in saving the boy's life. He felt that he had a share in the good work Billy was doing.

God is continually saving us in some spiritual way in our lives. When God offers gifts to us, God does not give them for ourselves alone. God wants us to share these gifts to build up the world. God sees in us an extension of the work of Christ here on earth. When we act, Christ acts; when we build, Christ builds; when we share, Christ shares. Through the sacraments, God touches us in a very special, intimate way so that we may reach out and touch others with the gifts of Christ's love.

For Scripture reflection and discussion concerning this chapter, see **Journeying in His Light,** *"The Sacraments and Love."*

8 Sacraments of Initiation, Part 1: Baptism

Introduction

Many towns in the United States are named after families that originally owned the land and all the stores in the town. One town in the Midwest, however, bears the name of the family that settled in the town with nothing but a wagon, a horse, and some scrap furniture. The family had originally intended to move on farther west, but the friendly welcome they received in the town soon changed their minds. The mother and father, along with the five boys, ranging in age from thirteen to three, found a plot of land outside the town and began to farm the land. Within three years, the family suffered tragedies: first, the father was killed by a runaway horse, then rains completely washed away any hope for a harvest. The older boys went to work in town to raise enough money for more seed. The townspeople joined forces to bring food to the family so that they could save their money for seed. Within three more years, the boys had saved enough for more seed and had reaped a successful harvest. They, in turn, invited some of the poor of the town to come to their farm and take what they needed. As their farm continued to produce, an invitation went out once each year to all the poor of the town. The boys even began to plan extra plantings to care for the poor. Although the family never owned a store in the town and had very little invested in the town bank, the townspeople wished to preserve the memory and spirit of such good people. A special town meeting was called, and the townspeople voted to change the name of their town to the name of this family. As a testimony to some good people who settled in that area, the name of the family still lives on in this small midwestern town.

In this chapter, we reflect on the Sacrament of Baptism. Through baptism, we receive a new family name in memory of the person of Jesus Christ who died and was raised that we might live. We receive the name *Christian* through this sacrament, and, once we receive this name, we have the responsibility of keeping the memory and spirit of Jesus Christ alive in the lives of all people.

1. What is the Sacrament of Baptism?

a. Baptism is a sacrament that brings us into a new life in union with Christ and the Christian community.

To the members of the early Church, the manner of baptizing signified their belief in what was happening. The one being baptized would step down into a pool of water and be completely submerged in the water. He or she would then come out of the water (usually on the other side of the pool) as a symbol of his or her entry into a new life. This was considered an entry into the death and resurrection of Christ. In the Letter to the Romans, Paul expresses the belief behind this practice when he writes:

> *Do you not know that all of us who have been baptized into Christ Jesus were baptized into his death? Therefore we have been buried with him by baptism into death, so that, just as Christ was raised from the dead by the glory of the Father, so we too might walk in newness of life. For if we have been united with him in a death like his, we will certainly be united with him in a resurrection like his (Romans 6:3–5).*

Just as Christ entered a new life through his resurrection, so a person enters a new life in union with Christ and the Christian community through baptism.

b. Baptism is one of the Sacraments of Initiation into the Catholic Church.

At the outset of the baptismal ceremony, the sign of the cross is made on the forehead of the person entering the Church, and the presider, in the name of the community, welcomes the one being baptized into the community. Through the Sacrament of Baptism, a person becomes a member of the Christian community and shares in the gifts and duties of the community. Because the community commits itself to the newly baptized at the time of the baptism, and because the newly baptized, in turn, commits himself or herself to the community, the Church urges that the ceremony take place in the presence of the assembled community.

In speaking to the Corinthian community, Paul reminds them that they all belong to the one body of the Church through their baptism. We read, "For just as the body is one and has many members, and all the members of the body, though many, are one body, so it is with Christ. For in the one Spirit we were all baptized into one body—Jews or Greeks, slaves or free—and we were all made to drink of one Spirit" (1 Corinthians 12:12–13).

c. Baptism is a sacrament which brings us into the reign of God.

When Jesus began his mission, he proclaimed, "The time is fulfilled, and the kingdom of God has come near; repent, and believe in the good news" (Mark 1:15). With the coming of Jesus and his death, resurrection, and ascension, the reign of God became a living reality on earth. The people of the Old Testament saw God as reigning over all, but, with Jesus, this reign entered the world in a new way. Through union with Jesus, a person enters the reign of God.

When Nicodemus, a Pharisee, sought instruction from Jesus during the secret hours of the night, Jesus told him, "Very truly, I tell you, no one can see the kingdom of God without being born from above" (John 3:3). Nicodemus asked if a person could enter his mother's womb and be born again, but Jesus explained this new birth into God's reign in a special way. Jesus told him, "Very truly, I tell you, no one can enter the kingdom of God without being born of water and Spirit" (John 3:5). In this text, Jesus is speaking not of life hereafter, but of the reign of God which is existing on earth and which will reach its fulfillment in eternity. Unless a person is born of water and the Spirit, he or she does not enter this special union with Christ, known as the reign of God even on earth.

Although the Church reveals the presence of the reign of God on earth in a visible way, the Church and the reign of God are not one and the same. The Church belongs to the reign of God on earth, but the Church does not exhaust the total meaning of the reign of God. Through baptism, a person not only enters the Church, but also the reign of God which is "at hand." Through their lives, baptized Christians make the reign of God a continual, living reality on earth.

d. Baptism is a sacrament by which all one's sins are forgiven.

Since baptism signifies a dying to one's old life and a rising to new life, it also signifies death to all sin which had control over our life in the past. In union with Christ, a person enters a new life of grace. In Paul's Second Letter to the Corinthians, we read, "So if anyone is in Christ, there is a new creation: everything old has passed away; see, everything has become new! All this is from God, who reconciled us to himself through Christ, and has given us the ministry of reconciliation. . ." (2 Corinthians 5:17–18). The use of water in the sacrament further underlines this idea of leaving the slavery of sin behind. Just as the Israelites passed from slavery to new life through the waters of the great sea, so we pass from sin to new life through the waters of baptism.

e. Baptism is a sacrament which draws us into a new covenant with God through Christ.

In the Old Testament, God made a covenant with Abraham, Isaac, Jacob, Moses, and other great leaders of ancient Israel. This promise was the hope and expectation of all the Hebrew people from the time of Abraham, and they looked toward the coming of the messiah. Christians believe that the Messiah came in the person of Jesus Christ, and that union with Christ and his Church through baptism draws one into this covenant made with Abraham and his successors. In his Letter to the Galatians, Paul tells us:

As many of you as were baptized into Christ have clothed yourselves with Christ. There is no longer Jew or Greek, there is no longer slave or free, there is no longer male and female; for all of you are one in Christ Jesus. And if you belong to Christ, then you are Abraham's offspring, heirs according to the promise (Galatians 3:27–29).

Just as we have two parties to every covenant and certain promises and responsibilities on the part of both parties, we must recognize that the baptized share not only in the many gifts of Christ, but they also have certain responsibilities to fulfill as Christians.

2. What is the common priesthood of the faithful?

a. As baptized Christians, we are called to worship God the Father in the name of Jesus.

An expression commonly used in some areas is the *common priesthood of the faithful*. Christ is priest, prophet, and king. Through baptism, all Christians share in the gift of Christ's priesthood. We should not confuse the term *priesthood of the faithful* with the *ordained priesthood*, which refers to those who have celebrated the Sacrament of Holy Orders. The priesthood which comes through our baptism calls us to worship God in the name of Jesus Christ. The Church attempts to help us realize this gift by urging us to active participation in worship, through singing, praying, and serving in specific ministries during worship. In becoming one with Christ, a Christian shares in the gift of Christ's priesthood.

b. The Church has established the ministries of lector and acolyte and has invited lay Catholics to share in these ministries.

At one time, only those who were candidates for ordination would share in certain ministries within the Church. In recognition of the priesthood shared by all people at baptism, Pope Paul VI opened the ministry of "lector" and "acolyte" to lay Christians along with those preparing to receive ordination. Through the institution of lector, a person is committed to reading the word of God, with the exception of the gospel, at liturgical celebrations. The lector is also called to prepare others for the proper reading of Scripture and to instruct the faithful for the worthy reception of the sacraments. Through the institution of acolyte, a person is called to assist the deacon or presbyter at liturgical clebrations and to see to the proper preparation for service at the altar. In addition, the acolyte is to have a good grasp of Eucharistic theology. The acolyte distributes the Eucharist at liturgy and brings the Eucharist to the sick.

c. The laity actively participate in liturgical celebrations and perform various ministries in the celebration of the Eucharist.

Installation into a ministry is permanent and limited to those who fulfill the proper requisites for this installation. In specific circumstances, the Church also calls for the laity who are not installed in these ministries to serve as readers and Eucharistic ministers, to serve in worship, to preside over liturgical prayer, and to baptize. When the laity are installed in permanent ministries, we refer to them as lectors and acolytes. When we are commissioned for certain functions, we are referred to as readers, Eucharistic ministers, or servers, depending upon our particular ministry.

Through their baptism, the laity have the right and obligation to participate in the common celebration of worship and to discharge certain tasks proper to their state. During the Eucharistic Celebration, their ministries include the role of readers, Eucharistic ministers, servers, ministers of music, etc. Many of these duties belong properly to the laity. When a number of ordained priests are among those celebrating, the ordained serve as Eucharistic ministers. The laity perform their ministries not because the presider allows them to do so, but because of the rights and obligations which flow from their baptismal commitment. Major areas of ministry for the laity in their daily lives touch upon the important areas of evangelization and social justice.

d. A minister should share in only one special ministry within a single liturgy.

The reader should be concerned solely with reading the word of God and should not distribute the Eucharist at the same liturgy. Nor should a minister of the Eucharist distribute the Eucharist at more than one celebration on any given day. The reason the Church makes these requests in worship is to avoid confusion of ministries, as well as to protect the special value of each ministerial function. The ministers should share fully in the service in which they are ministering.

3. What do we mean by our baptism as prophets?

a. Jesus Christ is a prophet.

Earlier in this book, we learned that a prophet was one who spoke or acted on the name of God. In the Gospel of Luke, the author presents Jesus not merely as a prophet, but portrays him as **the** prophet. Jesus not only preaches in the name of God, but preaches as God. As his opponents proclaim throughout the Gospels, he speaks as one having authority and not as one who depends upon the wisdom of past teachers. In Luke's Gospel, Jesus begins his journey to Jerusalem declaring, "I must be on my way, because it is impossible for a prophet to be killed outside of Jerusalem" (Luke 13:33). Jesus sees the fulfillment of his mission as accepting death as a prophet.

b. As baptized Christians, we are called to share in the prophetic mission of Christ.

In the baptism of a child, the ordained minister touches the child's ears and mouth, praying that the child will hear God's word and speak God's word. The duty of sharing this word of God is given to the disciples and all the Church in Jesus' words at the time of his ascension. Jesus tells his disciples, ". . . [teach] them to obey everything that I have commanded you. And remember, I am with you always, to the end of the age" (Matthew 28:20). As people who hear and spread the message of Christ, we share in the gift of Jesus as prophet.

c. We share in the prophetic mission of Christ whenever we act or speak in God's name.

The Church calls upon the baptized to serve as teachers of religion to the young as well as to adults. In the Rite of Christian Initiation of Adults, Christians become sponsors and companions to those on the journey into the faith, sharing with them God's word and example

163

through their lives. Through learning about Christ and speaking out courageously on issues pertaining to Christ's message of love and concern for all people, Christians live as prophets in this world.

4. What do we mean by our call to share in the reign of God?

a. Jesus Christ is king.

Jesus, as king, did not sit upon a golden throne, but came astride a donkey as he entered Jerusalem for the last time and ended up on the cross as his throne. Throughout his life, Jesus preached a reign of service, not one of dominion. Although Jesus did not deny that he held a dominant and unique position in creation and that he was truly a king, he claimed that his kingdom was not of this world. The author of the Gospel of John shares an insight into Jesus' kingship when he describes Jesus' discourse with Pilate. When Pilate asks Jesus if he is a king, Jesus answers, "My kingdom is not from this world. If my kingdom were from this world, my followers would be fighting to keep me from being handed over. . . . But as it is, my kingdom is not from here" (John 18:36).

b. As baptized Christians, we are called to serve those in need.

Paul saw his mission as one which continued the service of Christ on earth. He writes, "I am now rejoicing in my sufferings for your sake, and in my flesh I am completing what is lacking in Christ's afflictions for the sake of his body, that is, the church" (Colossians 1:24). Jesus showed his concern for others during his life, and he was willing to suffer for others. Paul recognizes that his own suffering continues the presence of Christ on earth in service to others. Jesus gave us an example of service in washing the feet of the Twelve at the Last Supper, and he told a story of service in the parable of the Good Samaritan who cared for a man who was robbed and beaten. Jesus is considered a king, but his reign differs from worldly reigns. Jesus' kingship is shown in service. In writing to the Galatians, Paul tells them, "For you were called to freedom, brothers and sisters; only do not use your freedom as an opportunity for self-indulgence, but through love become slaves to one another" (Galatians 5:13). Through service to others, we share in the gift of Christ as king.

c. Through the Sacrament of Baptism, a Christian must confront all divisiveness and sin in the world and work toward unity.

Just as Jesus came to confront the power of evil and to bring the world into one in himself, so the newly baptized must work toward the same goal. The Christian must continually make evil uncomfortable in the world, never allowing an evil attitude toward life to overcome the message of Christ. Through his death and resurrection, Jesus overcame the power of evil in the world, and the Christian must use the gifts of baptism to continue this confrontation of evil.

In overcoming evil, the Christian continually works toward a unity of love in the world. The Christian realizes that all are called to be one in Christ, and with the assurance of Christ's guidance, the Christian must work toward this unity. In Paul's Letter to the Ephesians, we read, "There is one body and one Spirit, just as you were called to the one hope of your calling, one Lord, one faith, one baptism, one God and Father of all, who is above all and through all and in all" (Ephesians 4:4–6).

5. What is ministry?

a. Ministry is a special call to serve in the name and spirit of Jesus.

Jesus Christ traveled across the land of palestine, preaching the good news of the reign of God and healing spiritual and physical ills. He had nowhere to lay his head, but neither did many of the people he served. At the Last Supper, he gave a further sign of his service by washing the feet of the apostles. Throughout his life, Christ gave an example of the type of ministry he calls us to live. His was a ministry of servanthood. He allowed himself to be led to the cross, to be crucified, and even to die as part of his ministry to confront evil. Christ was the obedient servant. Through our baptism, we received a call to follow the example of Christ and to serve in the name and spirit of Christ.

b. Ministry is a special call to serve as a member of the Church.

We are members of Christ's body, and, as such, we are members of his Church. After Christ's resurrection and ascension, the apostles began to share his ministry with others. In the name of Jesus, the cared for the poor, cured the sick, and preached the message of the reign of God. The Acts of the Apostles proclaims the call of the disciples to serve as ministers in many different ways. We are told how some in the Church shared in the ministry of preaching and the ministry of serving. As the early Church saw new needs arise, it would call upon its members to fill those needs. As members of the Church, Christians reached out to others and to one another. They recognized their ministry as a special call to serve as a member of the Church. Through the Sacrament of Baptism, we are called to ministry. Paul speaks about the various ministries given by Christ and reminds us that they are given for the build-up of the Church, the Body of Christ on earth. Paul writes, "The gifts he gave were that some would be apostles, some prophets, some evangelists, some pastors and teachers. . ." (Ephesians 4:11).

c. Ministry is a special share in the gifts of the Holy Spirit.

In calling us to ministry, Christ oes not call us to act alone. In the Gospel of John, he tells his apostles, "I will not leave you orphaned; I am coming to you" (John 14:18). Christ continually shares his gifts with us through the power of the Holy Spirit. These gifts enable us to carry out our ministry as Christ and the Church would have us carry it out. Paul writes of the gifts of the Holy Spirit that help us to live our call to ministry.

> Now there are varieties of gifts, but the same Spirit; and there are varieties of services, but the same Lord; and there are varieties of activities, but it is the same God who activates all of them in everyone. To each is given the manifestation of the Spirit for the common good. To one is given through the Spirit the utterance of wisdom, and to another the

166

utterance of knowledge according to the same Spirit, to another faith by the same Spirit, to another gifts of healing by the one Spirit, to another the working of miracles, to another prophecy, to another the discernment of spirits, to another various kinds of tongues, to another the interpretation of tongues. All these are activated by one and the same Spirit, who allots to each one individually just as the Spirit chooses (1 Corinthians 12:4-11).

Some refer to their special gifts of the Spirit as *charisms.*

d. All baptized Christians are called to ministry in Christ.

Through our baptism, we are all called to ministry. When Christians reach maturity, they have an obligation to share their ministry with others. A passive Christian, looking to save his or her own soul with no concern toward serving others, is not fully responding to the baptismal call to share the light of Christ with others. Paul, writing to the Colossians, tells us that we were baptized not only into Jesus' death, but also into his life, and it is this living presence of Christ which we are called to share through our ministry. Paul writes, ". . . when you were buried with him in baptism, you were also raised with him through faith in the power of God, who raised him from the dead." (Colossians 2:12). Through our baptism, we are called to minister to the worshiping community, and to minister to those outside the worshiping community. We are meant to hear the word of God and to share it by word and action.

Paul goes on to remind us of the virtues involved in our ministry. He writes, "As God's chosen ones, holy and beloved, clothe yourselves with compassion, kindness, humility, meekness, and patience. Let the word of Christ swell in you richly; teach and admonish one another in all wisdom; and with gratitude in your hearts sing psalms, hymns, and spiritual songs to God. And whatever you do, in word or deed, do everything in the name of the Lord Jesus, giving thanks to God the Father through him" (Colossians 3:12, 16–17).

6. Who may be baptized?

a. All adults who have not yet shared in the Sacrament of Baptism and who believe that Jesus Christ is the Son of God become human and who wish to follow his message as lived through the Catholic Church may receive the Sacrament of Baptism in the Catholic Church.

Before adults celebrate the Sacrament of Baptism, they must first profess their belief in Jesus Christ as the living Son of God, come as a human being, and now resurrected and ascended to the Father. They must also profess a belief in the Holy Catholic Church and commit themselves to live out the teachings of Christ as reflected in the Church. The community renews its vows along with the candidates. When the people heard Peter preaching on Pentecost, they believed that Jesus was the Messiah, and they asked Peter what they must do. Peter answered, "Repent, and be baptized every one of you in the name of Jesus Christ so that your sins may be forgiven; and you will receive the gift of the Holy Spirit" (Acts 2:38).

b. A person already baptized in another Christian faith who wishes to enter the Catholic faith cannot be baptized again unless there is a reasonable doubt concerning the fact of the first baptism.

If a person has shared in baptism in a Christian Church under the formula, "I baptize you in the name of the Father and of the Son and of the Holy Spirit" and has received sprinkling, pouring of water, or immersion in water, then that person has celebrated a true baptism. In carrying out these words and using these actions, other Christian Churches are acting in unity with the message of Christ as understood by the Catholic Church. Once we receive the Sacrament of Baptism, we cannot receive this sacrament a second time. A previously baptized person wishing to enter the Catholic faith must make a profession of faith before the community. In case of doubt, the priest confers this sacrament in a conditional way, that is, he prefaces the words of baptism: "If you are not already baptized, I baptize you in the name of the Father and of the Son and of the Holy Spirit."

c. Parents who are faithfully living out their baptismal commitment may have their child baptized in the Church.

At the time of the child's baptism, the parents take upon themselves the responsibility of sharing the faith with their child, both by practicing the faith and by providing a Catholic up-bringing and education of the child. If the parents are not willing to fulfill this obligation, the minister of the sacrament should delay the baptism of this child. In conferring all sacraments, the minister must have some positive hope that the baptized person will understand and live out the calling of that sacrament. If the parents are baptized and show no concern in living out their baptismal vows, the minister may conclude that the child will not receive a proper education in the living out of the baptismal promises. In this case, the minister of this sacrament should delay the baptism.

d. Any child in danger of death may be baptized.

Although an adult in danger of death must show some desire to celebrate the sacrament, a child cannot show such a desire. In danger of death, a child may be baptized. In this case, the religious conscience of the parents should be considered.

7. Who may baptize?

a. In the Catholic Church the ordained minister is the ordinary minister of the Sacrament of Baptism.

Because baptism is a community event even when the major part of the community is not present, the ordained minister, as representative of the community, should confer this sacrament of initiation into the Church community. A presbyter or deacon, both ordained ministers, share this ministry of baptizing in the name of the Church. The minister of this sacrament is responsible for the proper preparation for the sacrament. Instruction or preparation should precede the celebration of this sacrament. Parents should plan far enough in advance so that the presbyter or deacon may arrange some time for instruction and preparation for the Sacrament of Baptism.

b. In danger of death, anyone may baptize.

If a person foresees that death may occur before the proper minister of the Church can arrive, that person may baptize. If the person in danger of death is an adult, he or she must make some sign of desiring the sacrament. A person may not baptize oneself. A simple way of baptizing is to pour the water on the forehead of the person to be baptized or on any part of the body that might be exposed while pronouncing the words, "I baptize you in the name of the Father and of the Son and of the Holy Spirit."

8. What happens to those who are not baptized?

a. If a person believes that Jesus Christ is God become human, that he shared his sacraments and message with us through the Church, and that we are obliged to receive the Sacrament of Baptism, that person has an obligation to receive the sacrament.

Jesus invites us to follow him. For those who recognize this invitation as coming through the Sacrament of Baptism, the sacrament becomes an obligation. To refuse this sacrament while realizing the obligation is to commit a serious sin against God. It is to turn down Christ's invitation "to come follow" him. For those who seem to believe that this sacrament is necessary, yet do not respond, we cannot easily judge their motivation, nor can we easily say that they have sinned. Perhaps their belief is not as strong as it appears on the surface.

b. A person who does not know Jesus Christ or does not know or believe the necessity of baptism, but follows conscience as perfectly as possible, is not obliged to receive the Sacrament of Baptism for salvation.

Many wonderful and good Jewish people will never share in baptism, since their faith does not believe in the necessity of this sacrament. These people and others who lead a good life without seeing the necessity of baptism are not obliged to receive this sacrament. If these people truly believed in the necessity of baptism, they would most likely receive the sacrament. Some have called this "baptism of desire." In the early Church, we read of cases where people who had not yet received the Sacrament of Baptism died for Christ. Some claimed that these people received "baptism of blood." Neither the baptism of desire nor the baptism of blood can be considered a sacramental baptism. The sacrament demands the signs of water and the saying of the words of baptism.

c. The Scriptures do not tell us what happens to infants who die without the Sacrament of Baptism.

As we mentioned earlier in the chapter, Jesus told Nicodemus, "Very truly, I tell you, no one can enter the kingdom of God without being born of water and Spirit" (John 3:5). The Church accepts this text as assuring the immediate entrance into heaven of a child who dies after baptism, since the child has committed no personal sin. The Scriptures, however, say nothing about the child who dies without the Sacrament of Baptism. In the past, some believed that the text "no on can enter into God's kingdom" seemed to exclude an unbaptized child from the external happiness of heaven. But the Church now realizes that the kingdom of heaven is not just life hereafter, but life here on earth. To enter the community of the Church is to enter the reign of heaven here on earth. Because the text could be referring to the reign of God and not merely to life hereafter, we cannot speak of any rejection of a child who dies without the Sacrament of Baptism. Knowing a merciful and loving God, it is hard to accept a state of just natural happiness without God or even worse a state of eternal rejection. That these unbaptized children are

171

invited to eternal happiness with God does not destroy the need for baptism. Baptism is celebrated that Christ may continue to work in the world through baptized Christians.

9. What is a sponsor or godparent?

a. The Rite of Christian Initiation of Adults calls for a person to act as a sponsor on behalf of the Church.

As people make their journey into the faith, they will have many questions and need to have some type of personal link with the parish family. Besides their relatives and friends who guide them in these areas, they should also have a sponsor, chosen by the parish family, to serve as a guide and spiritual companion during the period of the catechumenate. The sponsor should have a good grasp of the Catholic faith, have shown some involvement in the parish family, and have an open manner of sharing personally with another. Besides acting as a companion during the discussion sessions, the sponsor accompanies the catechumen through the rituals of Christian initiation and can serve as a friend in introducing the catechumen to other members of the parish family. Some parishes have special sessions to prepare sponsors serving in this privileged role on behalf of the Church. Sponsors are called upon to witness to the readiness of those seeking membership in the Church.

b. Godparents are those who commit themselves to assisting the newly baptized, or, in the case of infants, parents of the newly baptized in their specific duties.

A person becomes a godparent through the special witness given at the time of the celebration of baptism. Although adults may choose to have their sponsors (chosen by the parish) as their godparents, many of them will have others from among their friends or relatives serve as godparents. Godparents for adults commit themselves to helping the newly baptized in their duty as Christians.

Godparents for children do not commit themselves to the child, but to the parents of the newly baptized, stating that they are willing to help the parents in their duty as Christian parents.

c. Godparents and sponsors are to be Catholics in good standing who have celebrated the three Sacraments of Initiation.

The godparents and sponsors are to have a grasp of Catholic teaching, be living a life consistent with the faith, and be mature enough to fulfill this responsibility (a person sixteen years old or older is presumed to have the requisite maturity), be initiated with the Sacraments of Baptism, Confirmation, and Eucharist, be neither the mother nor the father of the candidate, and be canonically free to fulfill this office. Ordinarily there are two godparents for a child and one or two for an adult. At least one godparent is to be a Catholic who fulfills the requirements mentioned above. Another person, a baptized and believing Christian not belonging to the Catholic Church, may serve as a Christian witness along with a Catholic godparent, if the parents so desire. In the ceremony, the godparents profess their faith with others, and promise to be witnesses to that faith.

10. Why is the sign of water chosen for the Sacrament of Baptism?

a. One of the uses of water in life is for cleansing.

In the Sacrament of Baptism, all sins of the adult candidate will be washed away. This symbol of cleansing from sin is considered a major symbol in the use of water in this sacrament. More recently, the use of water has received its deeper scriptural meaning.

b. Water in the Scriptures often symbolizes sin or chaos or death.

In the beginning of the story of creation, we read that the world was a watery mass, and everything was in chaos. Into this watery mass and chaos, God brought order by creating the world. Later, in this same Book of Genesis, we read another story concerning water. God sends a flood upon a sinful world. Out of this water of the flood, new life emerges. From this sin comes a new creation in the person of Noah and his family. In the Book of Exodus, the people were caught in the chaos of slavery in Egypt, and God led them into the desert through the waters of the Reed Sea. Christ begins his public life by going down into the waters, being baptized by John the Baptizer. When Jesus hung upon the cross, the sign of new life occurred as the soldier ran a spear through his side, and blood and water flowed forth. Through these signs used in the Scriptures, the authors expressed the symbol of water as signifying death followed by new life. Water symbolizes sin, chaos, or death. Coming out of water shows an entry into a new life.

c. Water in baptism symbolizes a dying and rising with Christ.

In the early Church, people were baptized by stepping down into a pool of water. The deacon of deaconess would submerge the candidate and pronounce the words "I baptize you in the name of the Father and of the Son and of the Holy Spirit." A newly baptized person would then come out of the water sharing a new life, a new beginning. Baptism by immersion, that is, complete submersion in the water, is still used in the Church. Also used is the pouring of water upon the forehead of a person. It has the same symbol of dying and rising, going down into the water and coming out with a new life, life in union with Christ.

11. How is the Sacrament of Baptism celebrated?

a. From the time of the early Church, certain characteristics continually appeared in the celebration of the Sacrament of Baptism.

The initiation process in the early Church was often a journey of several years which involved certain rituals along the way. Today, this journey takes place during the process of inviting adults into the faith. Children, however, cannot make this journey, since they do not have the ability to make the decisions necessary for the fulfillment of the process. In the case of infant baptism, the preparation time is often shorter and the learning of the faith and its renewed commitment takes place throughout the life of the child. In every baptismal process, however, certain basic ingredients are always present to the degree possible or permissible. These elements include the proclamation and acceptance of the word of God, a profession of faith, the Sacrament of Baptism itself, and the celebration of Confirmation, followed by Eucharistic Communion.

b. The celebration of the Sacrament of Baptism properly takes place within the celebration of the Eucharistic Liturgy.

Just as families choose to celebrate a birth in the family setting of one's home or with one's family or closest friends, so the Church community chooses to celebrate spiritual birth within the major community celebration which is the Eucharistic Liturgy. During this liturgy, the proclamation of the word of God takes place as members of the community and the presider at Eucharist celebrate the baptism of a new member into the Body of Christ. As the family rejoices in the spiritual birth of their child, the community also rejoices in the spiritual birth of a new member.

The presider prays on behalf of the community, expressing the community's joy in accepting this new candidate for the Sacraments of Initiation. When Jesus chose his disciples, he said, "If you will be my disciples, pick up your cross and follow me." The presider invites the parents and sponsors to make the sign of the cross on the forehead of the child as a symbol of this commitment to discipleship. In the case of an adult celebrating the Sacraments of Initiation, the presider invites the sponsors to trace the sign of the cross on the candidate's forehead.

During the Eucharistic celebration, the elect themselves or the parents of the child join with the community in making a profession of faith. This is the faith of the Church expressed in the midst of the liturgy, and it is the faith which the elect or the parents of the child seek in baptism.

175

c. The parents and godparents make specific commitments during the baptismal ceremony.

In the case of the baptism of a child, the presider greets the parents and godparents at the beginning of the Eucharistic Liturgy. The greeting of adult candidates takes place much earlier during the RCIA process. In this greeting, the presider asks the parents, candidates, and sponsors if they clearly understand their commitment.

The Church recognizes that parents, as primary teachers of the child, have a major role in the baptism of the child. Besides viewing baptism from the point of the child, the Church also views it from the point of the parents who declare in the ceremony that they understand their duty and commit themselves to carrying out this duty. Although it is the child who is baptized, it is the parents who make the major commitments in the baptismal ceremony. For this reason, the parents are the ones who hold the child (if necessary) during the celebration of the Sacrament of Baptism.

The godparents, acting on behalf of the community, commit themselves to nurturing the faith-life of the parents and the child. The commitment of the godparents is not directed toward the child, but toward the child's parents. In the ceremony, the godparents promise to help the parents of the child in their duty as Christian parents. Implied in the godparents' commitment is the promise to pray for the child and to offer the child and parents support in living the Christian life.

d. Anointings with blessed oil signify the role of the Spirit in the life of the newly baptized.

Anointing with oil had human origins before the time of the early Church. Athletes often covered their body with oil before some important athletic event. In some cases, oil symbolized a spiritual commitment. In the baptismal celebration, the presider makes use of oil at two separate points. Before the time of the baptism, the presider anoints the child or the candidate with oil to show that this person is about to become the newly anointed one. The title *Christ, Messiah,* or *Anointed One* given to Jesus designated his role in creation. The newly anointed person in baptism now shares in Christ's ministry in creation through the power of the Holy Spirit. The newly anointed one is now ready to "run the race" through life, carrying the message of Christ.

After the celebration of the Sacrament of Baptism, adult candidates celebrate the Sacrament of Confirmation. The presider anoints the candidates with oil which confirms and completes the baptismal anointing. When the Church celebrates the Sacrament of Baptism for children, the presider anoints the child with the same oil the bishop uses in the Sacrament of Confirmation. The actual celebration of the Sacrament of Confirmation takes place later. The anointing reminds the child's family that the journey of full initiation still lies ahead with the celebration of the Sacraments of Confirmation and Eucharist.

e. The presider blesses the water to be used in the sacrament.

During the Easter season, water blessed at the Easter Vigil should be used for the Sacrament of Baptism. This shows that baptism is actually a Passover event, that is, a dying and a rising. Outside the Easter season, the presider blesses the water at each ceremony. This symbolic use of water is a sign that the newly baptized person is dying to his or her old life and rising to a new life in union with Christ.

As the presider pours the water over the forehead of the candidate or immerses him or her in the water, the presider pronounces the words of Christ as given in the Scriptures, baptizing ". . . in the name of the Father, and of the Son, and of the Holy Spirit." At the moment of baptism, the presider calls the candidate by name.

f. A white garment is placed on the newly baptized and a lighted candle is held by one of the parents or godparents (for the child) or by the newly baptized adult.

The white garment or baptismal robe, as well as the lighted candle, symbolize that Christ has come into the world. The newly baptized has clothed himself or herself in Christ, and the child's parents or the newly baptized adult are told to keep the light of Christ burning brightly in the life of their new baptismal commitment.

At the Easter Vigil, which is the appropriate time for welcoming new members into the community, the community of the baptized hold lighted candles from the beginning of the ceremony. The candidates, however, do not light their candle until after their baptism, when they become a light to the world in union with Christ.

g. The presider touches the ears and the mouth of the newly baptized, praying that he or she will hear God's word and preach God's word.

Through the Sacrament of Baptism, we are called to discipleship. We are called to evangelize or to be a witness to Christ's message. Many have left this to the ordained priest, ministers, or sisters in their particular Churches. But the obligation to understand and witness to the gospel message comes to us through the Sacrament of Baptism.

h. The community joins along with the parents, godparents (sponsors), and the newly baptized in the prayer given by Christ by which we address God in the most intimate way as "Our Father."

When Christ taught the apostles how to pray, he addressed God under the Hebrew title of *Abba*. The original meaning of this word could be translated more closely by the word *Daddy*. It is an informal, personal greeting of one's true father. Through the Sacrament of Baptism, we now share so closely with Christ that we dare to say "Our Father (Dad)" in a most personal relationship. Since the Lord's Prayer represents the prayer of the community, the parents along with their newly baptized child, or the newly baptized adults, stand in a dominant place around the table of the Lord as they join together as baptized Christians in praying the prayer of the Church.

i. The celebration of First Eucharist concludes the Sacraments of Initiation.

In sharing the Sacrament of Eucharist for the first time, the new members of the Catholic family complete the celebration of the Sacraments of Initiation. After the final prayer, the presider may invite the members of the assembly to unite their happiness with that of the new members of the Catholic Church by applauding. In this way, the members of the assembly express their joy and support of these new members who are now fully initiated into the Catholic family.

j. The celebration ends with a blessing for all the baptized.

The solemn blessing concludes the celebration, with a special blessing for the parents if it is a baptism of a child. The newly initiated adults then receive the commission to "Go in peace," which means they are now sent out with the rest of the community to live their faith in the world.

Conclusion

The family in the introduction of this chapter moved into a town that welcomed them and eventually took their name. The sole reason for the change of the name was goodness and love. Jesus comes into our lives looking for a welcome. He never forces his way into our lives, but comes and, at times, waits. Through the Sacrament of Baptism, we welcome Jesus, and we begin to bear his name in the title Christian. *If the town that bore the name of this family ever forgot the spirit of the family and became self-centered and destructive, the family might wish that the town had not chosen to take their name.*

If we, as Christians, do not live up to the goodness, love, and sharing demanded in baptism, Jesus could wish that someone more deserving would have accepted his name through baptism. In the name and spirit of Christ, we receive his gifts and name at baptism and share these gifts in building God's world. This is our call in bearing the name of Christ.

For Scripture reflection and discussion concerning this chapter, see **Journeying in His Light, "Sacraments of Initiation, Parts 1 and 2."**

9 Sacraments of Initiation, Part 2: Confirmation

Introduction

A playful five-year-old boy watched the smoke swirl up from his father's cigarette. He ran across the room to where his father sat, playfully cupped some of the smoke in his hand and ran off to the corner of the room with his treasure. He opened his hands in the corner and, to his surprise, he found no smoke in them. He immediately ran back to where his father sat smoking, cupped more smoke in his hands and slowly moved toward the corner as though he were carrying eggs. Again, he found no smoke when he opened his hands. He looked confused for a moment, but immediately ran off to play another game.

At times in our lives, we become like that playful five-year-old boy. We believe in God, we go to church, and we try to treat our neighbor well. But events happen in life that try our faith and belief in a caring God. Like that child, we think we have our faith in the palm of our hands, but just when we open our hands to find it, it has eluded us. We believe in God, but where is God when an innocent child dies or a spouse dies? We believe in God, but why did we have to lose this particular job? We believe in God, but where is God in this world? The challenges come, and we open our hands looking for faith. Some of us find it, and some do not. To live as an adult Christian in the world takes more than courage, it takes a special gift of God. God shares a very special gift with us when God offers us the Sacrament of Confirmation. Christ is alive, Christ is loving, Christ is sharing—in us. The Sacrament of Confirmation enables us to open our hands and find our faith as well as witness to our faith. In confirmation, we live our baptism more fully.

181

1. What is the Sacrament of Confirmation?

a. Confirmation is one of the Sacraments of Initiation.

As we mentioned in the chapter on sacraments, the three Sacraments of Initiation are Baptism, Confirmation, and Eucharist. Through these three sacraments, a person becomes one of the Catholic faithful. Through the Sacrament of Baptism, a person belongs to the community of the Catholic Church, but the Sacrament of Baptism is really the beginning of the journey into full sharing in the Church. Through confirmation and Eucharist, a person journeys into a deeper sharing in the gifts given by Christ to the Church.

In a document from the Second Vatican Council, the Church insists that we recognize the Sacrament of Confirmation as one of the Sacraments of Initiation. The Church wanted this unity to be preserved when the new rite for confirmation was completed. In the "Constitution on the Liturgy," we read, "The rite of Confirmation is to be revised . . . so that the intimate connection of this sacrament with the whole of the Christian initiation may more clearly appear" (Vatican II, "Constitution on the Sacred Liturgy," number 71).

b. The Sacrament of Confirmation emphasizes the full presence of the Holy Spirit in our lives.

In celebrating the sacrament, the presider prays that the newly confirmed person will receive the gift of the Holy Spirit. Although the Church recognizes that the ritual for the Sacrament of Confirmation draws us into a greater awareness of the Holy Spirit in our lives, we must be careful not to leave the impression that we are receiving the Spirit for the first time in confirmation. In the Sacrament of Baptism, we are baptized in the name of the Trinity (Father, Son, and Holy Spirit), and we have the Trinity dwelling in us. Through our baptism, we have received the gifts of the Spirit. Through confirmation, however, the Church pays special attention to these gifts of the Spirit and prays that we might enter more fully into a living unity with the Spirit. The emphasis on the gift of the

Spirit coming to us at confirmation reminds us that the Spirit works in different ways at different times and that all our human activities continually depend upon the activity of the Spirit in our lives.

c. The Sacrament of Confirmation confirms the presence of the baptismal gifts and calls us to live a Christian life in a responsible manner.

In reality, the Sacrament of Confirmation confirms the presence of the baptismal gifts in a person. In the past, we might have said that a person reaches a mature age and is then, as an adult, able to confirm his or her commitment to God. This idea does not seem to have any foundation in Church history, even when the sacrament was part of the baptismal rite. A caution with such an emphasis lies in the danger that we might view baptism as only a sacrament of the moment, an entry into union with Christ and the community, rather than as a lifelong commitment to living a faithful Christian life. In baptism, we receive gifts of the Spirit which call us and enable us to witness to Christ in a mature manner in our daily lives. In confirmation, we continue to share in these gifts of the Holy Spirit, and the confirming or sealing means that we continue to become members of the community, sharing in its privileges and responsibilities for life.

d. The Sacrament of Confirmation emphasizes the unity of the Church in its mission.

When the bishop celebrates the Sacrament of Confirmation before the community, the rite reminds us that the Church reaches beyond our small community to the entire world. Even in cases where the priest confirms, the oil used for the anointing must be blessed by the bishop, thus emphasizing unity. In witnessing in the name of the Church, the presider recalls that he does not speak for a small community of Christians, but for the universal Church. Because of this, a Christian is not free to preach his or her own message, but the message of Christ as given through the Church.

2. How did confirmation develop?

a. The early Church celebrated the sacrament now known as confirmation along with the Sacrament of Baptism.

The members of the early Church did not consider confirmation as a sacrament separate from baptism. The person was baptized, anointed by the bishop (confirmation), and brought to share in the Eucharist. The early records tell us how adults went through these steps to enter the Church community, and we must presume that the children somehow accompanied their parents through this process. In the early Church, whole families came into the community together.

The first records of the baptism of children come from the early third century. A century later, the people of the Roman Empire followed their emperor, Constantine, into Christianity and the baptism of children became more common. Many of the converts of this era became Christian for economic and political reasons, but many more sincerely became members of Christianity, and they brought their children to the church for baptism.

The one being baptized would go down into a pool of water, and the minister would submerge the person, using the words for baptism. The newly baptized would then come out of the water, put on a white robe, and come before the bishop and the assembled community. The bishop would place his hand on the head of the newly baptized and anoint the person with oil, praying as he did that the Holy Spirit would continue to work through the newly baptized. From these records, we realize that the bishop's action was not seen as something separate from the baptism, but as a continuation of the ritual of baptism.

b. By the fifth century, the role of the bishop became separated from the baptismal ceremony.

In the fifth century, the number of people entering Christianity was rapidly growing, and the bishops were no longer able to assist at every baptism. Another influence upon the number of baptisms, especially of infants, came from St. Augustine's teaching on original sin. St. Augustine claimed that a person needed baptism in order to enter eternal, spiritual happiness. Parents naturally wanted their children baptized as soon as possible. Eventually, the role of the bishop in the celebration of the Sacrament of Baptism changed.

The Christian Church of the East solved the problem by having the baptizing presbyter continue with the anointing ordinarily performed by the bishop. They saw this action and the celebration of the Eucharist as inseparable rites of initiation. The Christian Church of the West solved the problem by allowing baptisms to take place without the presence of the bishop with the idea that the ministry of the bishop would take place at a later and more convenient time. Eventually, large crowds of people would gather whenever the bishop was present, and the bishop would lay hands on and anoint those who had not yet shared in this rite.

c. With the separation of the rite performed by the bishop from that of baptism, the rite performed by the bishop eventually came to be seen as the sacrament now known as confirmation.

Within the first thousand years after Christ, the rite performed by the bishop was gradually separated from the rite of baptism, and it received a new name, the *Sacrament of Confirmation*. With the separation of the Sacrament of Confirmation from the Sacrament of Baptism, much study and discussion centered around the specific place that confirmation had in the Church. The conclusion was that the Sacrament of Confirmation is a special sacrament, flowing from baptism, but at the same time, distinct from the Sacrament of Baptism.

3. Who may administer the Sacrament of Confirmation?

a. The bishop ordinarily administers the Sacrament of Confirmation.

A bishop of a diocese has the right and duty to oversee the confirmation of all members of his diocese. As successors of the apostolic tradition, the bishops' role in the celebration of this sacrament underlines more clearly the unity of the Church and the Church's link with the early apostles.

b. The ordained priest, who baptizes or receives an adult into the Church through a profession of faith, also confirms the new member of the community.

Because confirmation properly belongs to the Ritual of Initiation, the Church celebrates the Sacrament of Confirmation immediately after the baptism of an adult. The ordained priest celebrates this rite, even if the bishop is expected to come to the parish in the near future to celebrate the Sacrament of Confirmation. In doing this, the Church preserves the proper order of the Sacraments of Initiation, baptism, followed by confirmation, followed by Eucharist. At the time of professing communion with the Church, the adult, whether baptized previously or not, celebrates the Sacrament of Confirmation.

If a child of grade-school age is received into the Church and the child has not yet reached the acceptable age for confirmation, the ordained priest may not confirm the child. But if the child has reached the acceptable age for confirmation, the child is baptized, confirmed, and celebrates First Eucharist during the same Eucharistic celebration.

c. The bishop may share the privilege of celebrating the Sacrament of Confirmation with designated ordained priests.

In places where there are a large number of people to celebrate this sacrament, the bishop may designate other ordained priests to assist him in the celebration of the Sacrament of Confirmation. In areas where Confirmation has returned to its proper order in the initiation process, the bishop, for various reasons, may not be able to assist at all celebrations where children are to celebrate this sacrament prior to the celebration of their First Eucharist. When this occurs, the bishop may delegate pastors to celebrate this sacrament in the parish. When the unconfirmed is in danger of death, an ordained priest should celebrate the Sacrament of Confirmation with that person, regardless of the person's age.

4. Who may be confirmed?

a. Before celebrating the Sacrament of Confirmation, a person must already have celebrated the Sacrament of Baptism.

The Sacrament of Baptism is the first Sacrament of Initiation and the sacrament which must be received before all others. Through the Sacrament of Baptism, the Holy Spirit establishes a new relationship with the new Christian. The Sacrament of Confirmation builds upon this gift of baptism. In order to share in a growth in the Spirit, a person must already have received the Spirit in one's life and be disposed toward this growth. In the Acts of the Apostles, we have a single incident which seems to say that baptism does not bring with it the gift of Spirit, but this incident must be read in relationship to other instances of baptism in the Scriptures which speak of the gift of the Spirit at baptism. The incident, however, emphasizes the value of "laying on of hands," and is often used as an example of confirmation in the early Church. The Book of Acts tells us, "Now when the apostles at Jerusalem heard that Samaria had accepted the word of God, they sent Peter and John to them. The two went down and prayed for them that they might receive the Holy Spirit (for as yet the Spirit had not come upon any of them; they had only been baptized in the name of the Lord Jesus). Then Peter and John laid their hands on them, and they received the Holy Spirit" (Acts 8:14–17).

b. The candidate for the Sacrament of Confirmation.

In the United States, the bishop of each diocese is free to choose the age he feels most appropriate for this sacrament. In the United States, the age varies from prior to First Eucharist to high school. The Code of Canon Law states that a child must have reached the age of discretion, although the conference of bishops may agree on a later age. Unless there is danger of death, it is required, if the person has the use of reason, that the person be suitably instructed, properly disposed, and able to renew his or her baptismal promises. In the Eastern Church, children celebrate the Sacrament of Confirmation immediately after their baptism. Because of the close link between the Sacraments of Baptism and Confirmation, it is fitting that a person retain his or her baptismal name, rather than choosing a new name.

5. Who may be a sponsor for confirmation?

a. Sponsors must be baptized and confirmed Catholics who will help the candidates in the fulfillment of their Christian commitment.

Sponsors should help prepare the candidates for the sacrament and see that the candidates act as true witnesses to Christ and faithfully fulfill the obligations that come with the sacrament. They accompany the candidates and present them to the priest or bishop for the reception of the sacrament. If the candidates are adults, they present themselves by name. Each sponsor must be a practicing, baptized Catholic who has celebrated the Sacraments of Baptism, Confirmation, and Holy Eucharist; be canonically free to carry out this office, has completed the sixteenth year. Sponsors may be either male or female for any candidate.

b. The godparents at baptism should, if possible, be chosen as sponsors at confirmation.

Throughout the first part of this chapter, we spoke of the close link between the Sacrament of Baptism and the Sacrament of Confirmation. The liturgy should teach as well as share the blessings of Christ. The use of the same sponsors shows the close relationship between these two sacraments. Another reason for choosing the same sponsors arises from the sacraments themselves. Since confirmation is another aspect of initiation, the godparents in baptism should be the ones to continue the ministry of sponsoring in confirmation.

6. How is the Sacrament of Confirmation conferred?

a. The bishop or ordained priest places his hands on the head of those to be confirmed.

The gift of the Holy Spirit is often invoked in the Scriptures through the laying on of hands. The action of passing on the Spirit comes through this imposition of hands. The bishop or ordained priest makes a reference in prayer to the Sacrament of Baptism, showing the link between baptism and confirmation. He then prays that the candidate may receive the special gifts of the Holy Spirit:

Give them the spirit of wisdom and understanding,
the spirit of right judgment and courage,
the spirit of knowledge and reverence.
Fill them with the spirit of wonder and awe in your presence.
We ask this through Christ our Lord. R. Amen.

b. The actual conferring of the sacrament takes place through the anointing with oil accompanied by the short prayer invoking the Holy Spirit.

The bishop dips his thumb in holy oil (a special perfumed oil known as *chrism)* and makes the sign of the cross on the forehead of the candidate to be confirmed. At the same time, he repeats the words:

N., be sealed with the gift of the Holy Spirit. [The newly confirmed responds:] Amen.

In this response, the newly confirmed is proclaiming acceptance of the hopes and the responsibilities that this sacrament brings.

7. What are some ways of witnessing to the faith?

a. A person witnesses to the faith by openly professing and living out a belief in Jesus Christ.

Some people seem to apologize for their belief in God. We are called to profess openly our belief in Jesus through our life and through our words. We witness not only by speaking of Christ and his message but by living that message, for example, by treating our neighbor in a loving way, by reaching out to those in need, by accepting ridicule in the name of Christ, by being concerned for peace and justice throughout the world. Paul gave us an example of how we should witness to Christ when he said of himself, "To the weak I became weak, so that I might win the weak. I have become all things to all people, that I might by all means save some. I do it all for the sake of the gospel, so that I may share in its blessings" (1 Corinthians 9:22–23). When Paul found someone in need or someone who was weak, Paul acted as though he were the one in need or the weak person. For the sake of the gospel, Paul shared in the sufferings and needs of all in order to help them.

b. We witness to Christ by speaking out against the social ills of our society.

Whenever a Christian sees the dignity of a human person destroyed by society, the Christian must speak out against this sin. A Christian must confront racism, poverty, and injustice. To be a witness is not to allow things to happen and say nothing. It calls us to join our voices with others so that all together we can raise the consciousness of people to a greater concern for the dignity of the human person and for justice in every segment of society.

In the Gospel of Matthew, we read a parable told by Jesus concerning the final judgment. In this parable, we learn that whatever is done to others is done to Christ. Jesus calls to heaven those who gave him food when hungry, drink when thirsty, shelter when homeless, clothing when naked, comfort when sick, and visits when imprisoned. He tells them that anyone who treated the least of his people in this way treated him in this way. In the second part of this parable, Jesus condemns those who refuse to provide and care for others in need. He tells these uncaring people that they rejected him when they neglected to help those in need. As we treat others, so we treat Jesus. This includes speaking up for the indignities heaped upon other human beings.

c. We witness to Christ when we reach out to our neighbor by daily acts of love.

Taking time to visit the sick and sharing with them a kind word or taking time to sit down with a lonely person are ways of witnessing to Christ in the world. As we look through the Scriptures, we not only hear the message of Christ, we also see the compassion of Christ. In the Sacraments of Baptism and Confirmation, we make Christ present in the world. The message of Christ and the compassion of Christ must continue in each one of us. Jesus called his disciples "the light of the world," chosen to help others give praise to God through their actions. In the Gospel of Matthew, we read these words of Jesus, "In the same way, let your light shine before others, so that they may see your good works and give glory to your Father in heaven" (Matthew 5:16).

8. Is the Church called to work toward justice in the world?

a. The Church is called to live and teach the gospel message of love of neighbor, and this love implies justice.

A Pharisee approached Jesus to ask which commandment of the Law was the greatest. "He said to him, 'You shall love the Lord your God with all your heart, and with all your soul, and with all your mind.' This is the greatest and first commandment" (Matthew 22:37–38).

Justice demands that we recognize and respect the dignity and rights of our neighbor. When we do this, we are living out the call of Christ to "love our neighbor as we love ourselves." Shortly after

Pope John Paul II was elected pope, he proclaimed that he would work to overcome oppression in the world. From his own background, he could recall the indignity and lack of love that allowed leaders of governments to deprive people of their human rights. In his love and concern for all peoples of the world, Pope John Paul II echoed this goal to work for justice.

b. The Church has proclaimed its work toward justice as essential to its ministry.

In 1971, the third international Synod of Bishops met in Rome to discuss the issue of justice in the world. In a statement to the world, approved by Pope Paul VI, they described the work toward justice as a "constitutive element" in the Church's ministry. The expression *constitutive element* refers to a work that is essential or at the root of the ministry of the Church. The Synod of Bishops was stating that the work toward justice is not something extra the Church can undertake in the world, but rather that the work toward justice is on the same footing as celebrating the sacraments and preaching the word of God. There is no more powerful way to remind all members of the Church that the work toward justice is essential to the ministry of the Church. To be true to the Church in living out its call, we must continually work toward justice in the world.

c. The Church is called to work toward social justice.

In our lives, we are surrounded by many outside influences that control our ability and ease in loving our neighbor. We live under certain political systems and organizations that often dictate custom, law, and even the use of our human rights. The economic structures of a society and its many organizations that control money and property often influence the rights of a just wage, good working conditions, or the ownership of property. Wherever we turn, we find ourselves living and working within systems and structures that we often do not even understand. When we speak of social justice, we refer to justice on these broader levels that control our lives. We are speaking of justice within a society rather than the simple idea of one person respecting the rights of another.

Because the Church is called to work toward justice for all people, the Church must work toward **social** justice. If the systems of government, the economic powers of business, and the structure of organizations are unjust, the individual's rights and dignity suffer. The Church must speak out against all social injustice and work toward justice on the social level. We are social-minded people, called to live together in society and to grow and enable others to grow through our society. Even on the level of social justice, the Church must recognize this ministry to seek justice as a "constitutive element" of its mission.

d. Working toward justice includes working toward peace in the world.

In an historic pastoral letter on peace, entitled *The Challenge of Peace: God's Promise and Our Response,* the United States bishops carefully considered the challenge of peace in our nuclear society. They presented the scriptural basis for peace and discussed those occasions when a just war would be possible. In this letter, the bishops pointed out that some can accept the idea of a just war and rightly serve in the protection of their country or the human rights of others, but others may choose, in conscience, to be totally opposed to a particular war or to all war. The bishops supported the right of conscientious objectors in the Church, and they went on to examine the situation of nuclear war. Because of the extensive damage of nuclear war and the inability to avoid killing thousands or millions of innocent people, the bishops could in no way support nuclear war as acceptable in accordance with the just war theory. They proposed that all nations work toward a positive approach to peace which recognized the dignity of all life and the hope for peace which comes through prayer and trust in God.

Because of their stand against nuclear war, the bishops faced criticism from many who stated that they should not interfere in politics. The bishops, however, recognize their call to guide the moral consciences of those who wish to follow Christ. In the letter, the bishops state that they do not propose the considerations in the pastoral as laws to be followed, but as guidelines to help shape one's conscience.

In Matthew's Gospel, Jesus tells his listeners during his Sermon on the Mount, " 'Blessed are the peacemakers, for they will be called children of God' " (Matthew 5:9).

9. What is evangelization?

a. Evangelization is the sharing of the person and message of Jesus Christ with all people of the world.

In the Gospel of Matthew, Jesus directs his disciples to reach out to all people of the world to invite them into discipleship: " 'Go therefore and make disciples of all nations, baptizing them in the name of the Father and of the Son and of the Holy Spirit' " (Matthew 28:19). The Church, as a source of the message and gifts of Jesus Christ, has the call to share these blessings with the whole world. Evangelization is this sharing of the good news of Jesus Christ with all people of the world. Pope John Paul I, during his short term as pope, proclaimed evangelization as a major call of the Church. Through our baptism and confirmation, we share in this special mission of the Church to "make disciples of all the nations." Through these sacraments, every Catholic is called to evangelization.

b. Evangelization reaches out to the unchurched.

Millions of people throughout the world have never heard of Jesus Christ. Some have heard the name, but know nothing else about Jesus. Many of these people claim no Church affiliation. The mission of the Church reaches out in a special way to these unchurched that they might hear and know the message of Jesus and the gifts shared through his life. The unchurched have a right to this knowledge, and the Church has the privilege and duty of sharing this good news of Jesus Christ. In Paul's Letter to the Romans, we have some very direct questions from Paul which challenge us in our sharing of the faith. Through the Sacraments of Initiation, we receive a gift worthy of being shared with others, but Paul asks us, "But how are they to call on one in whom they have not believed? And how are they to believe in one of whom they have never heard? And how are they to hear without someone to proclaim him?" (Romans 10:14). All of us are called to share the message which we have received in faith from Christ.

c. The call to evangelization involves the whole community of believers.

The Church invites the unchurched to share in the family of believers. In this family of the Church, a new member should be able to recognize a deep concern for each member of the Church community. Included in this call to evangelization is a call to reach out to former members of the family. The Church should continually invite these nonpracticing members home to the community.

Another aspect of the call to evangelization is the call to the Church community to live fully the good news of Jesus Christ that it preaches. When a family invites others to share in its family activities and celebrations, the family presumes that others will enjoy sharing with them. In the same way, the Church family should strive to live the good news of Jesus Christ in such a way that others will find support and joy in living and celebrating this good news with the community. The full call to evangelization consists not only in reaching out to the world, but also consists in reaching inward to examine and keep alive the living message of Jesus Christ within the community.

Conclusion

How surprised we would be if the child in the introduction ran to the corner of the room, opened his hands, and let out a puff of smoke! We would not believe we saw the smoke, and, if we did believe it, we might want to experiment ourselves to see if it is possible.

In the Sacrament of Confirmation, we open ourselves to surprises. If we do not stifle the Spirit in our lives, we shall always be open to the surprises of the Spirit. We must have confidence in the Spirit within us, and we must accept our call through confirmation to witness to Christ. Then the surprises begin to happen.

For Scripture reflection and discussion concerning this chapter, see **Journeying in His Light,** *"Sacraments of Initiation: Part 2."*

10 Sacraments of Initiation, Part 3: Eucharist

Introduction

When their mother celebrated her seventieth birthday, all ten of her children, ranging in age from the late twenties to the late forties, wanted to make this an occasion she would never forget. She had proven herself a loving mother, and her children, her sons- and daughters-in-law, and her grandchildren crowded into a rented hall to celebrate her surprise party. Two of her daughters had lured her to the hall on the pretext that they were taking her out for a birthday dinner. From the moment their mother entered the hall till the party ended almost four hours later, the family centered all their attention on her, hugging her, singing to her, serving her, and presenting gifts to her.

At the end of the evening, when the family called for her to make a speech, she stood with a broad smile and said, "You have all been good to me, and given me many gifts. But the greatest gift of all is that you all love each other, and you joined together to share your love with me. I have been blessed."

In this chapter, we will be studying ways of showing our love for God. In recognizing God's great love, we want to share in that love and to celebrate it. God, like the mother in the story above, loves a party, a celebration, and God's joy abounds when the family comes together to celebrate that love. This chapter tells us about celebrating with God as a loving family.

1. Why do people worship?

a. Some people worship out of fear.

In ancient times, if a community suddenly experienced a tragic flood or a mighty storm, the people would seek to ward off the anger of the gods by offering the best of their animals for sacrifice. They hoped that these sacrifices would appease the gods: the storm gods, the wind gods, the sun gods, or whatever unknown god was causing this disaster. They worshiped these gods, even in time of peace, fearing that if they forgot about the gods, they would suffer a new disaster. In the Church today, there are people who worship God out of fear of going to hell. They go to Church not because they love God, but because they fear that at death they will suffer eternal damnation, eternal unhappiness.

This need to worship out of fear may be necessary for some as they begin to approach God. There is, however, another type of fear, a reverential fear, which is actually a result of love. The Old Testament tells us that the "The fear of the Lord is the beginning of wisdom; all those who practice it have a good understanding" (Psalm 111:10). The fear addressed here is a reverential fear, such as one would have in the presence of a great leader or a loving parent. This type of fear makes a person aware of the greatness of the person in whose presence he or she stands. Such a fear leads to worship out of love, rather than out of fear of what a person might do to us.

b. Some approach worship as a debt to be paid.

For some, the motive in this form of worship comes very close to worshiping out of fear. God has been good to us, and we must repay God, they say, as though we are returning a favor. Because God has given us great gifts in our lives, we have an obligation to repay the debt, to thank God for these gifts. In the Old Testament, the psalmist calls out to God and says, "What shall I return to the Lord for all his bounty to me?" (Psalm 116:12). Throughout the Scriptures, we are reminded of God's great love by providing for us, and our need to respond to that love.

c. Some worship God fully out of love.

Through the love shown by God throughout the Old Testament, through the loving words and actions of Christ in the New Testament, and through the gifts in their lives, people recognize God as a loving and compassionate God. The experience of a loving and compassionate God leads people to want to worship this God, to want to be able to say, "I love You." In the Letter to the Hebrews, the author expresses the love and gift of Christ who became a member of our human family and offered us a way of reaching out to God in love. The author writes:

> For we do not have a high priest who is unable to sympathize with our weaknesses, but we have one who in every respect has been tested as we are, yet without sin. Let us therefore approach the throne of grace with boldness, so that we may receive mercy and find grace to help in time of need (Hebrews 4:15–16).

2. Why is the scriptural image of a "memorial" important to our understanding of Christian worship?

a. Our ability to remember is basic to our humanness.

As human beings living together in a concerned society, we must have the ability to remember. Our whole life is shaped by our memories of our families, our friends, our memories of shared joys and tragedies, our recollections of birth and death. Someone once said that we are a story people. We play a part in the large story of life, and we look to the future because we recall the past, and shape our identities according to our memories. If we were to lose our memory, our story would end, because we would have nothing upon which to build the present and the future.

Historical religions such as Catholicism and Judaism depend very much upon their memories of God and the people with whom God related. We recall the promises of the past and we look with hope to the future because of these promises. Without our ability to remember, we would lose our identity as a people of God. In the psalms, we read about a man in exile in Babylon who asks God to curse him if he ever forgets his true home, Jerusalem. He writes, "If I forget you, O Jerusalem, let my right hand wither! Let my tongue cling to the roof of my mouth, if I do not remember you, if I do not set Jerusalem above my highest joy" (Psalm 137:5–6). The people of Israel remembered that Jerusalem was their true home, and they prayed that they would never forget their true homeland and the true meaning of Judaism. To forget Jerusalem would be to forget their link with God as the people of God.

b. Each year, the Jewish people recall the living memorial of their passover from slavery to the promised land.

Each year Israelite families would gather together to celebrate the great feast of the year, the Passover feast. They would recall that God had chosen them as God's special people, had freed them from the slavery of Egypt, had guided them through the desert, and finally had led them into the promised land. In loving gratitude, they remembered the gifts that God had given them and realized that God still guided their nation. On the Passover feast each year, they reenacted in a prayerful way a living memorial of an event that had taken place in past history, the blessing of which flowed down to the present moment. They would sacrifice a lamb to God in the temple, then take some of that lamb home to eat and share in the festival meal. This reminded them of the Israelites of Egypt, who killed the lamb, offered it to God, and painted the lamb's blood on their doorpost that the angel of death might pass over them. The family would celebrate this feast on the night called "the greatest of all nights," because it commemorated the passover from slavery to the freedom of the promised land. The family would sing psalms of praise and thanksgiving for God's protection in the past and guidance in the present.

In the Book of Exodus, we read that God directed the people to commemorate this event each year so that they would not forget what God had done for them. We read:

"You shall observe this rite as a perpetual ordinance for you and your children. When you come to the land that the Lord will give you, as he has promised, you shall keep this observance. And when your children ask you, 'What do you mean by this observance?' you shall say, 'It is the

passover sacrifice to the Lord, for he passed over the houses of the Israelites in Egypt, when he struck down the Egyptians but spared our houses.' " And the people bowed down and worshiped (Exodus 12:24–27).

This memorial event was not just a recalling of what happened in the past. The Israelites believed that the event was happening in the present in some way, as though the event and God's blessings remained timeless. In the Passover ritual celebrated today, one of the youngest in attendance asks the question, "Why **is** this night different from every other night?" The significance is that they do not ask, "Why **was** this night different?" For those celebrating the Passover meal, the night of the celebration, "this" night, is, even now, different from every other night.

c. At the Passover feast, Christ offered the Church a new living memorial of thanksgiving.

In his Gospel, Luke explains the feast of the Passover as celebrated at the Last Supper. At this Passover, Jesus offered himself in place of the lamb and offered a new memorial to the apostles. "Then he took a loaf of bread, and when he had given thanks, he broke it and gave it to them, saying, 'This is my body, which is given for you. Do this in remembrance of me.' And he did the same with the cup after supper, saying, 'This cup that is poured out for you is the new covenant in my blood' " (Luke 22:19–20). In the words, "Do this as a memorial of me," the Church sees Christ as offering to the apostles and their followers the gift of continually sharing in this new memorial. Just as Jesus changed bread and wine into his body and blood, so the Church believes that this gift and power are shared in the Church. The Church believes that even today this bread and wine become the living presence of the body and blood of Jesus during the Eucharistic liturgy.

d. Jesus realized the great act of faith needed to accept this teaching.

In the Gospel of John, the author tells how Jesus fed five thousand men in the desert. After telling of Jesus feeding them, the author shares a discourse on the bread of life which is the gift of Jesus' living memorial. Jesus realizes their need for faith and says,

So Jesus said to them, "Very truly, I tell you, unless you eat the flesh of the Son of Man and drink his blood, you have no life in you. Those who eat my flesh and drink my blood have eternal life, and I will raise them up on the

last day; for my flesh is true food and my blood is true drink. Those who eat my flesh and drink my blood abide in me, and I in them" (John 6:53–56).

A few seconds later, he says, "This is the bread that came down from heaven, not like that which your ancestors ate, and they died. But the one who eats this bread will live forever" (John 6:58). In this text, the author is showing the insights of the early Church into the message of Jesus. The response of the people reflects the need for faith in the early Church. Many of his followers heard this and said, " 'This teaching is difficult; who can accept it?' But Jesus, being aware that his disciples were complaining about it, said to them, 'Does this offend you?' " (John 6:60–61). Without the gift of faith, it was indeed difficult to accept the fact that Jesus gave his body and blood under the form of bread and wine. We read in the Gospel of John, "Because of this many of his disciples turned back and no longer went about with him" (John 6:66). To believe that Jesus would actually share with us his body and blood, under the form of bread and wine, simply must rest on the gift of faith.

e. Christ, through his death, resurrection, and ascension, offers us a living memorial by which we express our love for God in a perfect manner.

In his life, Jesus became obedient unto death even to death on the cross. Because of his confrontation of evil and his acceptance of obedience to death, Jesus was highly exalted by God. God the Father was pleased with Christ's offering. Through the resurrection and exaltation of Jesus, that offering of Christ became our offering. Every time we share in this living memorial of Christ's passion, death, and resurrection, we, the Church, worship God the Father. It is the most perfect way of worshiping God the Father and expressing our love for God. Paul writes, "For as often as you eat this bread and drink the cup, you proclaim the Lord's death until he comes" (1 Corinthians 11:26).

f. The name the Catholic Church gives to the celebration of this living memorial is the name Eucharist, *which comes from the Greek meaning, "to give thanks."*

Not only does the Church receive the gift of Christ to his Father, but the Church also celebrates this gift as a living memorial of thanksgiving. Many refer to this celebration as the *Mass,* but it is more truly called a *Eucharistic* (thanksgiving) *celebration.* By the gift of this Eucharistic celebration, we are thankful for all of the gifts of Christ, but most especially the gift of being able to worship God the Father in so perfect a manner and of being able to express our love for God as a community.

g. Catholics believe that the Eucharistic celebration is the source and summit of all Christian life.

Catholics find in the Eucharistic celebration the strength and encouragement for living the Christian life. All our endeavors, prayers, and activities, move toward the celebration of the Eucharist and flow from it. All the other sacraments lead to the Eucharist and derive their power from this gift. The Eucharistic celebration is central to the life of the Church. Through our baptism and confirmation, Christians share in the gift of priesthood which gives to us the right and obligation to enter more fully into worship. The Church calls upon its ordained priests to preside at Eucharist. Since every human activity has its source and aim in the Eucharist, the Sacraments of Baptism, Confirmation, Holy Orders, Anointing of the Sick, and Marriage find in the Eucharistic celebration an appropriate setting for their celebration. Although the Sacrament of Reconciliation does not take place within the Eucharistic celebration, it enables us to worship more faithfully as a holy and dedicated community.

3. Why is the scriptural image of a "meal" important to our understanding of the Eucharistic celebration?

a. In the time of Jesus, an invitation to a meal was considered an invitation into a person's life.

During the time of Jesus, invitations to meals were not given lightly. When people gathered for a meal, they ordinarily gathered with their "own kind of people." In a sense, the people could have said, "Show me whom you eat with, and I'll tell you what you are." Because of this attitude, the people of Jesus' day made their judgments of Jesus based upon the people with whom he ate. Many of the stories found in the Gospels center around Jesus' dining with sinners, tax collectors, and Pharisees. Each one of these meals had a significant message to teach.

In a story found in Luke's Gospel, Jesus invites himself to dine with a man named Zacchaeus (Luke 19:1–10). The underlying message of the story is that Jesus is inviting himself into the life of Zacchaeus, and this tax collector accepts Jesus into his life through an immediate change in his attitude. He repents of his past sins and seeks to reconcile himself with those whom he has hurt. This story offers a good example of the deeper meaning of inviting a person to a meal during Jesus' day.

b. Jesus chose a meal as the setting for the Eucharistic celebration.

When two friends meet who have not seen each other for some time, they often decide to discuss old times over a meal. At a meal, people come together in friendship, trust, and relaxation. According to the Scriptures, Jesus offers the Eucharist at a meal, a very special meal. At a Passover supper, Jesus offered his body and blood under the form of bread and wine.

Another reference for this Eucharistic celebration is the expression, *the Lord's Supper.* In Paul's letter to the Corinthians, he warns them about destroying the true meaning of the Lord's Supper when they do not think of others. He writes, "When you come together, it is not really to eat the Lord's supper. For when the time comes to eat, each of you goes ahead with your own supper, and one goes hungry and another becomes drunk" (1 Corinthians 11:20–21). He reminds the Corinthians of the love and sharing that should take place at the Lord's Supper. He tells them to be considerate of each other, as they gather for this meal: "So then, my brothers and sisters, when you come together to eat, wait for one another" (1 Corinthians 11:33).

The early communities of the Church also used the term *Breaking of the Bread* to designate their Eucharistic assembly and their unity with the one bread who is Christ. The author of Luke describes how two disciples of Jesus recognized the resurrected Christ at a meal, which is a reference to the Eucharistic celebration. He writes, "When he was at the table with them, he took bread, blessed and broke it, and gave it to them. Then their eyes were opened, and they recognized him; and he vanished from their sight" (Luke 24:30–31). Immediately, the disciples rushed to Jerusalem to tell the eleven about this experience of Jesus. And the simple narrative ends with the words, "Then they told what had happened on the road, and how he had been made known to them in the breaking of the bread" (Luke 24:35).

c. By telling us about the meals in which Jesus shared during his life, the Gospel writers are also telling us more about the Eucharistic meal.

As we read about Jesus and the meals he shared during his life, we learn about our sharing in the Eucharistic meal. Jesus did not dine just with "good people"; he dined with tax collectors and sinners. During a meal, Jesus heard some Pharisees complain to his disciples about their master eating with tax collectors and sinners, and Jesus told them, "Those who are well have no need of a physician, but those who are sick. Go and learn what this means, 'I desire mercy, not sacrifice.' For I have come to call not the righteous but sinners" (Matthew 9:12–13). The Eucharistic meal does not invite just those who are living close to God, but it calls those who are sinners that they might find love and change their lives.

During a meal, Jesus castigated some of the Pharisees for seeking places of honor and for tending only to themselves and not to others. The message tells us that the Eucharistic celebration allows no room for class distinction or for self-seeking. All come together as one for the sake of praising God.

4. Why is the scriptural image of "sacrifice" important to our understanding of the Eucharistic celebration?

a. The idea of "sacrifice" had many different meanings in the ancient world.

The basic notion behind sacrifice was a people's belief in a higher and more powerful force over creation. The ancient pagans would offer an animal or a portion of their crops, seeking to praise or appease their gods. The ancient Israelites offered animals or food to God to praise God and to thank God for blessings received. The reason food or animal sacrifice was offered to God (or the gods) was that these things were central to the life of the people. In this way, the sacrifice was seen as a sharing of one's life with God. The image which a people had of their gods would often determine the type of sacrifice and the meaning behind the sacrifice. The pagans, for instance, often sought to appease angry gods, while the Israelites more often wanted to praise God who was a loving God. In offering their sacrifice to God, the people of Israel recognized that their own life was fragile, and, through their offering, they acknowledged their dependence upon God.

A religious sacrifice as found in Israel is called a "cultic" sacrifice, and it connotes a religious context in which a priest acts as a mediator, making the offering on behalf of the people. The people of Jerusalem would bring their offering to the temple, and the priest would offer their sacrifice to God on behalf of the people by killing the animal upon the altar of sacrifice. The offering was then made sacred, and a portion would be taken home by the people for a sacred meal.

The cultic priests of the Old Testament protected the idea of a sacrifice which involved some type of blood offering. The prophets and wisdom writers would often remind the people of another type of sacrifice, the sacrifice of their own will to that of God's will. They told the people that God is pleased with their blood offerings, but God also wants them to live a life worthy of the chosen people of God. We read in the psalms, "Not for your sacrifices do I rebuke you; your burnt offerings are continually before me. Those who bring thanksgiving as their sacrifice honor me; to those who go the right way I will show the salvation of God" (Psalm 50:8, 23). In the New Testament, we see Jesus following these prophets and wisdom writers when he tells some of the Pharisees, "But if you had known what this means, 'I desire mercy and not sacrifice,' you would not have condemned the guiltless" (Matthew 12:7).

b. The sacrificial meal was a sign of unity with God.

Because the meal held such an important place among the Israelite people, it was natural that the sacrificial meal became the place where people were most conscious of God in their midst. At the Passover meal, the people of Israel celebrated with God by sharing together the lamb offered in sacrifice. During the meal, the life of the Israelite nation was again joined with the presence of the living God in the midst of people. The triple idea of meal, sacrifice, and memorial bonded the lives of the people of Israel with that of God. It is in the context of a sacrificial meal that Catholics bond their lives with that of Christ.

c. The sacrifice made by Jesus was to offer his will totally to the will of God the Father.

The Last Supper is found in the context of the passion narrative. Its place in the Gospels has a message for us; it reminds us that the Eucharist comes to us in the context of the sacrifice of Jesus' life for the sake of all people. In this offering of himself, Jesus draws us into the new covenant sealed in his own blood. In the Gospel of Matthew, we read:

> While they were eating, Jesus took a loaf of bread, and after blessing it he broke it, gave it to the disciples, and said, "Take, eat; this is my body." Then he took a cup, and after giving thanks he gave it to them, saying "Drink from it, all of you; for this is my blood of the covenant, which is poured out for many for the forgiveness of sins. I tell you, I will never again drink of this fruit of the vine until that day when I drink it new with you in my Father's kingdom" (Matthew 26:26–29).

When we read this passage, we see many of the characteristics of sacrifice. Jesus is offering his life for us; he is broken and killed. But this has a deeper message. It is the act of choosing to follow the will of God which makes Jesus' sacrifice perfect. It is the offering made in praise of God which makes the gift a true sacrifice.

In the letter to the Hebrews, the author lets us hear the words of Jesus when he says, "Sacrifices and offerings you have not desired, but a body you have prepared for me; in burnt offerings and sin offerings you have taken no pleasure. Then I said, 'See, God, I have come to do your will, O God' (in the scroll of the book it is written of me)" (Hebrews 10:5–7). In the agony in the garden, Jesus shows that it is the obedience to the will of God that is his true sacrifice. "Father, if you are willing, remove this cup from me; yet not my will but yours be done" (Luke 22:42). Because of this obedience of Jesus, Paul is able to write in his Letter to the Philippians, "Therefore God also highly exalted him and gave him the name that is above every name, so that at the name of Jesus every knee should bend, in heaven and on earth and under the earth. . ." (Philippians 2:9–10). Christ did not come into the world to be sacrificed as an offering of appeasement to a hurt God, he came to follow the will of God, wherever that will would take him. The will of God was that Jesus would overcome the power of sin in the world, and Jesus obediently followed this will, even to death on the cross. In his obedience to God's will, Jesus brought us salvation, and became for us the perfect sacrifice. In his sacrifice, Jesus did what no Old Testament sacrifice could do: Jesus offered himself fully.

d. In our sacrificial meal, we all share in this gift given to the Church by Christ.

In the New Testament, we do not have the same cultic priesthood as that found in Israel. The ordained priest of the Catholic Church does not offer a sacrifice on behalf of the people, he shares in the one sacrifice of Jesus Christ along with the people. The ordained priest presides at the assemblies and performs a major role in the celebration of the Eucharist, but all people worship as one in the name of Jesus Christ.

As we share in the Eucharistic sacrifice, we offer our lives as one with that of Jesus. In sharing in the sacrificial meal, we also share in the life and attitude of Jesus Christ. Jesus was obedient to the will of God, even unto death, so we proclaim our willingness through this sacrifice to be like Christ, obedient to the will of God, even if it should lead us to death.

5. What is the role of the Christian community in the celebration of the Eucharist?

a. The community celebrates a common memory.

When the community gathers for worship, it recalls its common heritage which has the life and message of Jesus at its center. The "memorial" for the Church is not an individual memory, it is a community memory—one that recalls how God first chose a people of God, a community, and prepared that community for the coming of the Christ. The "memorial" remembers Jesus and the Twelve, and how this message spread from the early, small community in Jerusalem to a community of people that reached to the ends of the earth. When we enter that community, we hear about Jesus shaping his community of followers and about the memorial of his body and blood, which Jesus left to the community. We begin to realize that the memorial of the Church is not a memorial of a particular apostle or follower of Jesus, but rather a memorial of a community accepting Jesus and his message, spreading that message, and welcoming new members into the community. Christ redeemed the community of all people, left a living memorial to the community, and invited us to share in the community and its living memorial.

b. The community celebrates a common ritual meal.

At the Last Supper, Jesus did not sit down with a group of individuals, but with a community, and he offered his body and blood "for you," meaning for the community. The community gathering together to celebrate the Lord's Supper is an important aspect of the living memorial, as is the presence of Jesus among us in the Eucharist. As we gather today for the Eucharistic meal, we do not gather merely as individuals praising God, but as a family, a community, worshiping in Christ's name. Because a meal involves giving and sharing, we should not assist with our mouths closed, but we should join in the praying and singing to the best of our ability. Some members will take part in serving the community as readers or distributors of the Eucharist. Just as we read about Jesus eating with sinners and tax collectors, so we can expect sinners (ourselves included) to join in our community banquet. We celebrate with the hope that our community meal will eventually lead us to a change of life, when necessary, as it changed the lives of so many others in the Gospels.

c. The community celebrates a common sacrifice.

In speaking about our unity with one another and with Christ and his sacrifice, Paul writes, "The cup of blessing that we bless, is it not a sharing in the blood of Christ? The bread that we break, is it not a sharing in the body of Christ? Because there is one bread, we who are many are one body, for we all partake of the one bread" (1 Corinthians 10:16–17). Paul recognizes that the call of the community to be one with Christ includes a share in the sacrifice of Christ. He later writes, "I appeal to you therefore, brothers and sisters, by the mercies of God, to present your bodies as a living sacrifice, holy and acceptable to God, which is your spiritual worship" (Romans 12:1). Although the community realizes that Jesus' sacrifice brought us salvation, we must still share that salvation with others. Because we are one with Christ, we must act in Christ's name. Paul sees his ministry as linked to Christ's life and sacrifice: "I am now rejoicing in my sufferings for your sake, and in my flesh I am completing what is lacking in Christ's afflictions for the sake of his body, that is, the church" (Colossians 1:24).

When we gather as a community to celebrate the Eucharist, we recall the sacrifice of Christ not only as an event which took place in the past, but, we believe, also as an event that is taking place in the present. It is the one, living sacrifice of Christ. Through our celebration of the Eucharist, we join our hearts with that of Christ, and we make our sacrifice one with his. The community shares in the one loaf, the one cup, the one sacrifice of the one Lord, and enables the living sacrifice of Christ to become more visible in the world today.

6. How is the Eucharistic celebration divided?

a. In the first part of this celebration, the assembly celebrates the Liturgy of the Word.

When people love each other, they share some of their deepest feelings with each other. They dare to share details about themselves that they would never share with any other person. In the Liturgy of the Word, we listen to God's word. Through these readings, God is revealing many of God's deepest secrets to us. Through the Liturgy of the Word, we come to know God a little more deeply. In the New Testament, we read that Jesus would often go into the synagogue, read a section from the Scriptures, and explain the Scriptures to the people. The Liturgy of the Word flows from the synagogue service, a service of sharing in the Scriptures.

b. In the second part of this liturgy, the assembly celebrates the Liturgy of the Eucharist or the sacrificial meal.

After listening to the word of God and getting to know God a little more intimately, the community now prepares to share this sacrificial meal. During this part of the liturgy, the bread and wine are prepared for the sacrificing meal; the bread and wine become the body and blood of Christ. The community shares in this gift by celebrating Communion.

7. How is the Liturgy of the Word celebrated?

a. The Liturgy of the Word begins with a short period of preparation or introduction.

As the presider approaches the table of the Lord, the assembly joins together in singing a gathering song. The presider makes a special reverence to the Lord's table, the *altar,* which symbolizes Christ. The altar should occupy the central position in the church. The presider then moves to a chair separated from the altar which is commonly referred to as the *presider's chair.* During the Liturgy of the Word, the presider does not return to the altar. The presider, along with the assembly, signs himself with the sign of the cross. After a short greeting and litany, the assembly joins in a prayer of glory and praise to God. The presider calls the assembly to prayer with the words, "Let us pray," pauses for a few moments of silent prayer, and then prays a prayer especially chosen for that day. Through these *introductory rites,* the assembly deepens the experience of community and is now prepared to hear God's word.

b. Readings from the Scriptures and a psalm between the readings form the main part of the Liturgy of the Word.

On Sundays and special feast days, the assembly listens to three separate readings. Ordinarily, the Church chooses the first reading from the Old Testament. A responsorial psalm—again from the Old Testament—ordinarily follows. The people respond at certain intervals during the singing or reading of the psalm. As a second reading, the Church chooses a reading from the Acts of the Apostles, the Letters (Epistles), or the Book of Revelation. At the conclusion of each of the first two readings, there is a short period for silent meditation.

A third reading, the most sacred reading of all, comes from the Gospels. The assembly stands during this reading. In the course of three years, a major part of the Bible will have been read during the liturgies on Sunday. If a person chooses to participate in the liturgy during weekdays, that person will hear a major part of the Bible every two years. Through these readings, we come to know God and to understand God's message more fully.

c. The homily also plays an important role in the Liturgy of the Word.

The *homily* consists of a message ordinarily shared by the presider of the Eucharistic liturgy. The homily explains the readings and shows how their message touches God's community even today. The presider is urged to share a homily at all liturgies, even liturgies celebrated with a small group of people throughout the week. Ordinarily, a short period of silence follows the homily.

d. The profession of faith and general intercessions complete the Liturgy of the Word.

The assembly prays together a *profession of faith* (Creed). This profession of faith had its birth at the Council of Nicea in 325 when people were denying that the Son of God was equal to God the Father. In this profession of faith, we proclaim that Jesus Christ is the Son of God and equal to the Father. The assembly then prays the *general intercessions.* In these prayers, the assembly prays for the particular needs of all people throughout the world. During the general intercessions, we must be careful not to make it a time of merely mentioning our own personal concerns. The Church reaches out to embrace all people in the world, and, in the general intercessions, we should express a consciousness of this universal outreach. We can attach our personal concerns to universal concerns. An example of this would be, "For all those suffering from sickness throughout the world, especially for . . . (name person)." We should avoid prayers of thanksgiving in the general intercessions, since the entire Eucharistic liturgy is a liturgy of thanksgiving.

8. How is the Liturgy of the Eucharist divided?

a. The Liturgy of the Eucharist begins with the preparation of the gifts of bread and wine.

The presider returns to the Lord's table for the first time since he reverenced it at the beginning of the celebration. Members of the assembly join in the Eucharistic celebration by bringing to the altar gifts of bread and wine. The presider then praises God for God's goodness in sharing these gifts which are used in the sacrificial meal. In the preparation of the wine, the presider adds a small amount of water and prays that, just as the Son of God came to share in our humanness, we too, by the blessings of his death, resurrection, and ascension, may share in his divinity. The presider invites the assembly to pray that this sacrifice will be acceptable to God the almighty Father. He then prays a short prayer over the gifts.

b. The Eucharistic Prayer begins more properly with a prayer of thanksgiving and an acclamation on the part of the people proclaiming God's holiness.

The presider then invites the people to lift up their hearts in a prayer of thanksgiving to God. The presider thanks God the Father for the gifts God has given through Jesus Christ and prays that the whole world may continually proclaim the glory of God. The assembly responds to this prayer, called the *Preface*, with an acclamation taken from Isaiah, a prophet of the Old Testament. They pray:

Holy, holy, holy Lord, God of hosts, heaven and earth are full of your glory. Hosanna in the highest. Blessed is he who comes in the name of the Lord. Hosanna in the highest.

This is the first of several acclamations that the assembly will pray together.

c. The presider takes the bread and wine and prays the words attributed to Christ at the Last Supper, "This is my body . . . this is my blood . . . do this in memory of me."

Catholics believe that at the moment the presider proclaims the words "This is my body" over the bread and "This is my blood" over the wine, he is proclaiming that the body and blood of Jesus is now fully present in the Eucharist under the forms of bread and wine. We refer to this part of liturgy as *the Institution Narrative*. Before the celebration of the reception of the Eucharist, Catholics should fast for one hour.

d. The assembly proclaims an acclamation of faith in Christ and continues to pray for all people throughout the world.

The assembly again proclaims an acclamation of faith in the death, resurrection, and coming again in glory of Jesus Christ. The Church prays for the pope, bishops, presbyters, and all living and deceased throughout the world. To show the special place of honor held by Mary, the Church honors her in the liturgy.

e. The Eucharistic prayer properly ends with the Great Amen of the assembly.

The presider holds up the body and blood of Jesus Christ to the people and praises God the Father in these words; "Through him (Jesus), with him (Jesus), and in him (Jesus), in the unity of the Holy Spirit, all glory and honor is yours, almighty Father, forever and ever." At this point, the assembly exclaims its "great amen." The "great amen" professes a belief and an acceptance of the Eucharistic gift of Christ.

f. The assembly prays the Lord's Prayer and shares a greeting of peace as they prepare for the celebration of the Eucharist.

Through the gift of baptism, we are able to pray to God in a very special and intimate way. To show this special intimacy and to show our oneness in worship, we pray together, "Our Father, who art in heaven. . . ." The presider then prays a short prayer for peace and invites the assembly to share a greeting of peace with one another. This greeting of peace flows out of the Lord's Prayer by which we seek forgiveness for our sins and promise to forgive those "who have sinned against us." As a sign of peace, we shake hands or exchange a kiss with the people around us, saying, "The peace of the Lord be with you." The people then join in a short litany, "Lamb of God, who takes away the sin of the world, have mercy on us. . . ."

g. The members of the assembly celebrate the reception of the Eucharist, or Communion, as it is sometimes called, under both kinds, bread and wine, and are sent forth to share their gifts with all people.

The "General Instruction" of the Roman Missal states: "The sign of Communion is more complete when given under both kinds, since in that form the sign of the Eucharistic Meal appears more clearly. The intention of Christ that the new and eternal covenant be ratified in his blood is better expressed as is the relation of the Eucharistic Banquet to the heavenly banquet" (#240). We are here encouraged to share in the Eucharist under the forms of bread and wine. During the Communion celebration, the assembly should sing a song of praise together as a visible sign of unity in sharing the "one sacrifice." The presider closes this portion of the liturgy by asking God's blessings on those who have shared in the banquet of the Lord. The *dismissal rite* follows upon the closing prayer. If any announcements are to be made, they should be made after the closing prayer and before the dismissal rite begins. The presider blesses the community, "In the name of the Father, and of the Son, and of the Holy Spirit," and sends them forth to "Go in peace" to share the love and service celebrated in the Eucharistic liturgy. The assembly prays the final, grateful response in the words, "Thanks be to God." The Eucharistic liturgy is ended.

9. Why do Catholics believe so strongly in celebrating the Eucharistic liturgy together on Sunday?

a. Along with the early Church, the Catholic Church celebrates Sunday as the day of Christ's resurrection.

The joys and gifts of Christ's resurrection affected the early Church so deeply that it celebrated the day of Christ's resurrection (Sunday) in place of the Jewish Sabbath (Saturday). Whenever the assembly came together on Sunday, it celebrated Christ's resurrection and all the gifts that flowed from the resurrection. Today the Church joins with the early Christian community in celebrating each Sunday as a little Easter.

b. In celebrating each Sunday as the day of resurrection, Catholics strive to make Sunday a special day in their week by sharing more fully in the perfect act of love, the Eucharistic liturgy.

If we love a person, we strive to understand how to express that love more perfectly. If our love is truly deep for a person, we wish to be with that person often, and certainly at least once a week. If a Catholic believes that the Eucharist is the best possible manner in which to express love for God and that the Sunday obligation is also an obligation to the community, and if a Catholic does not respond to these beliefs, the Church believes that this person is committing a serious sin. In the early Church, many saw the day of resurrection as beginning around sundown the day before. The Church, keeping this vision in mind, has allowed the community to share in the Eucharistic celebration on Saturday evening as well as Sunday

216

morning. Due to the many different hours that some people work in our society, this privilege also becomes a necessity. In addition to participating in the Sunday celebration, many Catholics share in the Eucharist each day during the week. However, the community comes together in a special way on Saturday evening or Sunday to express in a visible form the living, loving body of Christ, worshiping God in this Eucharistic liturgy.

10. What are some regulations concerning the Eucharist?

a. Catholics in serious sin should ordinarily refrain from receiving the Eucharist in Communion.

God shares the sacraments with us that we may be able to live more fully as a true image of Christ. The Eucharist should not be seen as a reward for being good, but rather as a help enabling us to reflect Christ by our life. Even if a person has many minor faults or sins, that person should still celebrate the Eucharist to seek God's help in overcoming these faults or sins. When people approach Christ in the Eucharist, they are not proclaiming their goodness to the community, but rather their need for God's help in their lives. People in serious sin, who have had an opportunity to reconcile themselves with God and the community and have not done so, should not celebrate communion. A person in serious sin should first celebrate the Sacrament of Reconciliation, which we shall treat in the next chapter.

b. Before the celebration of the reception of the Eucharist, Catholics should fast for one hour.

In general a person should fast one hour from food or drink before the reception of the Eucharist. This fast does not include medicine and water. In case of sickness, a person should try to fast for approximately fifteen minutes, if possible, but even this could be dispensed with if it becomes difficult. This fasting gives the person an opportunity to prepare in some small way for the celebration of the reception of the Eucharist. By fasting, a person shows special reverence for the Eucharist.

c. A Catholic who has been initiated in the Eucharist must receive Communion at least once during the Easter season each year.

Catholics refer to this as the *Easter duty*. The Easter season begins with the first Sunday of Lent and ends on Trinity Sunday, which occurs approximately sixty days after Easter. The fact that an obligation has been placed on Catholics to receive Communion once a year during the Easter season is one of the sad events of Catholic history. Because people lost the true value of celebrating Communion, this law had to be made. When people stopped receiving Christ in the Eucharist, the Church had to make the law in order for them to share in this great gift. The Spirit was lost, so a law took its place. Today most Catholics respond by celebrating the reception of the Eucharist as often as they celebrate the Eucharistic liturgy. Hopefully, this Easter duty law will gradually drop from usage as Catholics realize the great value and privilege of celebrating the reception of Christ in the Eucharist.

11. What do Catholics do with consecrated bread and wine left over from the Eucharistic celebration?

a. If any of the consecrated bread is left after the celebration of the Eucharist, the priest places this consecrated bread in a special container called a **tabernacle**. If consecrated wine is left, it is consumed by the ministers of the Eucharist or by some of the assembly.

The tabernacle contains the consecrated bread not consumed during the celebration of the Eucharist. In some churches. this tabernacle is in a room by itself, which is known as the *Blessed Sacrament chapel*. Often during the day, Catholics will come to the chapel to pray to Jesus Christ in his Eucharistic presence in the Blessed Sacrament. The act of genuflecting is a special act of reverence for the presence of Jesus reserved in the tabernacle in the sacramental form of bread. As Catholics enter the church, they customarily genuflect (touch the floor with the right knee), and, as they do this, they face toward the tabernacle. This custom has no basis in Scripture, but has simply developed as a Catholic practice.

b. If someone is sick, a priest or another minister of the Eucharist may bring the Blessed Sacrament to this person.

Sick people cannot always come to the church to share in the Eucharistic celebration. A priest or a minister of the Eucharist may bring the Eucharist to them at home or in the hospital. In this way, a sick person is able to share in the Eucharistic liturgy with the assembly.

c. Benediction of the Blessed Sacrament is a special service given by the Church to honor the sacramental presence of Christ.

While the community shares in prayers and songs of praise, the presbyter places the Blessed Sacrament in full view of the people. The consecrated bread is ordinarily placed in a glass container which is surrounded by ornate decorations and placed high enough on a stand on the altar for all to see. Benediction of the Blessed Sacrament flows from the Eucharistic celebration. *Benediction* means "God's blessing." This, also, has no basis in Scripture and is simply a form of worshiping God given by the Church. Although benediction of the Blessed Sacrament is a high form of worship, it can never claim to be a greater form of worship than the Eucharistic liturgy. In fact, the Church forbids benediction of the Blessed Sacrament immediately following the celebration of the Eucharistic liturgy. The Blessed Sacrament may be exposed immediately after the Eucharistic liturgy when adoration shall continue for several hours or days.

Conclusion

In the introduction to this chapter, we spoke of our desire to express our love for God. Once we discover the great goodness and love of God for us, we want to return that love. But we feebly look for ways to express our love in a satisfying way. As God has done so many times in our lives, God shares with us a gift to satisfy this desire. Through the Sacraments of Initiation—Baptism, Confirmation, and the Eucharist—we join with Christ in calling out to God in a most perfect way, "I love you." Through these sacraments, we have become part of the family. Even better, we have become one with Christ. In the image of the Son, the family of God calls out with the voice of Christ to proclaim to God, "We love you." This is the great gift of the Sacraments of Initiation.

For Scripture reflection and discussion concerning this chapter, see **Journeying in His Light,** *"Sacraments of Initiation: Part 3."*

11 Sacrament of Healing: Reconciliation

Introduction

Because Tom worked so well on all types of cars, the owner of the car shop had named him head mechanic. Over the years, Tom's reputation had gained many new clients for the owner. But on this Friday before the Labor Day weekend, even Tom had to admit that he could never finish all the cars by closing time. In a moment of weakness and weariness, Tom decided to take a short cut on an oil change ordered by his neighbor. In a few moments, Tom had poured enough oil in the engine to bring the gauge to the "full" mark. He drove the car out to the lot as though he had changed the oil. He knew his neighbor would never check to see if he actually had done the job. He would simply take it for granted.

Later that evening, as Tom drove home in a far better mood, he heard his neighbor shout as he passed, "Thanks for taking care of my car today, Tom." After supper, Tom thought of his neighbor's car and finally became disturbed enough to walk down to his neighbor's house to confess what had happened. Tom offered to change the oil in the driveway of his own house and to check the car for other possible repairs, all free of charge.

The neighbor was surprised, but pleased that Tom had offered to work on the car. When Tom had finished, he promised his neighbor that the next oil change would also be free of charge. The neighbor insisted that Tom have a piece of his son's birthday cake and a cup of coffee before he returned home. By the time he started home that evening, Tom realized that his neighbor had not only accepted his apology, but had even accepted his friendship by inviting him to share in his son's birthday celebration. Tom felt better the second time he returned home that evening.

221

1. What is conscience?

a. Conscience is a judgment by which a person decides whether a particular action agrees or disagrees with a fundamental way of thinking.

On the day that Tom cheated his neighbor, he felt bothered about it. His conscience had reminded him that he had acted contrary to his continual desire to do a good job for his customers. His conscience felt better as he headed home after working on the car because he had corrected his fault and had worked more in accord with his continual or fundamental way of thinking.

Whenever any of us act against our fundamental way of thinking, our conscience immediately reminds us that something is wrong. We are bothered. In the life of a Christian, any action or sin against God or neighbor should immediately trigger our conscience to remind us that we are sinning. By continually sinning, we gradually quiet our conscience so that we no longer allow ourselves to be bothered by our sins. As this happens, our fundamental option or way of thinking is also changing to a direction that accepts sin rather than God.

It is hard to imagine a person with no conscience. A parent who hurts a child should normally feel a pang of remorse and a sense of wrong-doing. However, for a person with no fundamental ability to love, conscience could easily be a stranger to that person's life. For most of us, conscience plays a major part in life.

b. For our conscience to form correct judgments, we must become aware of our Christian responsibilities.

A Christian forms a correct conscience by striving to understand the message of Christ and his Church. Tom's basic direction in life lies in being fair to his customers. We do not know how Tom formed this way of thinking, but we do know that he lives out the goodness demanded by the Christian message. Within our lives, we have certain responsibilities which affect our conscience. A parent who hurts a child will ordinarily feel a pang of conscience, whether that parent is a Christian or not. A Christian, however, should feel a pang of conscience when he or she strives to hurt even an enemy. Christ told us to love our enemies. As a Christian accepts and reflects on the message of Christ, a Christian is forming his or her conscience in line with this message. The message of Christ becomes the fundamental way of thinking. This is a Christian conscience.

c. Conscience does not consist merely in "feeling" that an action is wrong.

Even though we try hard, we may find some demands of the law of Christ difficult to accept, for example, some people reach a point of "feeling" no wrong in hating or hurting a neighbor who has spoken or acted against them. The basic direction of a person's life may be to live out Christ's message, and the very acceptance of that message enables the person to **know** that certain actions are contrary to this basic direction, even though the person may never **"feel"** that it is wrong or sinful.

2. What is a temptation?

a. A temptation is an attraction to choose a thought or action contrary to the love of God or neighbor.

A temptation consists in an invitation to sin. In the story of Christ's temptation in the desert by the devil (Luke 4:1–2), we see the devil inviting Jesus to perform certain actions that would be contrary to his mission. Instead of suffering and dying to show his messiahship, Jesus could simply have accepted the alluring solutions offered by the devil. Jesus rejected these temptations and won the battle against Satan. Temptations are an important part of our lives. Through temptations, we face the challenge of evil and the chance to conquer evil in the name of Christ.

b. Temptation is not a sin.

Christ, who committed no sin, was tempted. Only if a person accepts a temptation and intends to put the temptation into action does the temptation result in sin. When Tom felt the urge to cheat his neighbor, he committed no wrong. When he accepted the temptation and cheated his neighbor, Tom then committed a sinful action.

c. At times of temptation, we call upon God through prayer.

We shall never be tempted beyond our powers. When we recognize our weakness in temptation, we should call upon God for help. When St. Paul speaks of asking God to remove some physical weakness, God speaks to him and says, " 'My grace is sufficient for you, for power is made perfect in weakness.' [Paul continues,] So, I will boast all the more gladly of my weaknesses, so that the power of Christ may dwell in me" (2 Corinthians 12:9). By praying at moments of temptation, we will find that God's grace is sufficient for us. Through pra-yer and continual good actions, we are able to overcome temptations.

3. Can God alone forgive sins?

a. God alone has the power to forgive sins.

Throughout the Old Testament, the People of God constantly called upon God for the forgiveness of their sins. David sinned with Bathsheba, the wife of Uriah. Uriah was a soldier who served the Israelite nation in war and who refused to enjoy the pleasures of his home while his army was in the midst of battle. David had Uriah placed at the head of the army that Uriah might be killed in battle. After the death of Uriah, David took Bathsheba as his wife. When Nathan, the prophet, prodded David's conscience and reminded him of his sin, David responded, " 'I have sinned against the Lord.' [Then] Nathan said to David, 'Now the Lord has put away your sin; you shall not die' " (2 Samuel 12:13).

In certain Old Testament rituals, the people would seek forgiveness for their sins through some specially chosen sacrifice. Although the priest offered this sacrifice to God in the name of the people, God, not the priest, forgave the sins of the community. The priest simply turned the offering for sins over to God, asking God's forgiveness for the community. For the people of the Old Testament, sin was an offense against God, and only God possessed the power to forgive sins.

224

b. Jesus Christ, who is God, came forgiving sins.

A Pharisee had invited Jesus to dinner, but did not perform the customary ritual of cleansing before the meal began. A woman, known to be a sinner, came to Jesus with perfumed oil and, with her tears and the oil, washed his feet and dried them with her hair. We read in the Gospel: "Then he said to her, 'Your sins are forgiven' " (Luke 7:48). At this meal, Jesus professed his power to forgive sin. We read about a paralyzed man who was lowered through a roof in order to be cured. Elsewhere, the Scriptures continue,

> When Jesus saw their faith, he said to the paralytic, "Son, your sins are forgiven." Now some of the scribes were sitting there, questioning in their hearts, "Why does this fellow speak in this way? It is blasphemy! Who can forgive sins but God alone?" At once Jesus perceived in his spirit that they were discussing these questions among themselves; and he said to them, "Why do you raise such questions in your hearts? Which is easier, to say to the paralytic, 'Your sins are forgiven,' or to say, 'Stand up and take your mat and walk'? But so that you may know that the Son of Man has authority on earth to forgive sins"—he said to the paralytic—"I say to you, stand up, take your mat and go to your home." And he stood up, and immediately took the mat and went out before all of them; so that they were all amazed and glorified God, saying, "We have never seen anything like this!" (Mark 2:5–12).

The Gospels tell us that Jesus came forgiving sins, and at times, he even performed miracles as a sign of this power to forgive sins.

c. Jesus passed this power on to the Church.

Although God alone has the power to forgive sins, God shares this power with others. We read in the Gospel of John that, after his resurrection, Jesus shared this power with the apostles: " 'Peace be with you. As the Father has sent me, so I send you.' When he had said this, he breathed on them and said to them, 'Receive the Holy Spirit. If you forgive the sins of any, they are forgiven them; if you retain the sins of any, they are retained' " (John 20:21–23). According to the writings of the early Church, the apostles forgave in the name of Jesus Christ. They also shared this power with others. Although God alone has the power to forgive sins, God chose to share this power with the Church. The minister of the sacrament, the ordained priest, acts in the name of Jesus Christ and also in the name of the community. Ordained priests are strictly obliged not to reveal what is told in confession of sins.

4. What is the Sacrament of Reconciliation?

a. Reconciliation is a sacrament by which a person renews a love relationship with God and the community.

Whenever we sin, we weaken our deep relationship with God and the community. We no longer approach God as openly and freely as before. A need to reconcile ourselves with God and others becomes important. Through the Sacrament of Reconciliation, we are able to renew this love relationship. Reconciliation consists not only in confession of our sins, but also in a deep conversion of our whole life, a turning toward God. In the introduction, Tom not only confessed his fault, but he also offered his neighbor a greater gift than the offense. By offering work free of charge, he sought to reconcile himself with his neighbor. In the same way, when we sin, we seek to reconcile ourselves with God and the community. We do not look at our sin and merely tell God we are sorry. We strive, in the future, to become an even better person. Another name given to this sacrament is the *Sacrament of Penance.* The name *reconciliation*, however, includes not only the idea of confessing one's sins and performing an act of satisfaction, but also living out a change in life which draws God more deeply into our life.

A parable, known to many as the *Parable of the Prodigal Son,* has all the elements of true reconciliation, and it offers a warning to those who think they are following Christ by merely following his rules and not his spirit. In this parable, found in the Gospel of Luke (15:11–31), a son takes his inheritance and squanders it on a sinful way of life. When the son repents of his sinfulness, he returns to profess his unworthiness before his father and to ask his father's forgiveness for his sins. The father forgives him immediately and orders a celebration for his son, a repentant sinner who has returned home.

The father in the story represents God, who readily forgives anyone seeking forgiveness. Luke tells us that the father caught sight of his son at a distance and ran out to meet him. The message tells us that God is as anxious as the father to welcome repentant sinners.

The elder son, who kept all the rules, becomes angry with the father, who so readily forgives his sinful son. We discover in him a person who follows all the rules, but who has not grasped the spirit of the father. The elder son also needs reconciliation for his hard and unforgiving nature. The parable tells us not only that God is willing to share in reconciliation with us, but also that we should be quick to reconcile ourselves with those who sin against us, as the father in the parable did.

b. Through the Sacrament of Reconciliation, a person makes peace with the community.

As was mentioned in an earlier chapter, through our baptism, we are baptized into Christ which is the Church or the community of Jesus' people. We are so closely joined together in this community that our own sins affect the whole community. Paul writes, "If one member suffers, all suffer together with it; if one member is honored, all rejoice together with it" (1 Corinthians 12:26). Even our so-called private sins affect the whole community. Because we hurt the community by our sins, we seek forgiveness of the community by making peace through its representative. The ordained priest acts in the name of Jesus Christ and also in the name of the community. Through this sacrament we reconcile ourselves not only to God, but also to the community.

c. In the Sacrament of Reconciliation, a sinner celebrates God's forgiving love.

God's love is always an inviting love. In the Sacrament of Reconciliation, we celebrate God's call for our return to God's love and our response to that call. In our need for reconciliation, we recognize more fully our need for God's help and God's love. We also recognize and accept God's love for sinners. Because of God's love, we celebrate our return to God through the Sacrament of Reconciliation. In the parable of the prodigal son, the occasion of the son's confession of sins becomes the occasion for a celebration. The father says, "And get the fatted calf and kill it, and let us eat and celebrate; for this son of mine was dead and is alive again; he was lost and is found!" and Luke tells us simply, "And they began to celebrate" (Luke 15:23–24).

d. Through the Sacrament of Reconciliation, we receive help to live a better life.

By examining our conscience before the individual celebration of the sacrament, we pinpoint those areas of our life where growth must take place. We admit our need for help, and, through the Sacrament of Reconciliation, not only are our sins forgiven, but also we share in the blessings of God which enable us to live a better life. Through the Sacrament of Reconciliation, we promise in our weakness to strive to draw close to God, and God responds to our desire for conversion by sharing special graces or helps in order that we may live a new life. Paul writes, ". . . in Christ God was reconciling the world to himself, not counting their trespasses against them, and entrusting the message of reconciliation to us" (2 Corinthians 5:19).

e. Through the Sacrament of Reconciliation, even good people draw closer to God.

To celebrate the Sacrament of Reconciliation, we need not be in the state of sin. What is necessary for this sacrament is that we be able to recognize a sinful condition in life. This sinfulness does not mean that we must have committed a specific sin between the last celebration of this sacrament and the present celebration. It simply means that we recognize weak and sinful tendencies and recognize a need to draw even closer to God by celebrating this Sacrament of Reconciliation. Because of the special helps given to live a new and better life, we should periodically avail ourselves of this sacrament.

Whenever we are in serious sin, we should participate in this sacrament as soon as possible. The Church has established as law that any Catholic in the state of serious sin shall confess at least once a year. For those who continually strive to live close to God, such a law is never necessary.

5. How is the Sacrament of Reconciliation celebrated?

a. The rite begins with the reception of the penitent.

The reconciliation room is ordinarily a small room with at least two chairs, a small table, and a divider. The penitent may confess in privacy if he or she wishes. The penitent may also choose the chair opposite the ordained priest who is the minister of the sacrament. This allows the penitent to converse more fully concerning his or her spiritual failures and hopes. The minister greets the penitent. Both together make the sign of the cross. The minister then prays a short prayer by which he invites the penitent to trust in God's love and mercy. The penitent answers, "Amen."

b. A short reading of the word of God follows the reception of the penitent.

The minister or the penitent may read or recite from memory a passage of Scripture which speaks about God's mercy and the need for a change of life. The purpose of the reading is to enable both minister and penitent to reflect upon the loving mercy of God and to try to understand that love more perfectly. The penitent may choose a special reading that relates to some point the penitent wishes to emphasize in this celebration of the sacrament.

c. Encouraged by this word of God, the penitent then confesses how he or she has failed the Lord and the community by sin.

The penitent expresses failures as well as hopes for the future in the celebration of this sacrament. During this time, the minister gives assistance and advice. This is not a time for lengthy spiritual counseling or spiritual direction. If more time is needed, the minister and penitent should establish another specific time for continuing this direction.

d. The minister assigns an appropriate act of satisfaction for sin.

God's gift is one of forgiveness. It is unconditional and free. The purpose of satisfaction is to bring about a loving reconciliation between oneself and others, or even oneself and the Church, and to aid the person in becoming the one God is calling that person to be. The minister may suggest an action or some appropriate prayers to help the penitent carry out new hopes for the future.

e. The penitent prays a prayer of sorrow (contrition).

The minister invites the penitent to express in prayer an act of sorrow for sin. The penitent may do this in his or her own words or use a formal prayer. We commonly refer to this prayer as an *Act of Sorrow (Contrition)*. These words simply sum up and express verbally the sorrow which has already taken place (see appendix).

f. The minister prays the prayer of absolution.

The minister then lays hands on the head of the penitent, and prays the prayer of forgiveness or absolution. Placing a hand over or on the head of the penitent is an ancient gesture of invoking the Holy Spirit. In the prayer of absolution, the minister proclaims the gift of reconciliation existing between God and all people. This gift was accomplished by the death and resurrection of Jesus Christ. An important part of the reconciliation rite is the sending of the Holy Spirit among us for the forgiveness of all sins. The minister, in the name of Christ and as a member of the Church, prays "through the ministry of the Church" for pardon and peace and absolves the penitent. The words of absolution read:

God, the Father of mercies,
through the death and resurrection of his Son,
has reconciled the world to himself
and sent the Holy Spirit among us
for the forgiveness of sins;
through the ministry of the Church
may God give you pardon and peace,
and I absolve you from your sins

in the name of the Father, and of the Son, ✝
and of the Holy Spirit.

The penitent answers: *Amen.*

g. The minister and penitent praise God and the celebration is ended.

Acknowledging God's great mercy in the sacrament, the minister and penitent share a brief dialogue of praise of God. The minister prays the prayer: *Give thanks to the Lord, for he is good.* The penitent concludes: *His mercy endures forever.*

Then the minister dismisses the penitent who has been reconciled, saying: *The Lord has freed you from your sins. Go in peace.*

6. What is communal reconciliation?

a. Communal reconciliation *consists in a service by which the individuals of a community come together to recognize the social nature and harm of sin.*

In a communal celebration of the Sacrament of Reconciliation, the community shares publicly in a preparation for the Sacrament of Reconciliation. The reading of the word of God ordinarily read in the reconciliation room is now shared with the entire assembly. A brief homily usually follows the word of God. The minister or ministers then go to different areas to be used for the celebration of this sacrament. The penitents individually confess their sins and are absolved by the minister. They will often remain until all have celebrated the Sacrament of Reconciliation, and all will offer prayers of thanksgiving and praise for God's love and mercy. This may be done in word or song. Through this communal celebration, we realize that the sacraments are community celebrations, as well as the fact that all sins are offenses against the community.

b. Communal reconciliation at times includes general absolution.

Due to a large number of penitents and a lack of sufficient confessors, the Church allows the ordained priest to confer general absolution upon members of the community if the penitents are forced to be deprived of sacramental grace or Holy Communion for a long time through no fault of their own. The minister of the sacrament should do all in his power to see that the people are properly disposed for this sacrament and that they understand what is happening. Keeping in mind the spirit of reconciliation and the desire to use all means of deepening a relationship with God, the Church requires those in serious sin to discuss that particular fault at a future celebration of reconciliation. Reconciliation is more than forgiveness. It involves a new direction or conversion in life, and such direction becomes more firm when openly discussed in this sacrament.

7. What is necessary for the reception of this sacrament?

a. The penitent who shares in the celebration of this sacrament must have sorrow for sins.

In order for a person to celebrate this sacrament worthily, the penitent must be able to express some sorrow for sins. This sorrow for sins does not demand that a person come to the sacrament in tears nor with a deep, emotional feeling of sorrow. This sorrow can be a simple statement that a person seeks reconciliation for having offended God and the community. Sorrow does not necessarily express itself in tears but more in a change of life.

b. The penitent who celebrates this sacrament must also have the intention of never sinning again.

Overcoming sin and weakness is a lifetime task. God understands this, and God is ever present. God is always ready to renew the love relationship. The penitent should approach this sacrament with confidence and trust in God. To continue to confess sins that have already been forgiven in this sacrament is to show a lack of trust in the celebration of this sacrament. Once a sin has been confessed in this sacrament, there is no need to confess that sin again. God has already invited us to share more fully in God's life.

Conclusion

Ever since Tom confessed his guilt to his neighbor, he and his neighbor have become the best of friends. Tom's gratitude to his neighbor for accepting his simple apology and for accepting the extra work on the car has helped Tom realize the value of forgiveness. Not only has Tom's neighbor accepted the apology, but the neighbor has accepted Tom in a full and better way. This is a true sign of reconciliation.

Whenever we sin, we can turn back to God and the community and seek to draw closer to them in a new and better relationship. God is always accepting our friendship, always accepting our reconciliation. Each time we turn toward God, God does not bring us back into an old friendship, but rather brings us into a new and deeper friendship. In this new friendship, we realize God's love for us and our love for God.

For Scripture reflection and discussion concerning this chapter, see **Journeying in His Light,** *"Reconciliation—a New Beginning."*

12 Sacrament of Healing: Anointing of the Sick

Introduction

Virginia had never experienced sickness like this before. As she lay in the hospital bed, she looked anxiously to the doctor who was hurriedly examining her. The doctor finally stopped examining and said, "Virginia, we think you have had a slight heart attack. It really isn't serious, but we would like to keep an eye on you. Rest now."

It was only then that Virginia realized that the nurses and doctor had taped strange, round objects to her body. She knew that someone in another room was sitting by the monitor keeping an eye on the rhythm of her heart. She relaxed with a sigh, thanking God that it was no worse.

Throughout the rest of the day, a nurse occasionally stopped in, smiled, and asked if she needed anything. A nun with a bright, broad smile stopped by to pray with her. A priest had stopped by, and, as peacefully as one could imagine, had administered the Sacrament of the Anointing of the Sick. It was a pleasant experience to celebrate that sacrament. For years she had dreaded the moment a priest would stand over her "with the oils," but the experience was far different from her fearful expectations.

Virginia felt that she could never forget the kindness, gentleness, and blessings of all the people who shared her sickness. They made her feel very much at home, despite her illness. She told a friend some weeks later, "I suddenly understood what a healing touch of kindness and concern really was!" Virginia watches her diet and works a little more carefully now, but she still claims that those days in the hospital were the most pleasant days of her life.

1. How does the Church respond to sickness in the world?

a. The Church urges that we work with charity toward relieving the pain and suffering of a sick person.

Paul reminds us that when one member of the body of Christ suffers, all members suffer along with this one member. When any person is suffering here on earth, the whole of God's creation suffers along with this person. The Church urges that we use every means to alleviate the suffering of this person and to overcome the sickness of this person. It encourages the use of scientific means to draw a person back to health. It encourages all of us to treat the sick person with kindness and love, realizing that we are this suffering member. A person who is ill is encouraged to accept the illness as sharing in the suffering of Jesus Christ. However, the acceptance does not mean an acceptance of an illness that can be cured, but rather the acceptance of pain that often accompanies an illness even during the healing.

b. The Church urges that family and friends see themselves as a reflection of the Church in caring for those close to them.

The Church reminds the family and friends of the sick, as well as those who care for the sick, that they have a special share in the ministry of comfort. It is their task to strengthen the sick with words of faith and to pray with them. In case of sickness which keeps a person at home for some period of time, the family should consult the ordained priest so that he may respond to the needs of the person during the period of sickness.

c. The Church urges the presbyter to view visiting and care of the sick as an important part of his ministry.

The presbyter as a representative of the concerned Church, should show concern and visit the sick. The Church reminds the presbyter of his pastoral duty. In a case where sickness has kept a person at home, the presbyter should arrange to bring the Eucharist to this person. The Eucharist may be brought by the clergy or by a lay person.

d. All Christians are reminded to care for the sick with love and kindness.

Although the Church reminds the ordained priest of his pastoral duty to care for the sick as a representative of the Church, the Church also encourages all its members to reach out in charity to those who are sick. Each member of the community should show a deep concern for other members of that community, especially for suffering members. The presbyter should not be the only one within a parish to visit or care for the sick. Community members are to concern themselves with the sick of the community and respond to the sick person's needs by caring for them, helping the family, or simply reminding the sick that they are in our prayers.

All who show compassion for the sick participate in Christ's healing ministry. In writing to the Philippians, Paul tells them how much their support meant to him in his hardships. He writes,

> I rejoice in the Lord greatly that now at last you have revived your concern for me; indeed, you were concerned for me, but had no opportunity to show it. I know what it is to have little, and I know what it is to have plenty in any and all circumstances. I have learned the secret of being well-fed and of going hungry, of having plenty and of being in need. I can do all things through him who strengthens me. In any case, it was kind of you to share my distress (Philippians 4:10, 12, 13–14).

Paul trusted in the strength which came from Christ, but he admitted to the Philippians that their support meant a great deal to him.

e. In case of serious sickness, the family should call upon the presbyter to celebrate the anointing of the sick.

The Church urges that all people be made aware of the meaning of the Sacrament of the Anointing of the Sick and that they call upon an ordained priest to celebrate this sacrament in certain cases of sickness. Families should remember that a person need not be in danger of immediate death to celebrate this sacrament. The introduction to the rite states that "great care and concern should be taken to see that those faithful whose health is seriously impaired by sickness or old age receive this sacrament."

2. What is the Sacrament of the Anointing of the Sick?

a. The Sacrament of the Anointing of the Sick is a sacrament by which the Church continues the concern of the Lord himself by sharing with the sick special sacramental gifts passed on from Jesus Christ.

Throughout the Gospels, we read of Christ's continued concern for the sick and dying. He reached out to the sick and cured them. He looked upon them with kindness and shared a healing. In a story found in the Gospel of Luke, a leper comes to Jesus and states boldly, ". . . Lord if you choose, you can make me clean" (Luke 5:12). Although Jesus recognizes the presence of suffering and sickness in the world, he expresses a basic desire of God that all people will be healed. Jesus answers the leper as though he were answering all people, ". . . I do choose. Be made clean" (Luke 5:13). In the curing of the leper, Jesus is offering us an example of our need to cure others in whatever way we are able. The Sacrament of the Anointing of the Sick continues to show this loving concern of Christ for those whose health is seriously impaired.

b. The Sacrament of Anointing demonstrates the abiding presence of Christ and the Church, who offer hope and strength in time of sickness.

Through the Sacrament of Anointing, the sick recognize that Christ and the Church abide with them throughout their sickness, even to the point of death. The passion and death of Christ become an example of Christian suffering. In a unique way, the sick are consecrated through the Sacrament of Anointing to join their own suffering with that of Christ. Through this unity with Christ, the suffering endured by the sick becomes more meaningful, since it enables the sick to participate in the saving action of Christ.

The Church, in union with the communion of saints, never abandons the sick, but continues to pray and show concern for them. The sick, in uniting themselves with the passion and death of Christ and with the suffering of all people throughout the world, contribute to the sanctification of the People of God. Through this abiding presence of Christ and the Church, the sick can recognize that their suffering is not without merit, but that it can serve as a source of blessing for the people of the world.

c. Through this sacrament, the Holy Spirit shares the blessings of health, trust in God, and strength against temptation.

Through this sacrament, the Church shares with a person a new strength to bear suffering bravely and even to fight against suffering. At times, a return to physical health may follow upon the celebration of this sacrament. We should keep in mind that the sacrament always ministers to the whole person. It strives to bring about a deep inner healing and has the purpose of uniting the suffering of the sick person with the suffering of Christ and the hope that springs from faith in Christ. It also has the effect of forgiving all sins, even serious, when the sick person cannot share in the celebration of the Sacrament of Reconciliation. The terminally ill, who do not receive a physical healing from the anointing, receive spiritual help for their journey into eternity.

d. The beginnings of this sacrament are shown in the New Testament.

In the Gospel of Mark, Jesus draws aside the twelve apostles and sends them off two by two with instructions for their missionary journeys. During these missionary journeys, we read in the Scriptures, "They cast out many demons, and anointed with oil many who were sick and cured them" (Mark 6:13). At this time, we see the use of oil even by the twelve apostles as they are sent out by Christ.

In the Letter of James, we read about a custom of the early Church of praying over the sick and anointing them with oil:

> Are any among you sick? They should call for the elders of the church and have them pray over them, anointing them with oil in the name of the Lord. The prayer of faith will save the sick, and the Lord will raise them up; and anyone who has committed sins will be forgiven (James 5:14–15).

Through this Letter of James, we find a basis for this Sacrament of the Anointing of the Sick.

3. Who may share in this Sacrament of Anointing of the Sick?

a. Any person whose health is seriously impaired by sickness or old age should share in the celebration of the Sacrament of Anointing of the Sick.

The presbyter makes a judgment regarding the health of a person being seriously impaired and this judgment should be based on the spiritual and physical condition of the person. The presbyter should en-courage the faithful whose health is seriously impaired to celebrate the sacrament. At the same time, he should protect the sacrament from be-ing used in a trivial way. The Church does not refer to this sacrament any longer as the sacrament of the *last rites* or *extreme unction.* Elderly people who are in a weak condition may be anointed. For example, an elderly person who has the flu may be anointed, since that person could easily suffer a serious health problem. In a case where a serious illness is the reason for surgery, the person should be anointed. In the case of children, the anointing may take place if they have sufficient use of reason. The Sacrament of the Sick can be celebrated more than once by an individual.

b. Anointing may be conferred upon sick people who have lost consciousness or the use of reason.

If a person throughout life has freely chosen to celebrate the sacraments or has shown a desire to share in this Sacrament of Anointing in times of illness, this person may share in the sacrament even when unconscious or confused. Through an accident or aging, a person may lose the use of reason. Such a person may still share in this sacrament.

c. If a person has already died, the presbyter does not administer the Sacrament of Anointing.

At times, a presbyter is called to attend a person who is already dead. He should pray that God forgive the person's sins and that

God receive this person into God's love. The presbyter prays for the family and consoles them. However, he is not to administer the Sacrament of Anointing at this time.

4. How is this Sacrament of the Anointing of the Sick celebrated?

a. Bishops and presbyters are the proper ministers of the Sacrament of the Anointing of the Sick.

Bishops and presbyters are the proper ministers of this Sacrament of the Anointing of the Sick. With their pastoral responsibility of caring for the sick and preparing them for the celebration of all the sacraments, presbyters have the responsibility to share this sacrament with those capable of celebrating it.

b. The minister celebrates this sacrament by laying hands on the head of the sick person, offering a prayer of faith, and anointing the sick person with oil especially blessed for this occasion.

As in other sacraments, the ordained minister lays hands on the sick person's head in silence, then anoints the sick person on the forehead and the hands with oil. The minister prays:

Through this holy anointing
may the Lord in his love and mercy help you
with the grace of the Holy Spirit. R. Amen.
May the Lord who frees you from sin
save you and raise you up. R. Amen.

Although these actions confer the sacrament, the Church offers other prayers in preparation for the celebration of the sacrament. Through these prayers, the Church prepares the sick person and those who are taking part in this liturgy for the celebration of the sacrament. The prayers which follow upon this sacrament include the celebration of the Eucharist if the person is physically capable of sharing in this sacrament.

5. What is Holy Viaticum?

a. When a person at the point of death celebrates the Sacrament of the Eucharist, this person is receiving a special grace of the sacrament which is called Holy Viaticum.

The author of the Gospel of John links the importance of the celebration of the Eucharist with our resurrection on the last day. The person who shares in the body and blood of Christ has a pledge of Christ's resurrection: "Those who eat my flesh and drink my blood have eternal life, and I will raise them up on the last day" (John 6:54). The Sacrament of the Eucharist most closely symbolizes the death and resurrection of Jesus Christ. For this reason, the Church has chosen to make this a special sacrament at the moment of death.

Viaticum, rather than the anointing of the sick, is the true sacrament of the dying. The Church says that Viaticum is the true food for passage through death to eternal life. In some instances, when a person seems to be on the edge of death, a choice must be made, and, at such a time, the Church chooses Viaticum over the anointing. If time permits, a person may then share in the anointing after celebrating Viaticum. As anointing is the sacrament for the sick, Viaticum is the sacrament for the dying.

b. All Catholics who can physically celebrate Communion are to share in Viaticum as they near death.

Because of the strength and blessings which flow from this sacrament, the Church reminds all Catholics of their obligation to share in the Eucharist at the point of death. During the celebration of Viaticum, the Catholic should renew the vows of baptism by praying a profession of faith.

When persons near death, they are often conscious of their quickly fleeting life, and they wish to prepare themselves for their passover into eternal life. Some, trying to be compassionate, may tend to deny a person this time of preparation by not making Viaticum available to the dying person. This denial is contrary to the ideal of Christian life and preparation for death, and it deprives a person of a great gift for the passage into eternal life.

c. Where possible, Viaticum should be received during the celebration of the Eucharistic liturgy.

Since Viaticum shows in a special way a union in the mystery of the death of the Lord and his passage to his glory, the most appropriate context for the sharing in this sacrament would be within the Eucharist liturgy. When possible, the sick person should celebrate the Eucharist under both forms, that is, the form of bread and the form of wine. In some cases, where a person has difficulty swallowing, either a tiny piece of the consecrated bread or the wine may be given to the dying person.

6. What is communal anointing of the sick?

a. Communal anointing consists of groups of people celebrating this sacrament within the Eucharistic liturgy.

In certain cases, groups of people may celebrate this sacrament within a Eucharistic celebration. Elderly people and people whose health is seriously impaired should be urged to come and celebrate together in the Eucharistic liturgy. The Sacrament of Anointing of the Sick is an action of the community whereby all members are concerned for one another. As one member suffers, all suffer, and, as one member shares in the joy of a sacrament, all share in the joy of the sacrament. The group, coming together for communal anointing, manifests the great sign of a concerned community celebrating a joyful sacrament.

b. Others besides those who are to be anointed should share in the celebration of communal anointing.

Although those who are elderly or those who have certain illnesses are permitted to celebrate the Sacrament of the Anointing of the Sick, other members of the community should participate in this Eucharistic liturgy. The celebration of this sacrament is a special moment not only in the lives of those who share in this sacrament, but also in the lives of every member of the community. Others should come to share their concern, love, and support for those who need this sacrament. Active participation of the faithful in a communal anointing is certainly preferred because of its great sign of a community concerned for its members.

Paul tells the Romans that they should have an attitude of concern for all the brothers and sisters in the faith, whom he refers to as the "saints." Paul writes, "Look on the needs of the saints as your own; be generous in offering hospitality." Hospitality in this sense not only involves welcoming a person into one's home, but also treating a person with the love one would have for a close member of one's family. The fears and joys of the members of the Christian community become the fears and joys of all members.

Conclusion

When Virginia visits her friends in the hospital, she tries to share with them her own experiences of love and healing. She learned much from her own sickness and wants to share what she learned. As her sister lay dying some years later, Virginia came and sat quietly by her bed. The comfort of the anointing of the sick had helped her sister, but Virginia saw herself as an extension of that healing touch of Christ. She prayed with her sister, listened to her when she repeated those same stories over and over, and wiped her sister's forehead when her sister could no longer do these things for herself. Through her own sickness, Virginia had learned much about the healing touch of presence. The kind word, the thoughtful visit, the silent listening, the tender touch, and Sacrament of the Anointing of the Sick were all moments for the healing touch of Christ.

For Scripture reflection and discussion concerning this chapter, see **Journeying in His Light, "Anointing of the Sick."**

13 Sacrament of Service in the Community: Marriage

Introduction

Marie sat at the kitchen table, speaking with her mother about plans for the anniversary celebration. In only three months, Marie's mother and father would celebrate fifty years of marriage. While they talked, Marie noticed her mother relax just a slight bit when she heard the front door open and knew her husband had returned from his daily walk to the park and back. She reflected on the silent communication that existed between her mother and father after all these years of marriage. She would notice at other times a slight tension while she spoke with her father in the living room, especially if the kitchen seemed too silent for too long. But the sound of a pan banging in the sink would ease the tension as she noted that same slight relaxation in her father. She had learned of the concern that existed between her parents for each other, and how the sound of a door opening or a pan banging in the sink communicated that all was well. Through fifty years of struggling, adapting, and even arguing with one another, the two had gradually welded into one.

At the anniversary celebration, the four children, the ten grandchildren, and eight great-grandchildren stood as a living reminder of what this marriage had brought to the world. Through her parents' love and their family, Marie was able to understand the great ideal of marriage in God's creation. She smiled as she whispered to herself, "I guess God does know what He's doing."

1. How did the Sacrament of Marriage develop?

a. Throughout the Old Testament, we see a gradual growth in the understanding of marriage.

Many of the Israelites' marriage customs in early Old Testament times came close to those of neighboring groups. A man could have more than one wife. A man could divorce his wife, but the wife could not divorce her husband. A man committed adultery by having intercourse with another man's wife, but a married man could have intercourse with a woman who was not married and not commit adultery. In later Old Testament times, a deeper religious understanding of marriage gradually developed. We read in Genesis,

> So the Lord God caused a deep sleep to fall upon the man, and he slept; then he took one of his ribs and closed up its place with flesh. And the rib that the Lord God had taken from the man he made into a woman and brought her to the man. Then the man said, "This at last is bone of my bones and flesh of my flesh; this one shall be called Woman, for out of Man this one was taken." Therefore a man leaves his father and his mother and clings to his wife, and they become one flesh (Genesis 2:21–24).

In this reading, we see that God is the author of marriage and that marriage comes from the very basis of God's creation. At the moment of marriage, the man and woman grow so close together that they actually become one flesh. About four hundred and fifty years before Christ, the author of the book of Malachi cried out in prophecy,

> You ask, "Why does he not?" Because the Lord was a witness between you and the wife of your youth, to whom you have been faithless, though she is your companion and your wife by covenant. Did not one God make her? Both flesh and spirit are his. And what does the one God desire? Godly offspring. So look to yourselves, and do not let anyone be faithless to the wife of his youth (Malachi 2:14–15).

God no longer accepts sacrifice from these chosen people because God is unhappy with the one who has broken faith with his wife with whom he is one flesh. Malachi even went on to say, " 'For I hate divorce' says the Lord, the God of Israel, and covering one's garment with violence, says the Lord of hosts. So take heed to yourselves and do not be faithless" (Malachi 2:16). Statements such as Malachi's stand out in stark contrast against the thinking of the people of the Old Testament, even to the coming of Christ. Like John the Baptizer, the voice of Malachi on this point in the Old Testament could be called the voice of one crying out in the desert. With the coming of Christ, his voice would be heard more clearly.

b. Jesus brought a new awareness to the understanding of marriage.

In the Gospel of Matthew, we read that some of the Pharisees came to question Jesus about divorce. By the time Jesus had finished speaking, even the disciples wondered if they could carry out this law of Christ.

> *Some Pharisees came to him, and to test him they asked, "Is it lawful for a man to divorce his wife for any cause?" He answered, "Have you not read that the one who made them at the beginning 'made them male and female,' and said, 'For this reason a man shall leave his father and mother and be joined to his wife, and the two shall become one flesh'? So they are no longer two, but one flesh. Therefore what God has joined together, let no one separate." They said to him, "Why then did Moses command us to give a certificate of dismissal and to divorce her?" He said to them, "It was because you were so hard-hearted that Moses allowed you to divorce your wives, but from the beginning it was not so. And I say to you, whoever divorces his wife, except for unchastity, and marries another commits adultery." His disciples said to him, "If such is the case of a man with his wife, it is better not to marry." But he said to them, "Not everyone can accept this teaching, but only those to whom it is given" (Matthew 19:3–11).*

The fact that the disciples portray surprise at the words of Jesus shows that he is sharing with them a new teaching, one which is contrary to their way of thinking. Jesus points to marriage in this passage as a permanent union between a man and a woman. Elsewhere in the Gospel of Matthew, the Sacrament of Marriage is shown to be so sacred that even a person's innermost thoughts must respect the marriage of others. " 'You have heard that it was said, "You shall not commit adultery." But I say to you that everyone who looks at a woman with lust has already committed adultery with her in his heart' " (Matthew 5:27–28). Through the life, death, and exaltation of Jesus, marriage is raised to the high dignity of a sacrament.

c. The Letter to the Ephesians compares marriage to Christ and his Church.

In the Letter to the Ephesians we read,

In the same way, husbands should love their wives as they do their own bodies. He who loves his wife loves himself. For no one ever hates his own body, but he nourishes and tenderly cares for it, just as Christ does for the church, because we are members of his body. "For this reason a man will leave his father and mother and be joined to his wife, and the two will become one flesh." This is a great mystery, and I am applying it to Christ and the church. Each of you, however, should love his wife as himself, and a wife should respect her husband (Ephesians 5:28–33).

This letter portrays the high regard the early Church had for marriage. To compare the union of a husband and wife with the union of Christ and his Church is to use the highest comparison possible in the opinion of Christians. Just as Christ is his Church, the two become one flesh and share in this great union of Christ's love.

2. What is the purpose of marriage?

a. One purpose of marriage is to share in God's creative work of bringing new human life into the world.

One of the great gifts of God's creation resides in the gift of being able to give birth to a child. Because this event happens in our world every day, we often overlook the amazing miracle of birth. We can never forget that God has shared this gift with us: "So God created humankind in his image, in the image of God he created them; male and female he created them. God blessed them, and God said to them, 'Be fruitful and multiply, and fill the earth and subdue it; and have dominion over the fish of the sea and over the birds of the air and over every living thing that moves upon the earth' " (Genesis 1:27–28). In sharing this gift, God allowed a man and a woman to take part in the highest privilege of creation, namely the privilege of sharing as co-creators in bringing new life into the world. Not only does the privilege lie in giving birth to a child, but also in helping form the child for life. Christ reminds us through the Church of this privilege and obligation of the family. Marriage has as a primary purpose the bearing and rearing of children.

b. Another primary purpose of marriage is the development of mutual love between the husband and wife.

The development of love stands at the foundation of God's creation. Love should flourish in the family, and the love of a husband and wife shares first place in marriage along with the birth and education of children. Through sexual sharing, the husband and wife deepen their love for one another and bring to that sharing a complete giving of themselves in love. Through their daily life together, through joys and tragedies that they must face together, a husband and wife develop their love for each other. The commitment of marriage allows for trust and intimacy in which mutual love can continually grow. For this reason, mutual love is also considered a primary purpose of marriage.

3. What is a Christian marriage?

a. A Christian marriage is a sacrament in which a baptized man and a baptized woman pledge their love and faithfulness to each other through a special covenant.

Throughout the Old Testament, a key theme of covenant is often portrayed as a marriage between God and the nation of Israel. As was mentioned in an earlier chapter, a covenant differs from a contract. A contract usually refers to some work or action to be performed and concluded within a set period of time. A covenant, however, consists in a full personal commitment of one person to another for as long as the two live. When a man and a woman enter into marriage, they share in a deep personal covenant. The baptized man and woman share in a sacramental covenant, which we call a *sacrament*.

b. A Christian marriage is one which most fully reflects the love of Christ for his Church.

In the Sacrament of Marriage, there are really three people sharing: the baptized man and woman along with Christ. Paul referred to marriage as a reflection of Christ and his Church. In the Sacrament of Marriage, Christ enters most fully into the covenant. Before God and the community, and with the power shared by Christ's resurrection, two people fully commit themselves to each other for life, and Christ blesses this union by sharing the blessings and helps of a sacrament. The husband and wife enter into a deep relationship with each other and also into a deeper and more intimate union with Jesus Christ himself, as is the case in each of the sacraments.

4. Does the Catholic Church believe in divorce?

a. The Catholic Church does not allow divorce and remarriage.

If a person is truly married and has sought a legal divorce with the State, that person is not free to marry again. The Church takes strictly the words of Christ as found in the Scriptures, "But from the beginning of creation, 'God made them male and female.' 'For this reason a man shall leave his father and mother and be joined to his wife, and the two shall become one flesh.' So they are no longer two, but one flesh. Therefore what God has joined together, let no one separate" (Mark 10:6–9). In the eyes of the Church, marriage is a full giving of one's complete self to another for life. Once two people have entered this covenant, even if they separate, the covenant continues to exist. Later, in the same chapter of Mark, we read, "He said to them, 'Whoever divorces his wife and marries another commits adultery against her. . .' " (Mark 10:11). Even if a legal divorce should take place, Jesus does not accept this as a sign that the covenant has ended. In Mark, we read that a man or woman who separates and marries again commits adultery.

b. The Catholic Church does allow divorce or separation for a serious reason, but not remarriage.

There are times when people are better off separated than together. If a person suffers a violation of his or her human dignity within marriage, then this person certainly may seek a separation. However, even if a legal divorce is obtained, the person does not have the right to marry again. In the eyes of the Church, if a person is divorced and remarried, he or she may not share in the sacraments. The Church continues to invite the individual to share in worship. A divorced person who has remarried should not turn against the Church, but rather should continue to pray along with the Church that God will offer guidance and strength. A divorced person who has not remarried is ordinarily permitted to share in the sacraments. If a person has any doubts about his or her situation, he or she should consult the parish priest or parish associate(s) who deal with such situations.

c. A declaration of nullity consists in a declaration by the Church that no marriage ever existed.

In some cases, the Church will study the beginnings of a marriage to establish whether or not the marriage (as a sacrament) actually took place. There are certain demands a person must fulfill in order to enter a true marriage. A couple must have the intention of having children if they are physically able to do so. They must be a mature couple, capable of making a full commitment to each other. Reasons for a declaration of nullity can be physical or spiritual. A divorced person should consult a priest or some other person in the Church who has knowledge of marriage laws to look into their marriage for a possible declaration of nullity. Some marriages that eventually break up have their root cause of the break-up dating back to the beginning of the marriage.

5. What is necessary of a true (valid) marriage?

a. For the Sacrament of Marriage, a man or woman must be of mature age.

Ordinarily the Church requests permission of parents for anyone under eighteen years of age. However, when speaking about maturity, we must speak about more than age. A person can be immature at the age of twenty-one or twenty-five. The one witnessing the marriage in the name of the Church must often make a judgment concerning the maturity of the individuals entering this sacrament. In order for a person to make a commitment for life, that person must be mature. Immature people do not have the full ability to make a lifelong commitment.

b. There can not be a previously existing valid marriage.

Since the Church does not recognize divorce, a person who has previously married and who has received a legal divorce cannot enter the Sacrament of Marriage in the Church. The only exception to this rule would be a case when the spouse has died. If a previous marriage has been invalid, that is, if it has not fulfilled the demand for a true marriage, then a declaration of nullity must be received from the Church. A declaration of nullity simply declares that a previous marriage never existed.

c. A person entering marriage must be capable of sharing sexually.

The ends of marriage consist in procreation of children and in the mutual love between a husband and wife. Marriage is the sharing of one's full sexuality with another. For those who are physically capable, procreation is a necessity for a true marriage. In all marriages, people must be capable of sharing sexually. If a person does not have this capability, the person has a physical impediment to marriage. Sexual sharing is a symbolic sign of two becoming one and fulfills at least one of the primary ends of marriage, namely, mutual love between husband

and wife. A lack of this symbolic sign makes a person incapable of celebrating this sacrament.

d. A person must freely intend to enter a lifelong commitment.

When entering marriage, the couple commit themselves to each other for life. If they enter the marriage with definite openness to divorce and if certain conditions are not fulfilled, that marriage is invalid. If a person is forced into a marriage commitment, that person has not entered a true marriage. A marriage must be entered into freely and knowingly.

e. In order to enter into marriage, two people must not be closely related to each other by blood or by marriage.

A brother may not marry a sister, nor may close cousins marry each other. After the death of a partner, a brother-in-law may not marry a sister-in-law unless a special dispensation is granted. In all cases of any relationship, a person should confer with a priest before planning marriage.

6. What steps must a person take in order to enter marriage?

a. Before two people enter marriage, they must arrange with the priest for a period of premarriage dialogue.

Some dioceses demand that a couple confer with the priest before they even set a date for their marriage. During the preparation period, certain papers must be filled out in preparation for the marriage. The couple also should attend marriage preparation sessions. At these sessions, a married couple, a doctor, a priest, and others will share in preparing a couple for their marriage. Along with these instructions, the parish priest or a representative will continue to work with the couple to prepare for the marriage. During this time, they will discuss

253

matters that closely touch upon the life of a married couple. They will speak of communication in love, of sexuality, of pregnancy and child-bearing, and of the raising of a family. Extra preparation is demanded for teenage marriage. Teenagers should give themselves a sufficient amount of time before planning to enter marriage.

b. When a Catholic marries someone not of the Catholic faith, certain dispensations must be sought from the Church.

A person seeks a dispensation for marrying a nonbaptized person or a doubtfully-baptized person or a person baptized in another Christian Church. In such a marriage, the Catholic party promises to continue to practice the faith and to share that faith with his or her children. The partner must be aware of this promise, although the partner is not requested to sign any promises. Ordinarily, the Church freely grants such a dispensation once the promises are known and agreed to.

c. The names of those entering the Sacrament of Marriage are usually announced on three consecutive Sundays before the marriage takes place.

Three weeks before a marriage takes place, the names of the persons to enter marriage, as well as the parish in which they live, will be read in church or printed in the bulletin. The name for this announcement is *Banns of Marriage.* The purpose for reading the banns is to give people an opportunity to come forward if they know of any reason why the marriage should not take place, and also to announce to the Christian community that a marriage is to be celebrated. This is required only for the wedding of two Catholics, but is recommended for weddings where only one party is Catholic.

d. The Sacrament of Marriage should take place within the Eucharistic liturgy.

As with most of the sacraments, the appropriate place for the celebration of the Sacrament of Marriage is within the Eucharistic liturgy. The presbyter or minister, after the homily, will receive the marriage vows from the man and woman entering this sacrament. Although it is strongly urged that people share this sacrament within the Eucharistic liturgy, they may celebrate the sacrament at another time. Even in the case of a mixed-faith marriage, the Eucharistic liturgy may be celebrated.

7. Who is the minister of the Sacrament of Marriage?

a. The bride and the groom are the proper ministers of the Sacrament of Marriage.

In the Sacrament of Marriage, a baptized man and a baptized woman use their baptismal priesthood. They confer the sacrament upon each other. Because they have already celebrated the Sacrament of Baptism, they are able to celebrate this sacrament. If one of the parties has not celebrated the Sacrament of Baptism, the two people still enter a true marriage, but not a sacramental marriage. The marriage does not become sacramental until both parties have celebrated the Sacrament of Baptism. In this case, however, we still have a true and valid marriage.

b. Where one or both parties entering marriage are Catholic, they must exchange their marriage vows in the presence of an ordained minister of the Catholic Church.

Although the bride and groom are the proper ministers of the Sacrament of Marriage, Church law requires that an ordained minister, whether a bishop, presbyter, or deacon, ask for and receive the consent of the parties entering marriage if one is or both are Catholic. Two people who have not been baptized in the Catholic Church or who have not professed faith in the Catholic Church may validly marry before a minister or a state official who has the legal right to contract marriages.

c. A minister of another faith may be invited to participate in a marriage where only one party is Catholic.

With the permission of the bishop of the area and the consent of the appropriate authority of the minister of another Church, a minister may be invited to participate in a marriage where one party is not Catholic.

The minister may share in additional prayers or words of greeting. The ordained representative of the Catholic Church, that is, the ordained priest or deacon must accept, in the name of the Church, the vows of those entering marriage.

d. In exceptional cases, a dispensation may be granted for the minister of another faith to accept the vows of marriage in the name of the Church.

In some cases, a person of another faith may have a close relationship with a minister of the same faith. A dispensation may be received granting permission to a minister of another faith to act in the name of the Church in receiving the vows of those entering marriage. However, such a dispensation demands a special reason. In a case where a minister of another Church accepts the marriage vows, a Catholic priest may also take part by reading certain prayers, sharing blessings, or giving exhortations.

8. Why is sexual intimacy allowed only in marriage?

a. A result of sexual sharing is new life which is nourished most perfectly within the family.

One of the major purposes of marriage, as was mentioned earlier, is to share as a co-creator with God in bringing new life into the world. Through a special gift of God, a man and a woman are able to share in such a way that they conceive life. They must be open to the continuing care and development of this new life. The new life is most perfectly developed within the family which properly demands marriage and full commitment between a man and a woman. Through the Sacrament of Marriage, God shares special helps with a man and woman in the rearing of their children.

b. Sexual sharing is a high expression of mutual love and commitment between two people.

In God's plan, sexual sharing becomes a deep, loving communication between two people. In the introduction to this chapter, Marie noted how her parents communicated without words. They experienced each other's feelings and presence. In life, we communicate through words, actions, and even silence. When two people meet, they communicate their love to each other through sharing intimate details about their lives. Before the community, in the marriage ceremony, they communicate their trust and commitment to each other by the exchange of the marriage vows. In their sexual sharing, this communication should continue. True sexual sharing does not consist in one body sharing with another body, but rather one person communicating love and pleasure with another person.

When the angel in the infancy narrative told Mary that she was to conceive a son, Mary used an expression commonly used in that day to describe the sexual act. Mary's response was, that she did not *know* man. In the Scriptures, the expression *know* refers to sexual intimacy, and it carries with it the idea of communication. Even in our own day, we use an expression for sexual sharing that includes communication. We call sexual sharing *intercourse*. When two people share together sexually, it should include a deepening of their communication of trust and love with one another. Outside of marriage, the true meaning of sexual communication is lost and a full loving sexual sharing can never be achieved because two people lack the deepest form of communication, namely a lifelong commitment to one another.

c. Sexual sharing without full communication becomes destructive.

True sexual sharing is primarily directed toward giving and sharing. A continued sharing sexually, outside of a deep commitment, very often leads to a deep frustration. The act itself tends toward a deeper desire for communication and a desire to live and share together.

Love is so closely tied in with sexual sharing that a person who shares in the depth and commitment of marriage will often deepen in love toward his or her partner. On the other hand, sharing this act outside of marriage robs a person of a true ability to experience genuine love in this marriage act.

d. The Scriptures often speak of the dignity of sexual sharing in marriage.

Throughout the Old Testament, we find images in which God relates to the people of Israel as a husband to his wife. At times, the Israelites are like an adulterous wife. They turn to other gods; they prostitute themselves, and God punishes them for their unfaithfulness. In the New Testament, Christ continually points out that a person who shares sexually with another who is married commits adultery. He even says that a person who looks with lust on a woman commits adultery. In this way, Christ is telling us of the great dignity of sexual sharing within marriage. Paul writes to the Corinthians:

Do you not know that your bodies are members of Christ? Should I therefore take the members of Christ and make them members of a prostitute? Never! Do you not know that whoever is united to a prostitute becomes one body with her? For it is said, "The two shall be one flesh" (1 Corinthians 6:15–16).

In this writing, Paul proclaims that sexual sharing makes us one with our partner in this sexual act. If we share with a prostitute, we become one with the prostitute. If we share with another outside of marriage and outside of love, we become one with lust. Through a true sexual sharing in marriage, we become one in love with the person with whom we share as well as with God.

9. What sexual sins could a person commit?

a. When an unmarried man and an unmarried woman share sexually outside of marriage, they commit the sin called fornication.

Fornication occurs when a man and a woman, both unmarried, share sexually without the full, exclusive, lifelong commitment that comes through marriage. As with any great gift that comes from God, the gift of sexual sharing leads to certain responsibilities. It demands an exclusive, lifelong love that shares in all the joys and difficulties involved in married life. Sexual sharing is directed toward a deep expression of love and commitment to one another and the commitment to rearing children that flows from this expression of love. Through marriage, the couple commit themselves before God and the community to each other and their children. Fornication is sinful because it seeks sexual gratification without facing any of the responsibilities involved. Even if two people agree as "mature" adults to this mutual sexual sharing outside of marriage, they still "use" each other for their sexual gratification. It is using a great gift of God in a selfish and destructive way.

Where two people are planning to marry each other, they are still called to the ideal that flows from marriage, namely that a true, lifelong commitment does not take place until marriage itself. Engaged couples, deeply committed to each other, may break off their engagement with the right to commit themselves to another marriage. Although they see themselves as exclusively committed for life in their own eyes, engaged couples do not reach this stage until they have committed themselves to each other before God and the community through marriage. Otherwise, marriage would have no greater meaning than the engagement.

b. Adultery occurs when a married person shares sexually with another person who is not a spouse.

In the act of adultery, one or both parties may be married. When they are sharing sexually with a person other than their own husband or wife, they are breaking the commitment they made to their spouse before God, namely to not share in such an intimate, committed way with another. They have sinned against the exclusive nature of marriage and have sinned against God and their spouse. Adultery is often a sign that a marriage is in trouble. Not only does it destroy family life, but it also points to the fact that the family life has already started to break down. Some people show by adultery that they lack the maturity necessary for a fully committed marriage. If both parties in a marriage have faced the adultery, they should seek help in adjusting to "new beginnings" in correcting the problem. The very situation that led to adultery could still exist and must be faced for a long-lasting solution.

c. Masturbation consists in turning self-gratification in upon oneself.

Masturbation consists in giving sexual pleasure to oneself. In the past, every action of masturbation was considered sinful. Many hold the opinion today that some acts of masturbation do not have full consent of the will. In many cases, they become habits that are extremely difficult to overcome. Often masturbation becomes part of a growth process, a searching for sexual identity, that one may go through in adolescence. If it continues into later life, it should be a matter of concern, since it becomes a sign of sexual immaturity and perhaps a sign of escapism. People who have a habit of masturbation may not actually be committing sin. Simply to accept it, however, and not work against it in some way, would be to allow it to become a major weakness or sin in a person's life.

d. Homosexual orientation exists when a person's sexual desires tend toward a member of the same gender rather than a member of the other gender.

When the Scriptures speak against homosexuality, they often refer to a sin committed by people who could share sexually with a person of the other gender, but who choose to share sexually with a person of the same gender. Homosexuality, in itself, does not place a person in a condition of sin. There have been many insights into the question of homosexuality, and many attempts to understand it. In cases of morality, we ordinarily apply the same norms for a person with a homosexual orientation that would apply for sexual sharing between a man and a woman. Just as it is wrong for a man or woman not married to each other to share sexually, so it is wrong for a person to share sexually with a person of the same sex. Both of these cases are contrary to the nature and meaning of marriage.

Note: In all acts mentioned in this question (9), we must remember that we are speaking about actions that are contrary to the usual order of God's creation. We can never judge the degree of sinfulness of any person who performs any of these actions. The degree to which habit, psychological need, or life situation affects the freedom of the will should not be overlooked. People who continually find themselves unable to overcome any one of these actions should seek the guidance of an understanding confessor. The confessor will ordinarily suggest another type of counseling where he feels this is needed.

10. When is birth control permitted?

a. If a person does not have a serious reason for practicing birth control, that person should not practice birth control.

By birth control, we mean that the person controls the number of children the person will bring into the world. Some people would like to have an extra car in the garage or like to raise their standard of living by several levels beyond a level which is really necessary. In order to reach certain material success, they are willing to give up the idea of having children or to limit themselves to one child. In this case, birth control becomes sinful due to the selfish motive. Some sincerely feel in conscience that they cannot contribute to an overpopulation of the world. They may choose, for this reason, to limit the number of children. No one is allowed to practice birth control in marriage unless there is some good reason for choosing to control the number of children.

b. Natural birth control is allowed by the Church for special reasons.

In planning their family, parents may use natural means of birth control. A married woman shares sexually with her husband only on those days when she knows she ordinarily would not conceive. There are several methods of Natural Family Planning.

c. Parents should show a mature responsibility in planning and rearing their family.

The Catholic Church does not say that every parent should give birth to a child whenever the sexual act takes place. Often parents may decide how many children they can properly care for within their family. They consider their capability as well as their financial status and try to decide, to the best of their ability, the number of children they could reasonably rear. Having a large number of children is not necessarily the sign of a good Catholic family.

11. What are some forms of natural birth control?

a. One method, which does not seem to work for most, is known as the rhythm method.

This method involves charting the days between the menstrual periods. For most women, the time between periods is somewhere between twenty-eight and thirty-three days. Ovulation usually takes place fourteen days before menstruation. If a woman is consistent in the days between her period, she can determine when she and her husband can share sexually and when they must abstain. With this method, a couple must abstain a specific number of days before and after the estimated ovulation period. The problem with this method is that stress, sickness (even a cold), fatigue, change of diet, or any number of causes can change the cycle without the woman knowing it.

There are more effective natural methods which enable a couple to determine when the woman is most likely and least likely to conceive. The two most common methods which have proven effective are the Sympto-Thermal Method and the Ovulation Method, sometimes called the Billings Method. Training in these methods is held in many areas of the country, and a couple can ordinarily learn from the parish priest or from the Office for Family Life in the diocese where it will be held.

b. The Sympto-Thermal Method bases its program upon the changes in the woman's body around the time of ovulation.

A shift in the woman's basal temperature will take place shortly after ovulation. On the third day after this shift in the basal temperature, the infertile phase will begin. The method means a daily tracking of the woman's temperature throughout her cycle. Besides the shift in temperature, the method looks closely at certain symptoms which take place in the woman's body, for example, changes in the cervical mucus discharge, pain which identifies ovulation, and changes in the shape and texture of the cervix.

c. The Ovulation Method identifies the changes in the mucus discharge throughout the cycle, thus identifying the infertile, the less fertile, and the most fertile phases of a woman's cycle.

Right after her period, the woman will ordinarily enter a "dry phase," which means that she has no mucus discharge from the cervix. These are infertile days. This is followed by a mucus discharge which is at first sticky and cloudy, but which soon becomes clear, slippery, and able to be stretched without breaking. The final day of this last situation is called the peak, and ovulation usually occurs one day after the peak. In this method, the fertile period is determined to last from the beginning of the mucus discharge until the end of the third day after the peak. The woman is then considered infertile from the fourth day after the peak to the beginning of her next menstrual period.

d. Besides being helpful to families at a period when they do not wish to conceive a child, the Sympto-Thermal Method and the Ovulation Method are also helpful to families who wish to have children.

By knowing when the woman is most likely to conceive, a couple can share sexually at that time with a greater hope of conception taking place. The methods are not strictly birth control methods, as they are also methods of learning and understanding the woman's body. Whether or not a couple wishes to conceive a child at a designated time, the understanding of the gift and workings of one's body offer us a greater insight into God's creation.

e. The use of Natural Family Planning demands sacrifice on the part of the couple.

There will be certain phases during the cycle which will not allow for sexual sharing if the couple wish to avoid the conception of a child. The ability to make such a decision and abstain at will is a human and mature decision. Because marriage belongs only to the human family, it naturally requires sacrifice and dedication. Both spouses should enter the training for the use of any of these methods, since both will be making the decision. The woman should not be the only one who keeps track of the days when the couple may or may not share sexually. The value of using one of these methods lies in its avoidance of possible dangers from taking pills or placing objects within the body.

Some confuse the Sympto-Thermal Method and the Ovulation Method with the rhythm method. These are not other forms of the same method, but are scientifically studied and researched methods of natural family planning which have proved at least as effective as the pill in controlling birth. The methods simply learn about the body God gave women, and they call upon the love God gave to the husband and wife joined together in marriage.

12. When is birth control not allowed?

a. Church authority has often taught that artificial or contraceptive birth control is contrary to God's law.

By artificial or contraceptive birth control, we refer to pills or devices used to interfere with the conception of a child. Marriage is directed toward the giving birth and rearing of the child as well as toward the mutual love between the husband and wife. In the eyes of the authority of the Church, anything that interferes with either of these in an artificial way is contrary to the idea of marriage as found within our very nature. The use of artificial or contraceptive birth control methods brings about a direct interference in the conception of a child. By nature, a woman passes through periods when she cannot conceive. To set up situations where the woman is continually, or for a time, not able to conceive a child, or to make use of devices that hinder the possibilities of fertilization are seen to act beyond this law within the nature of the human act of marriage. In 1968, Pope Paul VI wrote a special letter to the entire world that affirmed the view that artificial birth control is contrary to the teaching of the Catholic Church.

b. Those in authority in the Church must continually call its members to the ideal of living a full, Christian life.

Like Christ, Church authority must present nothing less than the ideal. Pope Paul VI called the world to the Christian ideal of peace when he proclaimed before the United Nations, "No war! Never again!" Pope Pius XII, during the Second World War, also recognized the call to the Christian ideal of peace. But for situations when the ideal was not reached, he established certain norms for a "just war." Regarding artificial contraception, Church authority again calls all Christians to the ideal. Church authority is also conscious of the problem. In a document from the Second Vatican Council, we read:

> The Council realizes that married people are often hindered by certain situations in modern life from working out their married love harmoniously, and they can sometimes find themselves in a position where the number of children cannot be increased, at least for the time being. . . ("The Church in the Modern World," number 51).

Although the document goes on to state that only those means approved by Church authority may be used, it recognizes the high degree of virtue demanded in rejection of the artificial means of birth control.

> . . . in cases like these it is quite difficult to preserve the practice of faithful love and complete intimacy of their lives. But where the intimacy of married life is broken, it often happens that faithfulness is imperiled and the good of children suffers: then the education of children as well as the courage to accept more children are both endangered ("The Church in the Modern World," number 51).

The problem is well stated in this document.

Bishops' conferences throughout the world accepted the teaching of Pope Paul VI, but they reminded us that we could never judge the conscience of couples practicing artificial birth control. The judgment of conscience exists between the penitent and the confessor. Along with the pope, bishops' conferences have been unanimous in inviting those who find themselves in this situation to make continual use of the strength which comes from the sacraments.

c. Direct abortion is never allowed and is always sinful.

Abortion is the direct killing of a fetus or embryo, or causing the occasion that would bring about this death. To kill the fetus or embryo while it is in the womb or to cause an ejection of such before it is able to live outside the womb is abortion. This also includes pills or devices used to keep a fertilized egg from implanting in the womb. The Catholic Church considers life to be present from the moment of conception. Any act which directly kills the embryo or fetus is considered a violation of a person's right to life. As Christians, we have the obligation to speak out in the name of the unborn, since they do not have the voice to speak out for themselves. If we remained silent, these lives would continue to be quietly destroyed with no dissenting voice to defend their right to life.

d. Indirect abortion may be permitted.

A woman who discovers after becoming pregnant that she has a cancerous womb may have that womb removed, even though it will lead to the death of the embryo or fetus. The intention behind the removal of the womb is the saving of the life of the mother. Through this operation, the embryo or fetus will die, but this is not the intent of the operation. An indirect abortion occurs when the primary intent of any action is to save the life of the mother. This primary intent cannot consist in directly killing the fetus or embryo.

13. What obligations do parents have toward their children?

a. Parents have the obligation of rearing children in the Catholic faith.

Whenever we have something good to share, we wish to share it with those we love. A person who shares in all the gifts of the Catholic Church should desire to share these gifts with those close to them, most especially members of their own family. At the baptism of the child, the parents accepted the responsibility of rearing their child in the practice of the faith. Through the Sacrament of Marriage, the family is joined together by God for the sake of helping each member grow closer to God. The parents, by their life and example, are expected to teach the child as the child grows toward maturity. The parents will also share in preparing the child for the sacraments throughout the child's early life.

b. Parents must show love and respect for their children.

A child does not become the possession of a parent. A parent has the privilege of sharing life with the child and guiding that child in life. However, once that child is born, the child is an individual who depends very much upon the parents. As a child grows, the parents should share with the child all that is needed for a healthy growth through life. The parents should be open, at a certain point in life, to allow that child to walk freely when the child has reached a mature age.

c. Parents should show children the dignity of family life.

A child learns not just by being told things, but by the way he or she sees the parents act. Parents, who show love and respect for one another and who show love and respect toward the child, will fill that child with a loving formation in family life. Parents shall share time with each other and time with their children that all may be able to grow in deeper love and respect for one another.

Conclusion

After some years, Marie's father died, and her mother moved into a small apartment a few doors down from Marie's house. When Marie visits her, she tells Marie to cherish her husband and give time to her children. Marie sometimes resents the fact that her mother treats her like a child who needs directions about loving her husband and rearing her children. But then Marie remembers that her parents were really successful parents. They never had the riches that built new homes or bought new cars, but they had love. Their marriage was a true success. They had their tragedies, their doubts, their fights, and their joys. And through it all, they always had each other.

For Scripture reflection and discussion concerning this chapter, see Journeying in His Light, "Marriage and the Family."

14 Sacrament of Service in the Community: Holy Orders

Introduction

Father Damian came to Hawaii in 1864 to work in the missionary fields. By 1873, he had heard about the leper colony at Molokai that lacked any type of medical or spiritual help. Knowing that he might never again be accepted among the "normal" people of the Islands, Father Damian still volunteered to go to this colony. Leprosy was the dreaded disease that condemned people to a slow death on the island of Molokai, away from their families and friends. Father Damian brought the joy of Christ into those drab lives. He began by cleaning up the church building and painting some of its walls with bright paints. The dark colony soon came back to life under the enthusiasm of Father Damian. Father Damian took care of their spiritual and physical needs and brought to that colony a glimmer of hope. In the spirit of Christ's service to his people, Father Damian saw his life as one of continual service to the people of Molokai. He served the lepers for fifteen years and suffered with leprosy for the last three years of his life. He saw his disease as a gift from God. Not only did he serve the people, he now shared in their suffering. He had become one of them, a castaway leper on the colony of Molokai.

1. What is the ordained ministry?

a. The ordained ministry refers to bishops, presbyters, and deacons.

Through our baptism, we become a priestly people with a special call and power directed toward worship. This is a share in the priesthood of Jesus Christ and is known as *the priesthood of the faithful.* Through our gifts of priesthood, we worship God the Father "in . . . with . . . and through . . ." Christ, and in this way share in the highest form of worship.

There exists another participation in the life of Christ which comes through the Sacrament of Holy Orders and is known as "the ministerial priesthood." Those who share in this ministerial priesthood through ordination receive a sacred power and vocation to serve the faithful. The ordained ministry includes bishops, presbyters (ordained priests), and deacons. Since we are all priests through our baptism, a more exact term for the ordained priest would be *presbyter.* In the early Church, the ordained minister was not called a *priest,* but rather a *presbyter.*

b. The ordained ministry is a special call to the service of the word of God.

Ordained ministers are especially called to share Christ's message with all people. In order to share fully in his call to ministry, they should have an in-depth knowledge of the word of God and should be able to communicate that word in as clear and understandable a way as possible. Through their writing, preaching, and living, the ordained ministers should reflect the word of God in such a way that others will see in them a living reflection of this word of God.

c. The ordained ministry is a special call to the service of worship and celebration.

The ordained minister receives special gifts to share the sacraments given through Christ's resurrection. In the name of the Church, the ordained minister confers certain sacraments upon other members of the Church. He invites them into the community and shares with them the gifts of the community. The ordained minister calls the assembly to worship and leads the assembly in worshiping God the Father in the name of Christ.

d. The ordained ministry is a special call to the service of leadership.

Jesus came as a servant king. The reign he preached is far different from any earthly reign. The way to this reign is a way of service. The ordained minister is called to lead the way, but to lead the way as a servant to the people. The ordained minister is called to leadership within the community, but this leadership flows out of service and shows itself most perfectly in service to members of the community. Christ gave an example of this service when he washed the apostles' feet at the Last Supper. After Jesus washed the feet of the disciples, he told them, "Do you know what I have done to you? You call me Teacher and Lord—and you are right, for that is what I am. So if I, your Lord and Teacher, have washed your feet, you also ought to wash one another's feet. For I have set you an example, that you also should do as I have done to you. Very truly, I tell you, servants are not greater than their master, nor are messengers greater than the one who sent them. If you know these things, you are blessed if you do them" (John 13:12–17).

e. The ordained ministry is a special call to service through consecration to God.

A person enters the ordained ministry through a sacrament called *Holy Orders*. It is a special commitment and consecration by which the ordained minister is dedicated to minister with the people of God. The ordained priest lives a life which is set aside for the service of God to the community. This does not mean that they they live apart from others or have a life outside the everyday concerns of others, but they live a life totally dedicated to the work of the Church. As ministers of Christ, they must, as Christ did, share and witness to a life beyond this life on earth. They are not necessarily holier than others, nor free from weakness, but they represent in a visible manner the living presence of Christ in the Church. The presbyter is the public Church person.

f. Those ordained as presbyters in the Roman Western Rite ordinarily embrace celibacy and profess their intention of remaining celibate for the love of God's reign and the service of all people.

Celibacy in the Roman Western Rite means that presbyters bind themselves not to marry. The reason for celibacy in the ordained priesthood rests in the presbyterial commitment to dedicate one's life to the reign of God. It becomes a radical sign of a presbyter's dedication to service in the name and person of Christ, one which sacrifices the basic right to marry for the sake of serving the mission of Christ. Some see in celibacy the freedom necessary for dedicating oneself to a total service of others.

Celibacy is not essential for the presbyterate, but is Church law. The practice of celibacy began around the fourth century and became the law for the entire Western Church around the twelfth century. Because celibacy is Church law, the Church may dispense from this law. This has been done, for instance, in cases where a married minister of another denomination (such as the Episcopal Church) joins the Catholic Church and seeks, after a period of preparation, to become an ordained priest in the Catholic Church.

2. What are the different orders of ordained ministry?

a. One of the ordained ministries is the order of bishop.

A bishop shares in the fullness of the Sacrament of Holy Orders. Through this sacrament, the bishop becomes a member of the collegial college of bishops throughout the world and often heads a diocese. As one who shares in the apostolic office, the bishop shares in the mission of the total Church, under the authority of the pope. A bishop acts with certain powers or charisms which other ordained ministers do not share. Only a bishop may administer the Sacrament of Holy Orders and is the ordinary minister for the Sacrament of

Confirmation. Bishops share in the office of teaching, sanctifying, and governing the Church community.

b. Another ordained ministry is the order of presbyter (ordained priest).

With the bishop, the presbyter shares the duties of proclaiming the gospel, shepherding the faithful, and celebrating the Eucharist and other sacraments. A presbyter does not share in the power of conferring the Sacrament of Holy Orders. Presbyters are co-workers with the bishop, working in communion with and in obedience to the bishop. They form with the bishop a unified group called the *presbyterium*, ministering with the bishop in a particular area or diocese. Presbyters receive the charge of a parish community or a specific office in the local Church from the bishop. A presbyter belongs to a group (or order) of presbyters throughout the world, but more especially to the order of presbyters in the diocese under the bishop. As a sign of this unity, the presbyters impose hands after the bishop on the newly ordained during the ordination ceremony.

c. Another ordained ministry is the order of deacon.

With his ordination, the deacon receives the privilege of celebrating certain sacraments and sacramentals in the name of the Church. The deacon may baptize, preach, witness marriages, assist at funerals, and preside in the name of the Church at certain ceremonies. A deacon does not preside at the Eucharistic liturgy, nor does he have the power to forgive sins. In the early centuries, the order of deacon shared many varied activities, ranging from liturgical roles to leadership roles within the community.

3. What is the difference between a transitory and a permanent deacon?

a. A person who has been ordained a deacon and intends to move on to the ministry of presbyter is commonly called a transitory deacon.

The title, *transitory deacon,* is an unfortunate title for a deacon who wishes to be ordained a presbyter. When a person moves from one order to the next, the person does not erase the previous ordination. Even though they become presbyters, the order of deacon still remains with those ordained to this order. Each order, once conferred, is permanent. The term *transitory* became necessary to distinguish such a person from a *permanent deacon,* which is another unfortunate title.

b. A person who is ordained to the diaconate with no intention of going on to the ministry of presbyter is commonly called a permanent deacon.

All deacons, whether wishing to go on to the order of presbyter or not, are actually permanent deacons. When speaking of *permanent deacons* today, we are speaking of those who intend to serve in the ministry of ordained deacon with no intention of becoming presbyters. This office in the Church as a special and lifelong ministry was found in the early Church and has been revived in our present day. The permanent diaconate includes people of mature age, married as well as single, who have a particular work or profession in addition to serving as deacon. Through the Church, they share in the special charism of their ordination and reflect the presence of the Church in the world. They share all the duties of deacons as mentioned in the previous question.

4. How did the ordained ministry develop?

a. In the Old Testament, a priest was a mediator between God and the people of God.

In the Old Testament, we do not find an ordained ministry. We read that God set aside the family of Levi as the family of priests in ancient Israel. All the males born into this family would serve the rest of the tribes of Israel as their priests. Their function would be to offer to God in the name of the people the gifts and sacrifices the people of God brought before the altar. They would often receive the gifts from the people and offer them to God in the name of God's people. In this way, the priests functioned as mediators between God and the people.

b. The New Testament does not use the term **priest** to refer to anyone who holds a particular office or ministry within the Church.

When the New Testament applies the term *priest* to a single individual, it refers only to Christ. In the New Testament Letter to the Hebrews, we read, "You are a priest forever according to the order of Melchizedek" (Hebrews 7:17). The letter views Christ not only as an eternal priest, but an eternal High Priest, whose offering is his very own person. The author of the letter tells us, "For it was fitting that we should have such a high priest, holy, blameless, undefiled, separated from sinners, and exalted above the heavens. Unlike other high priests, he has no need to offer sacrifices day after day, first for his own sins, and then for those of the people; this he did once for all when he offered himself" (Hebrews 7:26–27).

c. When the New Testament refers to priests, other than Christ, it points to a particular group of people and not to individuals.

When speaking of the People of God, the author of the First Letter of Peter writes, "But you are a chosen race, a royal priesthood, a holy nation, God's own people" (1 Peter 2:9). The Book of Revelation also points to a group of people rather than a single individual as priests when the author writes, ". . . you have made them to be a kingdom and priests serving our God" (Revelation 5:10). According to the New Testament, there is only one priest, Jesus Christ. The faithful and the ordained faithful share in this one priesthood of Jesus Christ in a different way.

d. The New Testament portrays the apostles as the first chosen or ordained ministers of the Church.

Although the New Testament does not specifically use the term *ordination*, it does speak of specific ministers chosen by Jesus.

The apostles were the first chosen (ordained) ministers of the early Church. They served in the name of Christ by bringing Christ's blessings to the people and joining with the people in worshiping God the Father. They really showed no specific sign of acting in the same sense as priests in the Old Testament. They did not take the people's offering and place it before God. Rather, they preached the message of Jesus and they shared the gifts that Jesus shared with them.

e. By the end of the first century, there was a structure of orders in the Church.

By the end of the first century, we see bishops as separate from presbyters and presbyters as separate from deacons. Apparently, in the early Church, only bishops made up the ordained ministry. The eventual need to share some of their powers led to the establishment of the orders of presbyter and deacon. Through the imposition of hands and praying of a specified prayer, the bishop shared with others some of the powers of his office. After the first century, the distinction between bishop, presbyter, and deacon became more clearly defined and separated. The structure we know today developed through centuries of living and reflecting on the gifts of Christ to his apostles and to his Church.

5. How is the liturgy of the ordination of presbyter celebrated?

a. *The Sacrament of Holy Orders should take place within the context of the Eucharistic celebration.*

The Eucharist is the source of the ordained ministry as well as the aim of the ordained ministry. Ordination should take place before the community because the ordained minister is a person called forth from the community to serve the community.

b. *A person is called to a special ministry by the bishop.*

In the ceremony, the candidate for ordination is called by name by the deacon of the Eucharistic liturgy. The deacon calls out, "Let those who are to be ordained come forward." As each name is called, the person responds, "I am ready and willing." The bishop then asks if they are worthy, and a presbyter answers in their name, "I testify that upon inquiry among the people of God and upon recommendation of those concerned with their training, they have been found worthy." The bishop then responds, "We rely on the help of the Lord God and our Savior, Jesus Christ, and we choose our brothers here present for the office of presbyter." At this point, the people as a group share their approval either by applause or by responding together, "Thanks be to God," or both.

c. *The bishop then questions the candidates who are to be ordained.*

The bishop asks the candidates if they are willing to share with the bishop in caring for the Lord's flock. He asks if they are willing to share and celebrate the sacred mysteries, if they are resolved to preach the word worthily and with wisdom, and finally if they are willing to consecrate their lives to the salvation of all people. To each of these questions the candidates respond, "I am."

d. At this point in the ceremony, the candidates promise obedience to the bishop.

The bishop asks if they are willing to be obedient to their Ordinary (bishop). The candidates respond, "I am." The bishop then prays that God who began the good work in these candidates may bring it to fulfillment.

e. Ordination takes place when the bishop and presbyters lay hands on the head of the candidates, and the bishop prays a special prayer for ordination.

The bishop puts both hands on the head of each of the candidates in turn. Then all presbyters present impose hands on the heads of the candidates. After this, the bishop prays for God's help in this ceremony. In his prayer, he recalls God's special gifts to the people of the Old Testament, especially in the priesthood of Levi. He prays that God grant the dignity of presbyter to these candidates who, in turn, join with other ordained ministers in sharing Christ's message.

f. The bishop now brings the newly ordained into the community of presbyters by symbolic actions.

The newly ordained now receive the presbyter's garments for Eucharistic celebration. Their hands are anointed, and they are presented with a chalice in which wine and water have been poured and a paten on which rests bread to be consecrated. The bishop and all presbyters present give a sign of peace that symbolizes a welcome into the order of presbyter. As the liturgy continues, the newly ordained, along with the bishop, celebrate the Eucharist.

6. What are religious?

a. Religious are people who consecrate themselves to God by vows, or promises, of poverty, chastity, and obedience.

Christ proclaimed that the reign of God was here among us. Accepting this reality of Christ's presence in the world and Christ's wish to share this reign, men and women dedicate themselves, through special vows, to living out and sharing this presence of Christ's reign. They become a living sign of this reign on earth, while at the same time reminding us that the full experience of this reign is yet to come. With love of God, and with a living hope that love and service will reach fulfillment in the eternal reign of God, religious accept a life of service to all people.

By the vow of poverty, religious commit themselves before God to share in common their material possessions. The purpose behind the vow is to free them of all attachment to riches of this world and to remind them of the one great possession, Jesus Christ. By the vow of chastity, religious forego the right to marry so they may more readily show the world the continual presence of Christ and the willingness to belong to all who call upon them for the sake of the gospel. By obedience, religious offer themselves to the service of the Christian community. They commit themselves to serve the Church as this call comes to them through their community. Through these vows, religious commit their lives to God and to a specific way of living out their baptismal vows.

b. A religious is a person who ordinarily lives a common life within a religious community.

In vowing poverty, chastity, and obedience, the religious seeks to live in community with others. The vows enable the person to live this life more fully. A religious community ordinarily is founded for a specific work which may change as times and needs change. Today many different communities with a variety of ministries serve in the name of the Church.

c. A nun or a sister is a woman who belongs to a particular religious community.

A woman who commits herself to God by the vows of poverty, chastity, and obedience is commonly referred to as a *sister* or a *nun*. Sisters and nuns live together in community and share in common life. They may be called to teaching, social work, hospital work, work in the mission field, coordination of religious education programs, or pastoral ministry in a parish. Or they may be called to the contemplative life, to a life of prayer for all people. Sisters and nuns have responded to the many needs in the Church today.

d. A brother is a man who lives the religious life.

A man who vows poverty, chastity, and obedience and who consecrates himself to God through a specific community is referred to as a *brother*. Brothers also engage in various activities and ministries within the Church. They may serve as teachers, hospital assistants, administrators, and religious educators, or in other ministries to which they are called.

7. Do presbyters belong to religious communities?

a. Some presbyters belong to religious communities.

When a presbyter vows poverty, chastity, and obedience in a certain community, we refer to that person as an ordained *religious priest*. Communities of presbyters in the Church usually have a specific function or mission as a community. One community may be dedicated to teaching, while other communities may be dedicated to preaching or serving in mission fields. The presbyters who belong to these communities are usually assigned by the superior of their religious community. For pastoral appointments, recommendations are made to the bishop by the superior, and the bishop officially makes the appointment in his diocese.

b. A presbyter who serves in a particular diocese with a promise of obedience to the ordinary of that diocese is referred to as an ordained dioc-esan priest.

At the time of his ordination, a presbyter promises obedience to the Ordinary of the diocese and to his successors. The ordained diocesan priest usually serves in one diocese and accepts various appointments within that diocese. He does not belong to a religious community, and he is responsible for his own welfare.

Usually presbyters of the Latin Rite, whether religious or diocesan, do not marry. The law that forbids marriage for presbyters in the Western Church became a law of the Western Church around the twelfth century. Before that time, presbyters were permitted to marry.

Conclusion

Father Damian had accepted the ministry to the lepers, and, as a true presbyter of the Catholic Church, he led the people to Christ by service. He brought the word of God to these people, but he also brought the compassion of Christ into his work. He could look to Christ who became like us and rejoice because he became like the people he served. Through his life, Father Damian showed the world what the ordained ministry involved. He shared in a sacred privilege, and he used that sacred privilege to show us an image of Jesus Christ who came in service to all people. In the exaltation of Jesus, we look back into his life and see what his exaltation cost. Jesus became one with us, the Word became flesh who shared in our humanness. Father Damian, like Christ, found his exaltation in becoming one with those he served. Because he served so well, most remember him as Damian the Leper. *In both cases, these titles tell of their exaltation.*

For Scripture reflection and discussion concerning this chapter, see **Journeying in His Light, "A Ministry of Service."**

15 Death to Life

Introduction

When the doctor told Phil he was going to die, Phil scoffed at the doctor's appraisal of his health. He felt fine. A little more tired than usual, but still fine! As Phil lay in the hospital bed feeling more fatigued and frightened each new day, he became angry. Why should all those older people live when he had to die at such a young age? He had so much to give yet. Why not one of those people who spent their time begging food and drinking all day? He was not yet forty, and already he was dying. On another day, his anger turned to bargaining. He prayed, "God, if You give me a little more time, You won't believe how good I'll be. I'll go to church every day!" One day, Phil told his wife to leave him alone. He had fallen into a deep depression. His favorite television program, his new car, his daughter visiting from over two hundred miles away, and his wife who sat patiently day by day at his bedside—none of these seemed important to him. Finally, one day, Phil woke up and told his wife without emotion, "I'm ready." She tried to tell him that he would soon be up and around, but he shook his head and repeated, "I'm ready." Phil died peacefully a few weeks later.

A woman psychiatrist by the name of Dr. Elisabeth Kübler-Ross has studied the process of dying and has discovered stages that resembled Phil's process very closely. The dying patient goes through five steps. The first step is denial, where the patient objects, "No. Not me! Not yet!" The second step is rage and anger: "Why me?" The third step is bargaining: "A little longer, and I will really be good." The fourth step is depression: "don't bother me!" The fifth step is acceptance: "It's all right. I'm ready."

For many people, especially those who have no belief in life hereafter, death is the frightening moment that should be avoided as long as possible. This chapter looks to the hope that Christ's message gives us concerning death and beyond. For a Christian, death does not end life, but brings life to a fuller awareness of love and eternal fulfillment.

1. What is the Christian belief about death?

a. A Christian believes that there is eternal life after death.

Christians do not see death as the end of life, but rather as the beginning of a **new** life. The new life will be a different type of life and will last forever. Paul expresses it this way: "For we know that if the earthly tent we live in is destroyed, we have a building from God, a house not made with hands, eternal in the heavens" (2 Corinthians 5:1). At the point of our passing from this life into eternal life, we will face God and receive the reward or punishment flowing from the way we have lived our life. The Letter to the Corinthians continues, "For all of us must appear before the judgment seat of Christ, so that each may receive recompense for what has been done in the body, whether good or evil" (2 Corinthians 5:10).

b. Christ shares with all Christians a hope for a new life.

In the discourses in the Gospel of John, Jesus tells his disciples that he is going to prepare a place for them. All Christians should see in these words of Christ a message that extends beyond the apostles to every person:

"Do not let your hearts be troubled. Believe in God, believe also in me. In my Father's house there are many dwelling places. If it were not so, would I have told you that I go to prepare a place for you? And if I go and prepare a place for you, I will come again and will take you to myself, so that where I am, there you may be also" (John 14:1–3).

Throughout his life, Jesus told parables, stories, concerning a continual life hereafter. He tells of a rich man who would not share his food with a poor man. The poor man enters eternal happiness along with Abraham, Isaac, and all the prophets. The rich man lives a life of eternal pain. The Scriptures tell us that in the resurrection of Jesus Christ, we receive a new dawn, a new hope in his resurrection. Until the coming of Christ, people wondered about the idea of life hereafter. Through his death and resurrection, Christ showed us a glory that he will share with all of us.

c. Faith in the resurrection does not take away our need to grieve.

Although we accept in faith the idea that the deceased are now living in Christ and are born into eternal life, we still experience human grief. We should accept our human condition and realize that we feel lonely, lost, and deeply saddened when someone close to us dies. Grieving is a necessary and healthy aspect of our human condition. Through grieving, we too pass through the stages of accepting death, in this case, the death of someone close to us. In time, we learn to turn our grief into fond memories. A tinge of sadness will return now and then, but God has given us an ability to get on with life. Grief, accepted maturely, will gradually give way to a life continually open to new joys and new tragedies. Instead of a "piece of ourselves" dying with someone, a "piece of that person" will live on through us. The faith that leads to a hope for resurrection for all of us should serve as a source of strength through moments of grief in life.

In the Gospel of John, we read the story about Jesus raising Lazarus from the dead. Jesus had already proclaimed to Martha that anyone who believed in him would never die spiritually, although the person would die in the view of the world. Despite this belief, the sadness of the loss of Lazarus overcomes Jesus, and the Gospel tells us, "When Jesus saw her weeping, and the Jews who came with her also weeping, he was greatly disturbed in spirit and deeply moved. . . . Jesus began to weep. So the Jews said, 'See how he loved him!' " (John 11:33, 35–36). Some interpreters would claim that the weeping of Jesus showed how closely he followed the Father's will. They see the event as one which portrays Jesus as not yet certain that the Father would allow him to raise Lazarus from the dead. Like the rest of us who lose close relatives and friends in life, Jesus grieved for the loss of his friend Lazarus.

d. At the moment of passage from this life to the next, our time for gaining or losing merit has ended.

At the moment of our death, we stand before God as we truly are. We can no longer gain merit, nor can we lose the merit we have. At this moment, our whole attitude of mind suddenly brings us into a direct confrontation with God. We experience the great loving presence of God and judge our own worthiness or unworthiness of entering God's presence. God need not judge us because we judge ourselves. At this moment, we see ourselves as we truly are and realize most fully the goodness and love of God. We proclaim ourselves worthy or unworthy of this love as we look into our own attitude toward God. In the Gospel of John, we read the words the author attributes to Jesus, "I do not judge anyone who hears my words and does not keep them, for I came not to judge the world, but to save the world. The one who rejects me and does not receive my word has a judge; on the last day the word that I have spoken will serve as judge" (John 12:47–48).

2. What is the Catholic teaching concerning the taking of life?

a. Catholics, along with all those who profess faith in God, believe that God is the master of all life.

Since God is the creator and author of all life, God alone is the master of all life. Our human life, created in the image and likeness of God, is sacred, and, as such, shares in a special relationship with God. The fifth commandment forbids killing, since no one can claim the mastery over life necessary to directly destroy innocent life. The Catholic Church applies this law against killing to the totality of human life, **from the womb to the tomb,** that is, from conception to the point of a person's natural death. We live as stewards, not owners of our lives.

b. Occasions exist when a person has a right to legitimate defense.

Despite the general prohibition against life, situations exist when a person may kill an unjust aggressor in order to defend his or her life. In such an act, known as *self-defense,* the reason for killing another person is not the desire to kill, but the desire to defend one's own life against an unjust aggressor. This right to act in self-defense respects the basic idea of a person's right to life and true love for oneself.

Legitimate defense is not an exception to the prohibition against murder since it differs from murder, which has as its intention the killing of an innocent person. At times, legitimate defense can become an obligation when a person bears responsibility for the life of another or for the common good of the family or society. Such obligation could include a parent defending the life of a child, a nation protecting itself against an unjust aggressor, or a government protecting its citizens.

c. Governments have the right to impose penalties on unjust aggressors for the preservation of public order and the safety of others.

The purpose of punishment is for correction, not for punishment alone. It seeks the preservation of public order and the safety of others. In committing a crime, the aggressor forfeits his or her right to be treated as an innocent person. Legitimate public authority has the right to bestow a penalty that is just and balanced according to the gravity of the crime. In cases of extreme gravity, such as murder, legitimate authority may prescribe the death penalty, commonly known as *capital punishment.* If legitimate authority, however, judges that it can defend human life against an aggressor and protect the public order and safety without the taking of life, then such author- ity should avoid the taking of life. In doing this, public authority recognizes the dignity of every human person while fulfilling its role in protecting the common good.

A problem arises when public authority administers capital pun- ishment unevenly. In cases where minorities or the poor are more likely to receive the death penalty than those of the majority or wealthy class who have committed similar crimes, then public authority must correct these inequalities. Because of the gravity of capital punishment, justice demands that it be abolished if it is not distributed evenly.

d. No one has the moral right to commit suicide, that is, to take one's own life.

Only God has the right to end our earthly life. The natural end of life takes place through the process of aging, sickness, disease, accidental death, or some other situation that results in death. Meanwhile, we are stewards, not owners, of our own lives and have the duty to preserve and nourish all human life, including our own. Suicide is a rejection of God, because it is a rejection of God's gift of life. It often leaves survivors with feelings of guilt, anger, overwhelming grief, and confusion, and it often discourages them in their own task of living.

We should not immediately conclude that, when a person commits suicide, the person has condemned himself or herself to hell for all eternity. Suicide often results from grave psychological problems, or from some physical or mental distress that greatly reduce a person's ability to judge and choose properly. Although a person may appear to have chosen suicide with a clear and calm mind, it does not mean that the person is acting with a clear understanding of his or her situation before God and others. Because of this, the Church does not deny Christian burial for the person who has committed suicide.

e. Assisted-suicide and euthanasia are against the law of God.

Anyone who assists in suicide shares in the sin of suicide. *Physician-assisted suicides* exist where a physician provides a medical means for an apparently dignified and comfortable death for the suffering person. In this case, the suicide not only involves the person committing suicide, but also the physician or another person assisting in any way in the action. Even if a dying person requests help in committing suicide, an assisting physician, friend, or relative does not have a right to take from God the mastery over that person's life, even with that person's permission and encouragement.

Euthanasia is the direct killing of a sick or incapacitated person for the sake of ending the suffering of that person. A common term used for euthanasia is *mercy killing,* since it often arises out of compassion for the suffering of the sick or incapacitated person. Despite the good intentions of the person performing euthanasia, it still consists in a person taking to himself or herself a mastery over life which belongs to God alone, and for this reason is sinful.

f. It is morally acceptable to discontinue procedures considered extraordinary or disproportionate to the outcome of saving one's life.

In a case where medical procedures to prolong a person's life become burdensome, dangerous, disproportionate, or extraordinary, a patient, or one legally entitled to act for the patient, has the right to decide to refuse such treatment. The motive is not to cause the death of the patient, but to accept one's inability to impede death by prolonging life. This is not euthanasia or assisted suicide, but the act of allowing nature to follow its normal process in bringing about death.

The proximity of death does not relieve those attending the dying person from the ordinary care needed for comforting and supporting the patient in the process of dying. The use of painkillers to relieve the suffering of the dying person is permitted, even at the risk of shortening one's life.

g. Human beings have the right to kill animals for food or for some other good reason.

Animals, as creatures of God, give glory to God by their very existence. We read in the second story of creation in the Book of Genesis that God gives human beings dominion over animals. The author imparts this message by having Adam name the animals. The author of the Bible story believed that the ability to name something gave a person power over it. From this reading, we learn of the respect owed to animals as part of God's creation, and the role of animals in the life of human beings.

God entrusted animals to the stewardship of human beings, which gives us the right to use animals for food, clothing, work, companionship, and for reasonable medical and scientific experimentation.

These scientific experiments, however, must contribute to the care and saving of human life and must be performed with as little pain as possible for the animal. Where the number of animals could lead to abuse or to the lack of natural nutrition necessary to sustain the species, the hunting or killing of some of those animals may take place. The torturing or unnecessary killing of animals is contrary to human dignity and is sinful.

3. What is heaven?

a. Heaven is a full and perfect sharing in God's loving presence for all eternity.

When we attain heaven, we experience the great joy and happiness of being in God's presence and sharing fully and perfectly in God's love. The love we feel for any other person here on earth is only a shadow of the love that we will feel for God at the moment of our death. The happiness of heaven can never be expressed in words. Speaking of the glory of heaven, Paul writes, "What no eye has seen, nor ear heard, nor the human heart conceived, what God has prepared for those who love him" (1 Corinthians 2:9).

b. In heaven, the struggles and pains of life will cease.

Throughout life, we live through moments of sorrow, as for example when we lose those close to us. We experience pain, frustration, discouragement, and we continually struggle against temptations that seek to allure us from the main goal of our life. Once we reach heaven, all these sorrows and struggles cease to exist. We experience God's love, and that love so overwhelms us that all sorrow, suffering, and temptation can no longer touch us. In the Book of Revelation in the New Testament, we read about the new, heavenly Jerusalem. The author tells us that a voice from the heavens cries out:

See, the home of God is among mortals. He will dwell with them as their God; they will be his people, and God himself will be with them; he will wipe every tear from their eyes. Death will be no more; mourning and crying and pain will be no more, for the first things have passed away (Revelation 21:3–4).

c. Heaven is not a place, but rather a state of existence.

We build homes on a certain parcel of land. We look and live and walk in time and space. Our whole universe is a place. When we speak of heaven, however, we speak of eternal happiness in God's presence. It is a deep experience of the overwhelming presence of God, yet a presence which does not exist in a place, but really outside of place. What this state of existence really encompasses cannot be understood with the human mind. In this state of existence, we are somehow capable of loving God deeply and experiencing God's love for us. We are capable of knowing one another completely and of sharing together the great joy of eternal happiness.

4. What is hell?

a. Hell is a state of eternal rejection of God.

At the moment of our death, we experience a deep yearning to be with God. At that same moment, we face the truth of our lives and see ourselves as accepting or rejecting God by the way we have lived. The fundamental attitude of mind with which we meet death directs us to accept or reject God. When we choose hell, our attitude of mind tells us that we are not worthy of spending an eternity with God who is all loving. We see ourselves as unloving, turned selfishly in on ourselves and having rejected God during life. At the moment of our death, we continue that rejection and cast ourselves out of God's presence for all eternity. We actually cannot choose God. Our attitude of mind at that moment could never allow the humility and love needed for that choice.

b. Hell consists in a state of deep, burning loneliness or alienation from God.

In the Scriptures, we often read of hell as consisting of fire. In Matthew's Gospel, we read Jesus' parable about the sheep and the goats: "Then he will say to those at his left hand, 'You that are accursed, depart from me into the eternal fire prepared for the devil and his angels' " (Matthew 25:41). When Jesus spoke, he spoke in images that arose out of the experiences of his listeners. The image of fire as unceasing would have been familiar to those who knew the fire pits on the outskirts of Jerusalem—constantly burning trash and refuse. Today, an experience all of us share is the experience of a deep loneliness when someone close to us passes out of this world. Within our own hearts, we feel a burning sensation, a sensation brought about by loneliness or the experience of lost love. When we die, we will experience a deep yearning to be with God. The pain of hell consists in the burning sensation of loneliness and alienation from God and our own inability to accept God's love.

c. In hell, a person experiences a deep self-hatred.

In hell, a person accepts self over God, and this choice of self fills a person with deep self-hatred. When a person turns in upon himself or herself, that person finds only frustration and lack of love. In hell, people even hate others who are damned along with them. For all eternity, a person experiences loneliness, frustration, disappointment, and deep hatred, and suffers continually in this alienation from God.

5. Has Jesus ever spoken of anyone going to hell?

a. Jesus spoke about the experience of hell, but the Scriptures never tell us whether any person has ever been condemned to hell.

Jesus warns about the punishment of hell that awaits those who reject God throughout their lives. Neither Jesus nor the Scriptures speak of any specific person being condemned to hell. Even Judas, for his betrayal, is never explicitly mentioned as going to hell. The existence of hell is a fact that we believe as Christians. Whether anyone is in hell and who specifically is in hell can be known only by God.

b. The Scriptures tell us of Jesus promising paradise to a thief on the cross.

In the Gospel of Luke, we read about two thieves who were crucified on either side of Jesus. One of the thieves berated Jesus and challenged Jesus to save them. The other, however, rebuked his fellow thief, turned to Jesus, and said, " 'Jesus, remember me when you come into your kingdom.' He replied, 'Truly I tell you, today you will be with me in Paradise' " (Luke 23:42–43). In this text, Jesus promises the thief that he will share in the glory of eternal happiness. While the Scriptures do not tell us of a specific person going to hell, they do tell us of a specific person gaining heaven.

c. We are incapable of judging whether or not another individual enters eternal hell.

Jesus, during his life, warned us about judging others. He told us, "Do not judge, so that you may not be judged. For with the judgment you make you will be judged, and the measure you give will be the measure you get" (Matthew 7:1–2). We have no way of judging another person. We cannot enter into that person's conscience and understand why that person acts in any particular fashion. We can say that certain actions in themselves are sinful actions. Whether or not that person is guilty of sin is beyond our ability to judge. God warns us that if we dare to judge the sinfulness of another person, we must pass that same test.

6. What is purgatory?

a. Purgatory consists in the painful passage from this life into God's loving presence.

At our passage into new life, we yearn for an eternal presence in possession of God's love. We suddenly experience God and all God's love, and we painfully and shamefully face ourselves in our weakness. At this passover from death to eternal life, we must pass through the purifying fires of God's love and experience a deeper love of God than of our own selfish desires.

b. In the passage we call purgatory, we turn our love fully toward God.

Because of our selfish love and the continual turning away from God in many minor ways, we must suddenly confront God in our weakness.

293

We know that we have not cut ourselves off so completely from God that we condemn ourselves to eternal hell, yet we also see the painful attachments that we have chosen over God. At this very painful, purifying moment, we turn ourselves fully toward God and reject all our own selfish desires. The word *purgatory* has within it the idea of purging or cleansing. We simply purge ourselves of all selfish opinions that have drawn us away from a full love of God so that we may fully enter into an eternal happiness and a purified love for all eternity.

c. Purgatory is not a place.

Purgatory is not a place, and certainly not a place in which we spend a specific number of years. As with heaven and hell, purgatory is a state of existence. It is an experience of people who are saved and invited into God's presence for all eternity. Persons experience joy in this state because of the realization that they have gained eternal happiness with God, yet joined to that state of joy is a state of suffering. God wants us for all eternity in heaven, but God does not want us with our weakness and our self-centered attitudes. In the state of purgatory, this moment of passage, the self-centered attitude must painfully be purified for our entrance into an eternal happiness. Purgatory, although painful, is nothing like the eternal pain of loss in hell.

d. The Catholic Church teaches that our prayers can help others through this state of purgatory.

The Catholic Church teaches that those who have died may profit from our prayers as they pass through the state of purgatory. In the Book of Maccabees, we read that Judas, a leader of the people, went to gather the bodies of the slain. Scripture tells us:

> *He also took up a collection, man by man, to the amount of two thousand drachmas of silver, and sent it to Jerusalem to provide for a sin offering. In doing this he acted very well and honorably, taking account of the resurrection. For if he were not expecting that those who had fallen would rise again, it would have been superfluous and foolish to pray for the dead. But if he was looking to the splendid reward that is laid up for those who fall asleep in godliness, it was a holy and pious thought. Therefore he made atonement for the dead, so that they might be delivered from their sin (2 Maccabees 12:43–46).*

According to this Scripture reading, Judas would have been foolish to pray for the dead if there were no chance of a resurrection and no chance of those prayers benefiting the dead. When we see purgatory as a passage from the selfishness of this life to the full love of heaven, we must ask how our prayers can benefit an event that apparently has taken place in a flash of light. By the time we pray for someone already deceased, that person is enjoying the reward of God's full love, heaven. All we can say is that somehow our prayers affect the passage that took place in the past, even when we pray for that person today. The Church, in its reading of the Scriptures, believes that it is a "very excellent and noble" thing to pray for the dead. Our prayers benefit those who experience purgatory. We cannot explain how this happens, so we trustingly place our prayers in the hands of God and believe that it does happen.

e. On November 2 every year, the Church celebrates All Souls' Day.

On All Souls' Day, the church remembers all those who have made the passage from this life to eternity. On this day, we pray for our relatives, our friends, and others throughout the world that their passage to God was less painful. We pray in faith, realizing that somehow in God's goodness and in the mystery of eternity, our prayers are able to affect a moment of passage from this life to an eternal reward.

7. What is the rite of funerals?

a. The Rite for Christian Funerals includes the celebration of the Eucharistic liturgy.

When a Christian dies, the body is brought to the church where the Eucharistic liturgy is celebrated. At this liturgy, we celebrate the fact that someone who was baptized in Christ has now been raised in Christ. The symbols, prayers, and songs of this liturgy point toward spiritual joy, although the minds of those celebrating recognize the human sadness at the loss of someone close to them.

b. The symbols used in the Christian Funeral Rite refer to baptism, resurrection, and hope.

As was mentioned in reference to the Sacrament of Baptism, a white robe is placed upon the person being baptized, signifying a clothing in Christ. At the Christian funeral liturgy, the presider meets the casket at the door of the church and drapes a white cloth over it. This white cloth symbolizes the link between baptism, death, and resurrection. A person who has been baptized in Christ is now raised in Christ. At the time of baptism, the Easter candle stood near the baptismal font, reminding us of the day of Christ's resurrection. The Easter candle is also placed in a prominent place during the liturgy of Christian resurrection to again remind us of Christ's resurrection and our resurrection. The vestments worn at the liturgy are white vestments to symbolize the spiritual joy and hope of resurrection. In this way, the Church reminds us that we are celebrating a **Christian** funeral.

8. What is a saint?

a. The Catholic Church, after investigating the life of a good person and finding other signs of holiness, declares a person as worthy of the title **saint**.

When the Catholic Church declares that a person who has lived and died well is worthy of the title *saint*, the Church is actually using its authority, under the guidance of the Holy Spirit, to declare that the person is now sharing in the eternal presence of God. In other words, that person is now sharing totally in the resurrection and ascension of Christ. Before a person is declared a saint, that person's life undergoes intense scrutiny while some sign, usually in the form of miracles in that person's name, is sought of God. By this sign from God, the Church feels secure in naming a person a saint and declaring that person's life worthy of imitation. By honoring the saints, Catholics are really praising God for God's goodness in sharing holiness with our human condition. Without a good and loving God, no one would be able to become a saint. A saint points to this goodness and love of God.

b. All who have entered the eternal glory of God's presence, that is, heaven, are considered saints in the Catholic Church.

There are many people sharing in God's eternal glory whose names we do not know. Others are relatives and friends we have known in life who have passed on to God. Because the Church is not able to know by name all the people who have lived and served God well, the Church celebrates a feast in honor of all these saints. On November 1, the Church celebrates *All Saints' Day*. On this day, we celebrate the fact that many Christians have lived and died in God's love and are now sharing in God's eternal happiness. Some-day, the feast of All Saints, hopefully, will be our feast day. This is a special "holy day" for Catholics. On this day, we are reminded of our calling to eternal happiness. We are a pilgrim people who strive to live well that we may come to share in All Saints' Day.

c. We should strive to share God's glory out of love for God rather than a fear of hell.

Many Christians carry out the law of God because they feel that if they die in sin they will be condemned to eternal pain. The real meaning of heaven, however, consists in a deep experience of love. Through baptism, we begin the reign of God within our own per-son, and we grow in that reign as we grow in love through life. Our passage to eternal happiness will depend not on how well we kept the law, but rather on how well we loved God in keeping God's law.

9. What do we know about the end of the world?

a. The end of the world comes with the fulfillment of completion of God's creation.

The world in which we live will eventually come to its day of fulfill-ment. This does not necessarily mean that the world will be destroyed at the end of time, but that there will be a new heaven and a new earth; for, as we read in the Book of Revelation (21:1), "the first heaven and the first earth had passed away, and the sea was no more." We do not know exactly what this means, since the Scriptures speak about the end of the world in highly symbolic terms. Many interpret the words of Jesus who spoke of catastrophes as signs of the end of the world. Even Jesus, as did many of the people of his own day, used highly symbolic language when speaking of the end of the world. We know only that the world will end and that it will consist in the completion or final fulfillment of the reign of God in creation. As we read the Scriptures, we are reminded to look forward with hope to this day.

b. At the end of the world in time, all will share in the general judgment.

The word *judgment* has many meanings. At the end of time, there will be many who have already shared in the *particular judgment*, that is, the moment when they will have chosen or rejected God for all eternity. The *general judgment* consists in the final gathering when all of creation comes before God, not to be condemned or rewarded, but to experience as one, the fullness of God's creation. For those who have chosen a sinful attitude during life, the moment will be one of loneliness and rejection, while, for those who have chosen a loving attitude during life, it will be a time of fulfillment in joy and love.

During the early days of Paul's writings, the people expected the world to end soon, and they looked hopefully and expectantly toward this day. When it did not occur, they began to fear for those who had already died, wondering whether they had missed the second coming of Christ and thus missed eternal reward. Paul, in a letter to the Thessalonians, tells them that those who have died will indeed share in the final, general judgment. Paul writes:

> But we do not want you to be uninformed, brothers and sisters, about those who have died, so that you may not grieve as others do who have no hope. . . . For this we declare to you by the word of the Lord, that we who are alive, who are left until the coming of the Lord, will by no means precede those who have died. For the Lord himself, with a cry of command, with the archangel's call and with the sound of God's trumpet, will descend from heaven, and the dead in Christ will rise first. Then we who are alive, who are left, will be caught up in the clouds together with them to meet the Lord in the air; and so we will be with the Lord forever. Therefore encourage one another with these words (1 Thessalonians 4:13, 15–18).

c. At the end of time, Christ will turn over to God the Father the total gift of the reign which will have reached its fulfillment.

In the Gospel of John, we read that the Son of God, called the *Word* by the author of the Gospel, was with God the Father at the time of creation, and that all was created through the Word. The Word became flesh and was known to us in his human and divine nature as Jesus Christ, the one who brought salvation through his death, resurrection, and ascension. At the end of time, all creation will reach its perfection in Christ, and he will then offer the perfect and complete gift to God. In this way, we learn that the Son of God is central to creation from beginning to end and that the total fulfillment of the gift is finally directed to the Father.

In his First Letter to the Corinthians, Paul explains to his readers this wonderful mystery of creation. He tells them that everything, with the exception of the Father, became subject to Christ. At the time of perfect fulfillment, Christ will subject himself and the perfect gift to the Father. We read,

> *Then comes the end, when he hands over the kingdom to God the Father, after he has destroyed every ruler and every authority and power. For he must reign until he has put all his enemies under his feet. The last enemy to be destroyed is death. For "God has put all things in subjection under his feet." But when it says, "All things are put in subjection," it is plain that this does not include the one who put all things in subjection under him. When all things are subjected to him, then the Son himself will also be subjected to the one who put all things in subjection under him, so that God may be all in all (1 Corinthians 15:24–28).*

The final mystery of creation will unfold at the end of time, when the Son joyfully offers to the Father the perfect fulfillment of the reign of God. Our hope is that we will share in that loving and joyful fulfillment.

Conclusion

Given enough time, we too will pass through the five steps of dying. Many Christians, in a loving way, have already begun this process in their lives, not knowing whether they have five or fifty years ahead and not waiting for any specific illness. The reality of their eternal destiny is always before them. The apostle Paul was one who accepted the fact of his death and looked forward to that moment with longing:

> For to me, living is Christ and dying is gain. If I am to live in the flesh, that means fruitful labor for me; and I do not know which I prefer. I am hard pressed between the two: my desire is to depart and be with Christ, for that is far better; but to remain in the flesh is more necessary for you (Philippians 1:21–24).

Paul's love draws him to the eternal joy of God's presence and his duty and love for the people draw him to living out his earthly life. He has reached the point of acceptance and now awaits the fulfillment of his desire for God's presence. Death holds no fear for Paul.

For Scripture reflection and discussion concerning this chapter, see **Journeying in His Light, "Death to Life."**

Epilogue

At the beginning of this book, we read about a young boy going out at night for the first time to feed the horses. He slowly followed a circle of light that led him down the path and out to the barn. Now the years have passed. The boy has grown up, married, and is presently rearing his own children. One night, he decided that it was time for his oldest son to go out to the barn on his own to feed the horses. The young boy showed no fear. He simply stepped out onto the porch, pulled a lever on the side of an electric box, and watched the yard and barn leap into light. He easily accepted the chore of going out at night to feed the horses.

As the months passed, the father had grown accustomed to the boy's routine. But one week, he noted that the boy was coming in from the barn a little later than usual. He questioned the boy, and the boy admitted that he slipped out behind the barn after feeding the horses to sit in the dark and enjoy the stars. The son envied the simplicity of the father's young life, when electric lights never dimmed the beauty of the stars. The father smiled as he remembered his own fear of the darkness.

In our early pages, we expressed a hope of lighting up a path to understanding Catholic belief. Just as the boy moved toward the barn with his lantern, lighting up only small areas of the path, so we moved slowly toward an understanding of our faith, lighting up only small areas of the faith. Now, as we look back, we see a little more clearly the path we have traveled. As we make new discoveries in our faith and light up the path of understanding a little more, we must continually test these new discoveries against the background of the early Church and the Bible. Like the boy who slipped out of the barn into the darkness, we must never lose sight of the stars.

Prayers, Practices and Precepts

Throughout this book, we have shared some prayers and practices of the Catholic faith. This section will draw these prayers and practices together for quick reference, adding others that the reader may wish to know in living the Catholic faith.

Blessing with holy water on entering the church

In the Sacrament of Baptism, the minister of the sacrament baptizes "In the name of the Father and of the Son and of the Holy Spirit." As we enter the church, we bless ourselves with holy water. The blessing with the water reminds us that we enter the church as baptized Christians ready to share our baptismal gifts in worship of God.

As we enter the church, we dip the tip of our right hand in the holy water and bless ourselves with our right hand in the image of a cross by touching our forehead first, then our chest, then our left shoulder, and finally our right shoulder. While we make this sign of the cross, we pray the words: "In the name of the Father and of the Son and of the Holy Spirit. Amen."

Genuflection on one knee

If the Blessed Sacrament is present, Catholics show a special sign of reverence to this presence of Jesus. We genuflect (1) before taking our seat, (2) whenever we pass in front of the Blessed Sacrament, and (3) as we leave.

We genuflect by touching the floor with the right knee. Even if the Blessed Sacrament is exposed for benediction for special occasions such as Holy Thursday, we still genuflect on only one knee.

The Lord's Prayer

When the followers of Jesus asked him to teach them how to pray, Jesus taught them the prayer commonly referred to today as "The Lord's Prayer." Through our baptism, we enter into a close, intimate relationship with God. We no longer approach God in a most formal way, but rather with the intimate manner of a child approaching a concerned, loving parent. Because of this relationship, we can now call God *Dad* or *Daddy,* which is the real meaning behind the very formal translation of *Father* in the Lord's Prayer. In reality, we are simply saying, "Our Dad, who art. . . ." Through the gift of the resurrection and of our own baptism, we dare to say:

Our Father, who art in heaven,
hallowed be Thy name;
Thy kingdom come;
Thy will be done on earth as it is in heaven.
Give us this day our daily bread,
and forgive us our trespasses
as we forgive those who trespass against us;
and lead us not into temptation,
but deliver us from evil. Amen.

The Hail Mary

The Scriptures continually need to be translated into a more modern language so that we may more clearly understand their message. The first part of the prayer, "The Hail Mary," came from a previous translation of the Scriptures. In the infancy narratives, an angel appeared to Mary, called her "full of grace" and told her that the Lord was with her. When Mary visited Elizabeth, her cousin, Elizabeth proclaimed the blessedness of the "fruit of your womb." The Church added the name of "Jesus" to Elizabeth's greeting and added the second part of the prayer which is simply a request for Mary's prayers in the lives of its people.

Hail, Mary, full of grace!
the Lord is with you.
Blessed are you among women,
and blessed is the fruit of your womb, Jesus.
Holy Mary, Mother of God,
pray for us sinners,
now and at the hour of our death. Amen.

The Trinity Prayer

Besides making the sign of the cross in the name of the Trinity, the Church also makes use of a prayer of praise and glory to the Trinity. It professes a belief through prayer in God's glory, God's unity in three persons, and God's eternal existence.

Glory to the Father, and to the Son, and to the Holy Spirit. As it was in the beginning, is now, and will be forever. Amen.

The Apostles' Creed

The Apostles' Creed has its birth in the early Church and is a basic profession of faith in God and God's plan of salvation. Legend has it that there are twelve articles of faith mentioned in the Apostles' Creed and that each apostle added one of the articles of faith. This does not seem likely, although the Creed does go back to the early apostolic age of the Church. Longer professions of faith, such as the Nicene Creed used in the Eucharistic liturgy, are developments from the Apostles' Creed. Councils added more explanation to certain articles of faith and put them into the Creed. The Nicene Creed is actually the Apostles' Creed with further explanation of certain points that the Council of Nicea felt were necessary.

I[We] believe in God, the Father almighty,
creator of heaven and earth.

I[We] believe in Jesus Christ, his only Son, our Lord.
He was conceived by the power of the Holy Spirit
and born of the Virgin Mary.
He suffered under Pontius Pilate,
was crucified, died, and was buried.
He descended into hell.
On the third day he rose again.
He ascended into heaven,
and is seated at the right hand of the Father.
He will come again to judge the living and the dead.

I[We] believe in the Holy Spirit,
the holy catholic Church,
the communion of saints,
the forgiveness of sins,
the resurrection of the body,
and the life everlasting. Amen.

Act of Sorrow (Contrition)

In the Sacrament of Reconciliation, we pray an Act of Sorrow to express in words the sorrow we have already shown in the confession of sins. In this sacrament, we may choose to express our sorrow in our own words, or choose one of several different suggested acts of sorrow offered in the book of the *Rite for Reconciliation*. An example of an Act of Sorrow as found in the *Rite of Reconciliation* is the following:

My God,
I am sorry for my sins with all my heart.
In choosing to do wrong
and failing to do good,
I have sinned against you
whom I should love above all things.
I firmly intend, with your help,
to do penance,
to sin no more,
and to avoid whatever leads me to sin.
Our Savior Jesus Christ
suffered and died for us.
In his name, my God, have mercy.

The Rosary

The rosary stands out as one of the major devotions of personal piety for many Catholics. Although St. Dominic gave great impetus to the recitation of the rosary as far back as 800 years ago, the practice of the recitation of the rosary seems to predate even St. Dominic. Its origin lies in the shadows of the past, but its use among Catholics has made the rosary one of the best known forms of Catholic devotion. The rosary beads could easily go back to some of the ancient religious customs of counting prayers on beads. The Church, however, has placed certain blessings upon the use of beads which are blessed by an ordained priest. The rosary beads consist of a set of fifty beads, clustered together in groups of ten, called decades. A short chain with a single bead set in the middle separates the decades from each other. The chain is joined together to form a circle, and a small chain holding a crucifix, a single bead, and three beads grouped together extend from the circle. The praying of the rosary takes place as follows:

We bless ourselves "In the name of the Father, and of the Son, and of the Holy Spirit. Amen." We then pray the Apostles' Creed, holding the crucifix in our fingers. We pray the "Lord's Prayer" on the single bead and three "Hail Mary" prayers on the cluster of three beads. These prayers are recited for "an increase of the virtues of faith, hope, and charity." At the end of each cluster of beads, we pray the "Trinity" prayer. Each decade consists of one "Lord's Prayer," ten recitations of the "Hail Mary," and a single recitation of the "Trinity" prayer. At the beginning of each decade, we meditate on some event in the life of Jesus or Mary. When we finish praying the five decades, we again make the Sign of the Cross as an end to the prayer. The mysteries of the rosary are the following:

The Joyful Mysteries (Mondays and Thursdays)

1. The annunciation that Mary is to be the Mother of Jesus.

2. Mary visits her cousin Elizabeth.

3. Mary gives birth to Jesus.

4. Mary presents Jesus in the temple according to Jewish tradition.

5. Mary and Joseph find Jesus in the temple after three days.

The Sorrowful Mysteries (Tuesdays and Fridays)

1. The agony of Jesus in the garden on the night before his death.

2. Jesus is whipped by the Roman soldiers.

3. Jesus is crowned with thorns.

4. Jesus carries his cross.

5. Jesus dies on the cross.

The Glorious Mysteries (Sundays, Wednesdays, and Saturdays)

1. Jesus is raised from the dead.

2. Jesus ascends into heaven.

3. The Holy Spirit is sent upon the apostles.

4. Mary is taken into heaven.

5. Mary is crowned queen of heaven and earth.

The Rosary Beads

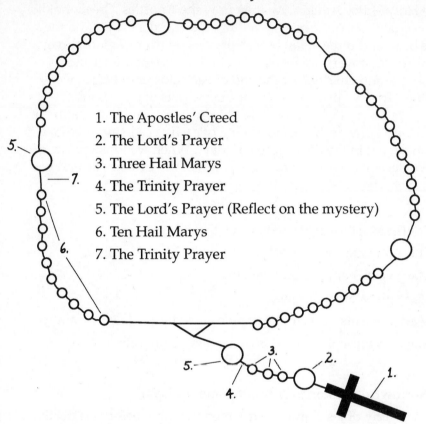

1. The Apostles' Creed
2. The Lord's Prayer
3. Three Hail Marys
4. The Trinity Prayer
5. The Lord's Prayer (Reflect on the mystery)
6. Ten Hail Marys
7. The Trinity Prayer

Stations of the Cross

A station is a place to stop or linger for some set purpose. In some cases, these places signify or recall some great event in history. In most churches, plaques which show pictures of Jesus on his journey to death are spaced along the walls. Each of these pictures or plaques is a station where the person praying will stop to meditate on the particular event portrayed in the picture. During the season of Lent, the Church meditates through its liturgy on the passion and death of Jesus, but always with an eye to his resurrection. The stations of the cross enable the Catholic to pray in a personal way, especially during the season of Lent, by meditating on Jesus' journey to his death and resurrection. There are traditionally fourteen stations, and they are as follows:

First station: Jesus is condemned to death by Pilate.

Second station: Jesus is made to carry his cross.

Third station: Jesus falls the first time.

Fourth station: Jesus meets Mary his mother.

Fifth station: Simon, the Cyrenian, helps Jesus carry his cross.

Sixth station: Veronica wipes the face of Jesus.

Seventh station: Jesus falls the second time.

Eighth station: Jesus speaks to the daughters of Jerusalem.

Ninth station: Jesus falls the third time.

Tenth station: Jesus is stripped of his garments.

Eleventh station: Jesus is nailed to the cross.

Twelfth station: Jesus dies on the cross.

Thirteenth station: Jesus is taken down from the cross.

Fourteenth station: Jesus is laid in the tomb.

Some books on the stations of the cross have added a fifteenth station to honor the resurrection of Jesus from the dead.

Fifteenth station: Jesus is raised from the dead.

Acts of Faith, Hope, and Love

The virtues that lie at the foundation of the Christian life are the virtues of faith, hope, and love. All other virtues flow from this foundation. When we pray these Acts of Faith, Hope, and Love, we are actually putting into words what we are already living. The following prayers are simply examples of ways of expressing our living faith, hope, and love.

Through an Act of Faith, we profess a belief in the Trinity and the work of the Trinity in our lives. We may express an Act of Faith in the following fashion:

Lord God, I believe that You are one God in three persons.
I believe that a new life opened for me through the death and resurrection
of Jesus Christ
and that Your love and guidance continue through Your Holy Spirit.
I believe in the truths taught by Your holy, Catholic, and apostolic church.
By responding in love to Your gifts,

I believe that I shall share in eternal joy with You.
This is my belief, Lord God,
and my belief is my joy. Amen.

Through an Act of Hope, we profess a confidence in God's promises as found in the Scriptures. We may express our Act of Hope as follows:

Lord God, trusting in Your deep love and goodness,
I hope to receive continued forgiveness for my faults
and Your guidance and help in avoiding sin.
My hope for eternal life and joy with You
fills me with joy and love each day I live. Amen.

Through an Act of Love, we express our love for God and for our neighbor. This is the greatest of the virtues because it gives life to all the virtues. Paul writes of love, "And now faith, hope, and love abide, these three; and the greatest of these is love" (1 Corinthians 13:13). We may express our Act of Love as follows:

Lord God, You continually share Your great love with me
through the gifts in my life.
In an attempt to imitate Your great goodness and show my love in return,
I will strive to love You with all my heart, all my mind, and all my strength,
and I will seek to love my neighbor as myself.
Lord, teach me to love even more. Amen.

Special holy days

In addition to Sundays, Catholics assemble together for special occasions or feast days at six other times during the year. These feasts may differ from country to country, although most countries retain the number of six holy days. The same obligation regarding one's participation in the Sunday Eucharistic celebration applies to these days also. The special holy days are:

1. Christmas Day—celebrated on December 25

2. Solemnity of Mary, the Mother of God—celebrated on January 1

3. Ascension Thursday—celebrated on the fortieth day after Easter

4. The Assumption of Mary—celebrated on August 15

5. All Saints' Day—celebrated on November 1

6. Immaculate Conception of Mary—celebrated on December 8

The bishops of the United States decided in 1991 that whenever January 1, the *Solemnity of Mary, the Mother of God*, or August 15, the *Assumption of Mary, the Mother of God*, or November 1, the *Solemnity of All Saints* falls on a Saturday or a Monday, the obligation to participate in the Eucharistic celebration on these days ceases. The bishops, however, urge the faithful to participate in the Eucharistic liturgy on these holy days.

Offerings for intentions of Eucharistic liturgy

The Eucharistic Liturgy is always celebrated in union with the Church throughout the world. It is also celebrated for the intention of the universal Church. In the early Church, the assembly would offer at the Eucharistic liturgy the necessary items for the celebration of the Eucharist, namely bread and wine. They would also make other offerings to be given for the poor or the support of the presbyter. The custom of making offerings for the support of the clergy continued for some time. In this way, the presbyter would be free to carry out the service of the Church to the community.

As time passed, people would make certain requests for prayers in making their offering. An offering for certain sacramental functions performed by the presbyter came to be called a *stipend*. In some places, clergy depended solely upon this stipend for their livelihood. Gradually, the prayer-request for which a stipend would be offered was announced, especially during the celebration of the Eucharistic liturgy. The custom most Catholics are familiar with today is the custom of making an offering to the presbyter or parish with the request that a special remembrance be given to the one "for whom the Mass is offered."

Actually, the Eucharistic liturgy is celebrated primarily for the universal Church. No amount of offerings can change this. But another intention can also be remembered—for specific persons or intentions. Besides making an offering for a specific intention, a person should not overlook the more important action of assisting at the Eucharistic liturgy for that intention. An offering for a Eucharistic celebration does not pay for someone else to pray in our place. It is an offering with the idea that the presbyter and the assembly will pray along with us. In many churches, the presbyter has stopped announcing the intention because the primary intention is the universal Church. This is done to avoid the impression that the

Eucharistic liturgy is primarily for the intention requested, which it is not.

If a Catholic wishes to have the presbyter remember someone in a special way at the Eucharistic liturgy, he or she simply calls the parish office and makes the request. An offering is ordinarily given. The pastor will often note the intention in the weekly bulletin.

Donations are given at the time of other sacramental celebrations, such as weddings, funerals, and baptisms. If an offering cannot be made, the presbyter may not refuse a sacrament. No one "buys" a sacrament and no one "buys a Mass."

The practice of fasting from food and abstaining from meat

The Church, as a community reflecting Christ, has often called upon its members to put themselves in union with the suffering of Christ by sharing in certain types of personal sacrifice. Because Friday is considered the day of Jesus' suffering and death, the Church asks that Catholics perform some type of personal sacrifice on Fridays in honor of the passion and death of Jesus.

During Lent, the Church obliges Christians to place themselves in union with the passion and death of Jesus by fasting and by abstaining from meat.

The obligation to abstain from meat binds Catholics on Ash Wednesday and on each of the Fridays during Lent. Those fourteen years and older are bound by this law.

The law of fasting allows for one full meal a day. It does not forbid the taking of food at the other two meals, but it ordinarily offers as a norm that the other two meals may not equal the main meal in quantity. Also, eating solid foods between meals is not permitted. The main meal of the day may be taken at whichever meal a person chooses.

The obligation to fast binds Catholics only on Ash Wednesday and Good Friday. This law binds everyone from eighteen to the beginning of their sixtieth year.

We fast because Jesus called us to prayer and fasting. In placing ourselves in union with the suffering of Christ, we place ourselves in solidarity with the poor and hungry of the world who are our suffering brothers and sisters. These acts of fasting and abstaining from meat should also be accompanied by works of charity and service toward our neighbors.

Symbolic offering of oneself at Eucharist

In many churches, a tray or basket filled with the bread to be used for the Eucharist is placed near the entrance. When Catholics enter the church, they take the bread from the tray or basket and place it in another container. It is this bread which will be used during the Eucharistic liturgy. In moving the bread from the tray or basket to the other container, Catholics are symbolically making an offering of their lives in this offering of bread. In the early Church, the people brought the bread and wine from home to be used during the Eucharistic celebration. After the general intercessions, these gifts of bread and wine are brought forward and are presented to the presider who prepares them for use in the liturgy of the Eucharist.

Manner of reception of the Eucharist

When Catholics share in the Eucharist, they celebrate the presence of Christ under the appearance of bread and wine. In the early Church toward the end of the Eucharistic celebration, the people would pass around the one bread and the one cup for all to share in the Eucharistic presence of Christ.

In receiving the Eucharistic bread, Catholics have two options. They may receive communion on the tongue by extending the tongue after they have arrived at the Eucharistic table. The presider or minister of the Eucharist will place the sacred bread on the tongue of those who approach the table in this manner, or Catholics may choose to receive the bread in the hand. This is an ancient tradition by which those approaching the presider or minister of the Eucharist extend a hand resting on the other, palm up, forming a type of cradle in which the presider or minister places the bread. Once the bread has been placed in the hand, the communicant steps aside, takes the consecrated bread from the cradle of the one hand with the other hand, and places the consecrated bread in his or her mouth. Those who are right handed place their left hand on top of the right with palm up when taking the consecrated bread, and those who are left handed place the right hand on top of the left one with palm up when taking the bread. In this manner, a person communicates himself or herself with the hand that person customarily uses for most activities in life.

The custom of all the faithful sharing in the consecrated wine was an ancient custom in the Church, now revived by the Church. Many churches use two ministers of the consecrated wine for every minister of the consecrated bread, thus avoiding lengthy lines for those sharing in the consecrated wine. The use of individual drinking cups should be avoided, since this destroys the symbolism of the sharing in the common cup. The one bread and one wine are a symbol of the one community in Christ.

When sharing the Eucharist, the presider or minister says "The Body of Christ" when offering the bread, and "The Blood of Christ" when offering the wine. The communicant responds "Amen" to each of these prayers.

In the Church, sacraments are meant to be presented through a minister. Jesus offered his disciples the bread and wine at the Last Supper (Luke 22:17–20). Except for the presider who takes, eats, and drinks, no one else, including the Eucharistic ministers, takes the Eucharist themselves. It is presented to them, and they respond, "Amen."

Indulgences

To understand the meaning of indulgences, we must reach back to the roots of the Church and the understanding of the Church as the Mystical Body of Christ. All the merits of Christ and the saints are now shared through the Church. By its authority, the Church has the power to share these gifts with others.

To help overcome the consequences of our sinfulness, the Church offers us help by sharing with us the merits which flow from Christ and the saints. This help is called *indulgences*. It may be a *partial indulgence* if it does away with part of the consequences of sin, or it may be a *plenary indulgence* when it does away with all the consequences of sin.

In the past, some have abused the idea of indulgences, and the Church is careful not to allow this to happen again. Pope Paul VI, in his "Apostolic Constitution on the Revision of Indulgences" (1967), spells out the types of indulgences used by the Church, and the occasions for these indulgences. Although we hear less about indulgences today than we did in the past, Pope Paul VI points out that the use of indulgences continues to be part of Church practice.

The precepts of the Church

Besides the Ten Commandments and the Beatitudes, the Church lists certain *precepts* which guarantee that the faithful will grow in the love of God and neighbor.

The first precept requires the faithful to participate in the Eucharistic celebration when the Christian community assembles one day each week which commemorates the resurrection of the Lord.

The second precept calls for the celebration of the Sacrament of Reconciliation at least once a year for those who are in serious sin.

The third precept calls for sharing in communion of the Eucharist at least once a year during the Easter Season, which usually includes the Sunday of Easter until the celebration of Trinity Sunday.

The fourth precept calls upon Catholics to participate in the Eucharistic Liturgy on certain designated feasts throughout the year which honor Jesus Christ, Mary, the Mother of God, or the saints (see the list of holy days on pg. 310).

The fifth precept calls upon Catholics to observe fasting and abstinence from meat on certain designated days throughout the year (see the times for fasting and abstinence on pg. 312).

The sixth precept calls upon the faithful to use their resources in providing for the material and spiritual needs of the Church and the world.

Index

A

Abortion, 266

Abraham, 34, 40, 46, 55

Abstaining from meat, 312–313

Acolyte, 161

Act of Contrition, 306

Acts of Faith, Hope, and Love, 309–310

Acts of the Apostles 50, 71, 85, 86, 112–113, 126, 166, 187

Adam, 31, 45, 55, 94
 sin of, 31, 94

Adultery, 97, 250, 259

Advent, 152

Agnostic, 16

All Saints Day, 297, 310

All Souls Day, 295

Angels, 43–44

Animal rights, 289–290

Annulments, 251, 252

Anointing of the Sick, 235–244
 communal, 243–244

Apostles, 59, 276
 mission of, 59
 received Holy Spirit, 85, 154–155

Apostles' Creed, 305

Ascension, 70–71, 154, 310

Ash Wednesday, 150, 153, 312

Assembly, 208, 210–216, 271

Assumption, 133, 135, 310

Atheism, 16–17

Augustine, 5

B

Banns, 254

Baptism, 157–180
 ceremony, 174–179
 minister, 161–162, 169–170
 of blood, 171
 of desire, 171
 of Jesus, 58
 symbols, 158, 173–174, 176–177

Beatitudes, 98–99, 193, 315

Belief in God, 8–22, 305

Benediction, 219

Bible (Old and New Testaments),
 anointing of the sick, 238–239
 baptism, 158–168, 171, 173–174, 175
 Eucharist, 198–210, 211
 God's self-revelation in, 24
 marriage, 246–248, 249–250, 258
 ministry, 165–167, 270–271, 275–276
 reconciliation, 104–106, 224–228
 revelation, 26–28

Birth control, 261–266

Bishops, 122–124, 126–127, 128, 130, 184–187, 270, 272–273, 276, 277–278

Blessing, 303

Body of Christ, 115–116

C

Cain and Abel, 32, 45, 94
Canon Law, 118
Capital punishment, 118
Cardinals, 124
Catechism of the Catholic Church, 119
Catechumenate, 148–149
Catholic, 117 and throughout
Charity (see Love)
Christ, Jesus, 50–63, 68–74, 176
  and prayer, 75–77
  as Lord, 49, 53, 62, 68–69
  baptism of, 58
  birth, 54–57
  coming, 54–57, 65–68
  crucifixion, 61–62, 65–67
  death and resurrection, 61–73,
    105–106
  followers, 59, 85, 165–167, 271
  genealogy, 54–57
  God, 84
  humanness of, 62–65
  love, 65, 67, 104
    message of, 60–61, 86
  Messiah, 56–58, 68–69
  miracles, 59–60
  mission of, 58ff, 66–67
  misunderstood by followers, 64
  morality, 84–88
  resurrection, 62, 68–70, 72
  second coming, 74, 297–299

source of knowledge about, 50
Christmas, 152–153, 310
Church, 111–136, 144
  and Scripture, 117
  and tradition, 117–118
  as Body of Christ, 115, 144
  as community, 114–117, 144
  as People of God, 114–115
  as symbol, 139–140
  as Temple of the Holy Spirit, 116
  definition, 114, 144
  early struggle, 112–114
  Eucharistic Prayer and, 213–215
  evangelization and, 194–195
  Mary and, 132–135, 304,
    306–308, 310
  mission, 119–122
  mystery, 116–117
  on resurrection of Jesus, 73
  precepts, 315
  structure of orders, 123–124,
    272–273
  teachings, 117–119, 123, 127–130
Code of Canon Law, 118
College of bishops, 124, 128, 130
Commandments, 36–36, 96–98
Confession (see Reconciliation or
  Penance)
Confirmation, 146–147, 149,
  181–196
Conscience, 222–223
Constantine the Great, 113
Contraception, 261–266

317

God

First through Third
Commandments, 36–37, 96–98

helping, 15

identity, 6–21, 36, 47

in relationship to life, 7, 20, 45,
106–109

intelligent, 13

knowledge of, 5–21, 23–48

love and, 8, 10, 13–15, 45

People of, 114–115

reign of, 60, 120, 159–160,
164–165, 279, 299

Spirit of, 79–90, 112–113,
115–116, 119, 129, 134–135,
155, 168–169, 174, 177,
182–184, 187, 189, 194

without beginning, 6, 11, 13

Godparents, 172–173, 178, 188

Good, 44–45

Good Friday, 154, 312

Gospels, 50, 52

differences, 52–60, 72

infancy narratives, 54–57

influenced by, 52–54

John, 52–53, 69–70

Luke, 52, 54–56, 64, 75–77

Mark, 52–53, 64, 67–68, 75–76

Matthew, 52, 54–57

Grace, 106–109

H

"Hail Mary," 134–135, 304

Healing, Sacraments of, 146,
222ff, 236ff

Heaven, 74, 290–291, 295

Hebrew Scriptures (see Old
Testament)

Hebrews (see Old Testament)

Hell, 291–293

Holy days, 310

Holy Saturday, 154

Holy Spirit, 79–90, 112–113,
115–116, 119, 129, 134–135,
155, 166, 168–169, 174, 177,
182–184, 187, 189, 194

gifts of, 87–88, 166, 182–183, 189

God, 82–84

prayer to, 88

Holy Thursday, 154

Holy Trinity, 82–84, 88–89

Holy Viaticum, 242–243

Holy Water, 303

Homosexuality, 260–261

Hope, Act of, 309–310

I

J

K

L

M

N

O

P

Other Books by the Author

Journeying in His Light

This formation guide presents thirty-five topics and session outlines. Using chapters from *In His Light* as background, sessions begin with a series of Scripture references and include questions for discussion and reflection. Space is provided for composing personal thoughts and prayers. Each session concludes with a simple prayer.

Journeying through the RCIA

This book is concerned with living the Christian life. Through information, Scripture texts, personal reflections, and discussion options, this book offers a reflective approach to understanding and experiencing the RCIA.

RCIA: A Total Parish Process

This book explains how to implement the RCIA in your parish. Reproducible worksheets offer suggestions for using the catechumenate as a source of renewal for the entire parish family. The book outlines ways of teaching, training, experiencing, sharing, and motivating within the process.

To order, send your name and address with the titles and order numbers of the books you wish to order. Please include $1.50 for postage and handling. Payment must accompany the order. Send to:

BROWN–ROA
P.O. Box 1028
Dubuque, Iowa 52004-1028